I0793069

POSTCARD HISTORY SERIES

# *Asbury Park Revisited*

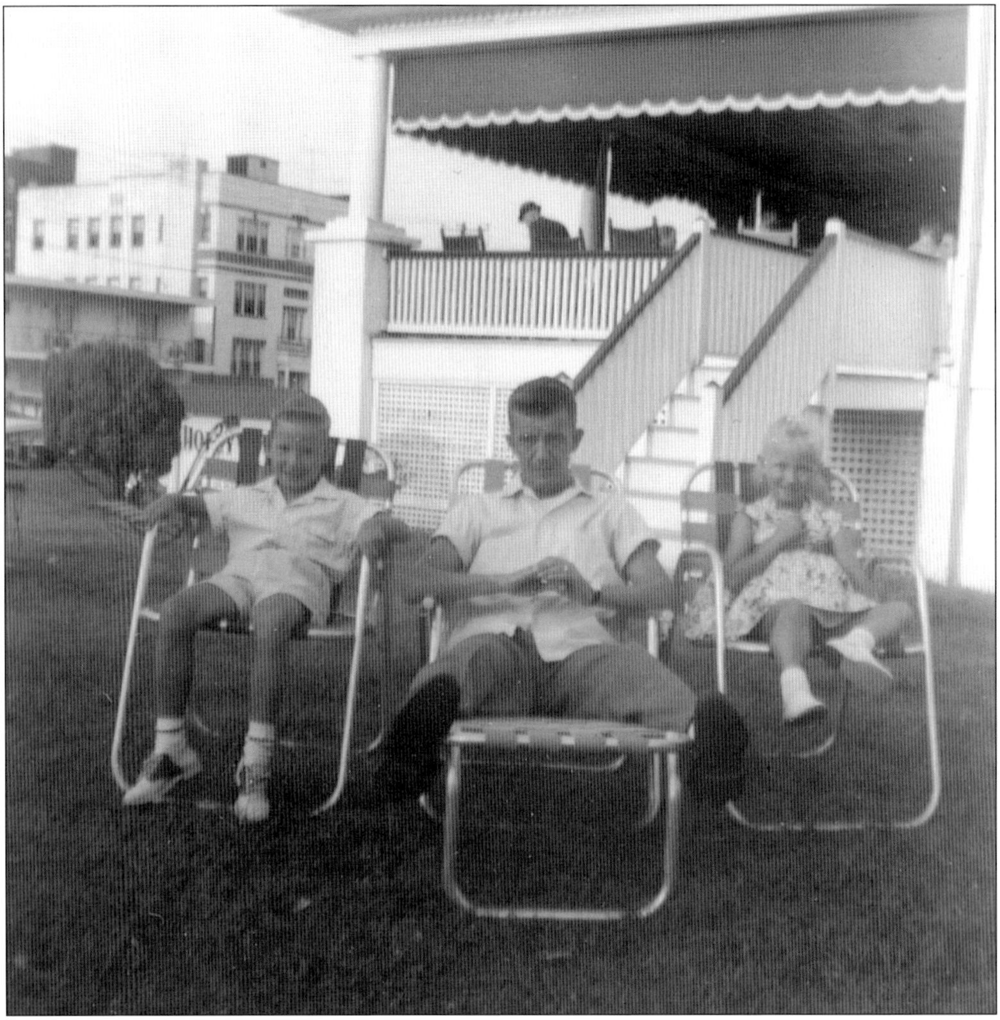

From left to right, the author's uncle Ray Hentze, grandfather Raymond Hentze, and mother, Laurie (Hentze) Steiner, enjoy a 1961 summer day on the lawn of Asbury Park's Hollywood Hotel, located on Fourth Avenue. (Courtesy of Carol Hentze.)

**ON THE FRONT COVER:** Riding in the swan boats on Wesley Lake was a favorite activity for visitors to Asbury Park in the mid-20th century. The boats provided views of both Asbury Park and nearby Ocean Grove. (Author's collection.)

**ON THE BACK COVER:** The Asbury Park views shown in this large letter–motif postcard include the boardwalk, beach, convention hall, new Casino, and heating plant. (Author's collection.)

POSTCARD HISTORY SERIES

# *Asbury Park Revisited*

*Lisa Lamb*

ARCADIA
PUBLISHING

ISBN 978-1-4671-3363-0

Published by Arcadia Publishing
Charleston, South Carolina

Printed in the United States of America

Library of Congress Control Number: 2015948603

For all general information contact Arcadia Publishing at:
Telephone 843-853-2070
Fax 843-853-0044
E-mail sales@arcadiapublishing.com
For customer service and orders:
Toll-Free 1-888-313-2665

Visit us on the Internet at www.arcadiapublishing.com

*For my guys—Mehow, Ack, and Doodle.*

# Contents

# ACKNOWLEDGMENTS

The work of a number of authors was instrumental in my research for this book. First among these is Helen Chantal-Pike, whose writing is as entertaining as it is informative. I strongly encourage anyone interested in Asbury Park, or the Jersey Shore in general, to seek out her book *Asbury Park's Glory Days.*

Peter Lucia's website noweverthen.com is extremely illuminating in providing the perspective of a teenager during Asbury Park's glory days.

Like virtually any city in America, Asbury Park has a complex history. I would be remiss if I did not acknowledge that the images in this book are not necessarily reflective of the experiences of all of Asbury Park's visitors or inhabitants. A very well-done examination of the history of Asbury Park relative to race and politics is *Fourth of July, Asbury Park* by Daniel Wolff.

I want to acknowledge Lisa Brahin Weinblatt, whose in-laws Martin and Sylvia Weinblatt owned the Metropolitan Hotel for many years. She was generous both in postage and her personal time, providing me with wonderful historical documents and insights related to this beautiful hotel.

The Ocean Grove Historical Society's digitized vintage newspapers and Princeton University's digitized Sanborn maps are incredible resources for exploring the history of Asbury Park as it happened.

I owe a huge debt of gratitude to the people who have contacted me through my website side-o-lamb.com over the years, whose shared interest in Asbury Park motivated me to continue to grow and share my collection of postcards and ephemera. I have tried my best to be accurate in both this book and on my site; if I have made an error, please contact me at lisa@side-o-lamb.com so that I may correct it.

To Kris, thanks for squeezing through that hole in the side of Palace Amusements with me. I know there were about 50 other things you would have rather done that day.

To Grandma and Aunt Bobbie, thank you for the photos.

To my boys, thank you for your patience while mama worked on this project.

Finally, to Mike—thank you for never bending the mail.

Unless otherwise noted, all images are from the author's collection.

# INTRODUCTION

On an overcast day in June 2004, a group of about 150 people gathered on the northwest corner of Asbury Park's Kingsley Street and Cookman Avenue. Across the street, a painting on a foot-thick piece of cinderblock wall attached to a partially demolished building was being framed in steel. News cameras recorded as a crane pulled the frame upwards. Applause broke out once the painting was free from the wall, and it was clear that it had remained intact. Normally, a construction project like this would not draw much of a crowd. On this day however, Tillie, the smiling de facto mascot of Asbury Park, was being salvaged from the side of Palace Amusements, an entertainment complex dating almost to the founding of Asbury Park.

A little more than 130 years earlier, James Bradley, a wealthy New Yorker who had made his fortunes in brush manufacturing, visited the Methodist retreat of Ocean Grove, New Jersey. Taken with the positive effect he believed the seashore had on his health, Bradley paid $90,000 to purchase 500 acres of oceanfront property north of Ocean Grove. He named his town Asbury Park after Francis Asbury, America's first Methodist Episcopal bishop. "Founder Bradley," as he was often called, had a vision for Asbury Park of polite cleanliness in both morality and physicality. The town would be a secular counterpart to Ocean Grove, where one could enjoy wholesome entertainment and healthful sea breezes. In order to make sure the atmosphere remained respectable, many of the restrictions in place in Ocean Grove would also be in place in Asbury Park: gambling and drinking were strictly prohibited, women were expected to be chaperoned and dress modestly, and businesses were closed on Sundays.

To say that Bradley was intimately involved in shaping the early direction of Asbury Park is an understatement. In addition to dictating the layout of the town's large lots, parks, and wide streets, Bradley served as the town's first postmaster and the editor of the town's first newspaper. He personally bankrolled the construction of the boardwalk as well as miles of sewer pipes for the town's sanitation system, which was the first of its kind in the area. Despite his civic-minded nature, Bradley was not completely beneficent. He posted signs along the boardwalk bearing prohibitions against what he perceived to be immoral behavior and hired special beach police who made sure people dressed and behaved respectfully. African Americans were not welcome east of the railroad tracks unless they were there for work. Lots were sold at Bradley's discretion, and he wrote restrictions into deeds to ensure that hotels and restaurants could not serve liquor. By the turn of the 20th century, Bradley's desire to keep the boardwalk free of commercial interests was at odds with local businessmen. In 1903, after years of contentious dealings with city hall over the direction Asbury Park should take, and facing a lawsuit that was likely to result in the city taking the waterfront, Bradley sold the boardwalk and sewer system to the city for less than a tenth of what it was worth.

In the early to mid-20th century, Asbury Park flourished. Grand hotels were constructed to house the thousands who came to spend time strolling the boardwalk and beautiful beachfront.

Buildings along the boardwalk offered music, dancing, and dining. The daily summer population was as high as 50,000 people, with more than 100,000 coming for events like the annual baby parade and carnival. A chamber of commerce was established in 1913 to promote the town, and due to its convenient rail service and multitude of downtown shops, Asbury Park became known as "the commercial center of Monmouth County."

Beginning in the 1950s, a number of factors came together to cause Asbury Park's popularity to wane. As highways allowed the public to travel farther and more quickly than before, day-trippers replaced people who would have come for the two-week stays that were common in the early 1900s. The boardwalk remained popular, but other towns with longer boardwalks, like the one at Seaside Heights, were easier than ever to get to. The Garden State Arts Center arena in Holmdel, with its ample parking and easy access to the parkway, drew bands that would have previously been booked at Asbury Park's convention hall. Disney World was a short plane ride away, and Great Adventure in Jackson, New Jersey, presented thrills beyond what any boardwalk could offer. The city's already declining tourism was made worse in 1970 when long-simmering racial tensions came to a head in riots that lasted for days, leaving 100 people injured and blocks of town destroyed. Downtown shopping fell out of favor as indoor shopping centers like Monmouth Mall in nearby Eatontown allowed consumers to make purchases in temperature-controlled comfort. In the late 1970s, a quarter of the commercial space on Cookman Avenue that had helped Asbury Park remain a year-round retail destination for so long was vacant.

By the time Bruce Springsteen began playing the Stone Pony, Asbury Park was well into a decline that has taken nearly 40 years from which to recover. At the turn of the 21st century, many of the buildings from Asbury Park's long history remained standing. Though they were dilapidated, one could look at the Albion or Metropolitan Hotel and imagine what it had been like to visit during Asbury Park's heyday. The Fast Lane, Charms Building, Baronet Theater, Palace Amusements, and Casino skating arena, though not open, were all still more or less intact.

On that day in 2004 when Tillie was removed from Palace Amusements, it felt like more than just a piece of a building was being salvaged; it was a tie to the past being preserved. Today, so many of Asbury Park's historic places exist only in memories and in images like those in this book. It is my hope that this book may bring back a memory for those who spent childhood summers here during her glory days and give those who never got that chance a glimpse into what they missed.

# *One*

# Greetings from Asbury Park

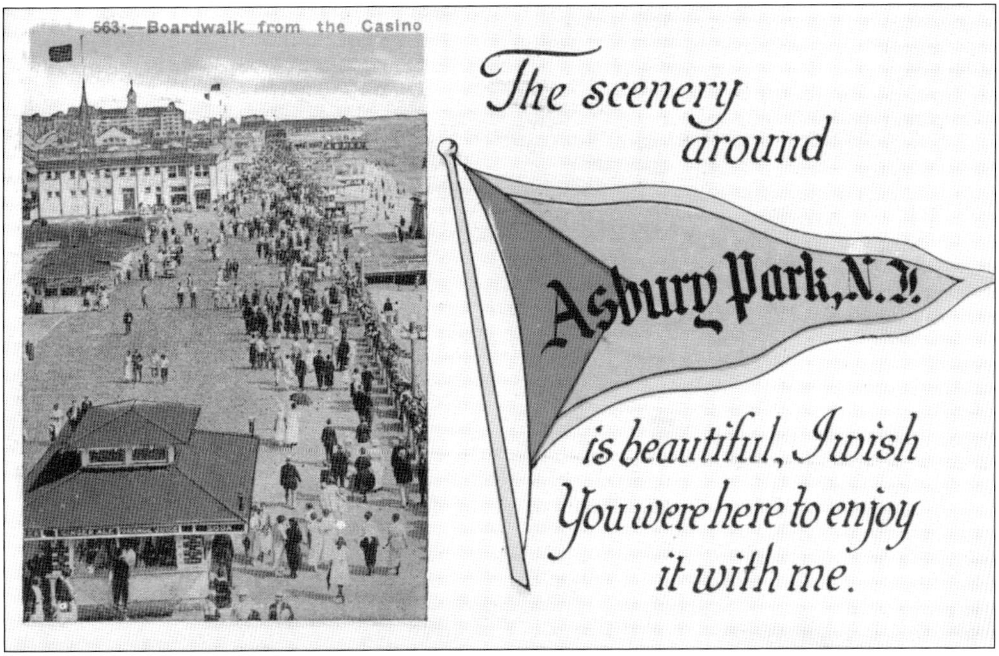


This 1920s view shows Asbury Park's boardwalk looking north from the second story of the Casino at Asbury Avenue. The Fifth Avenue Arcade, which like the Casino extended out onto the beach, can be seen in the distance. Along the right-hand side of the boardwalk are some of the octagonal pavilions that dotted the boardwalk in the early part of the 20th century, where patrons would enjoy the breeze coming off of the Atlantic Ocean.

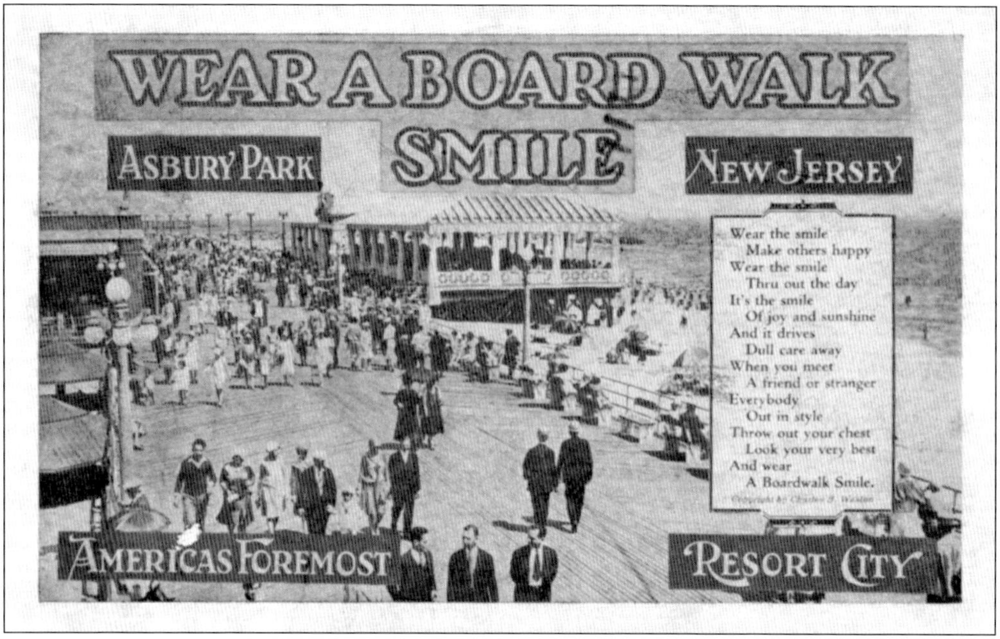


This postcard shows a view of the boardwalk in the late 1930s, with the lyrics to "Wear a Boardwalk Smile" by composer Charles B. Weston. This 1926 piano composition would be featured in the 2009 award-winning documentary *Greetings from Asbury Park*, which features local resident Angie Hampilos's fight to save her home from eminent domain.

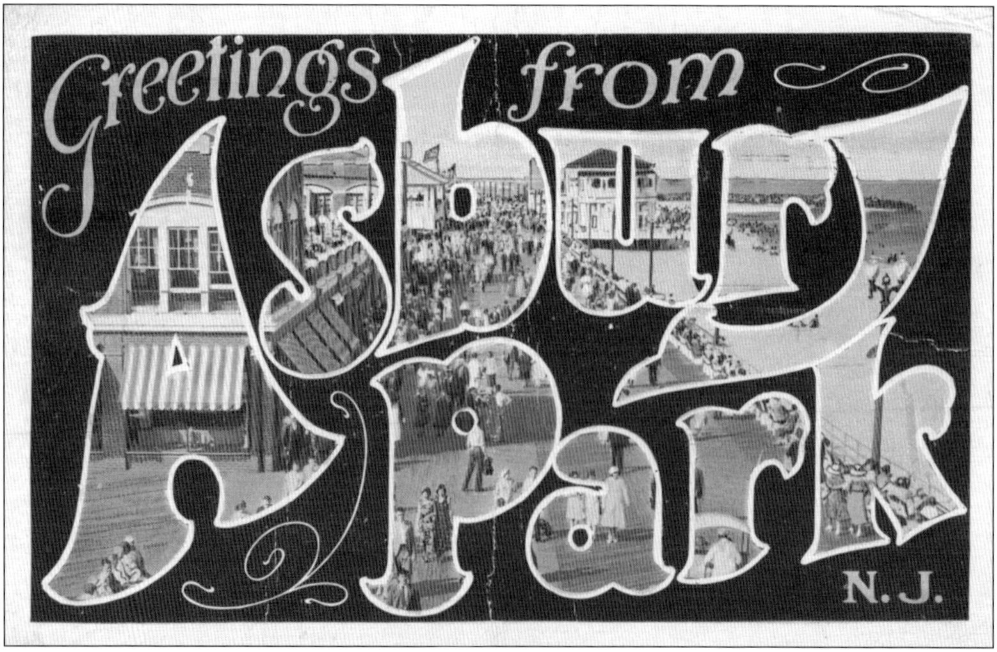


Large letter postcards like this one, which contained images of the locations people visited within the name of the place, were popular from the 1930s onward. This postcard, sent in June 1937, features the boardwalk, looking north from the convention hall. The Sunset Avenue pavilion is on the left, and the Seventh Avenue pavilion is to the right.

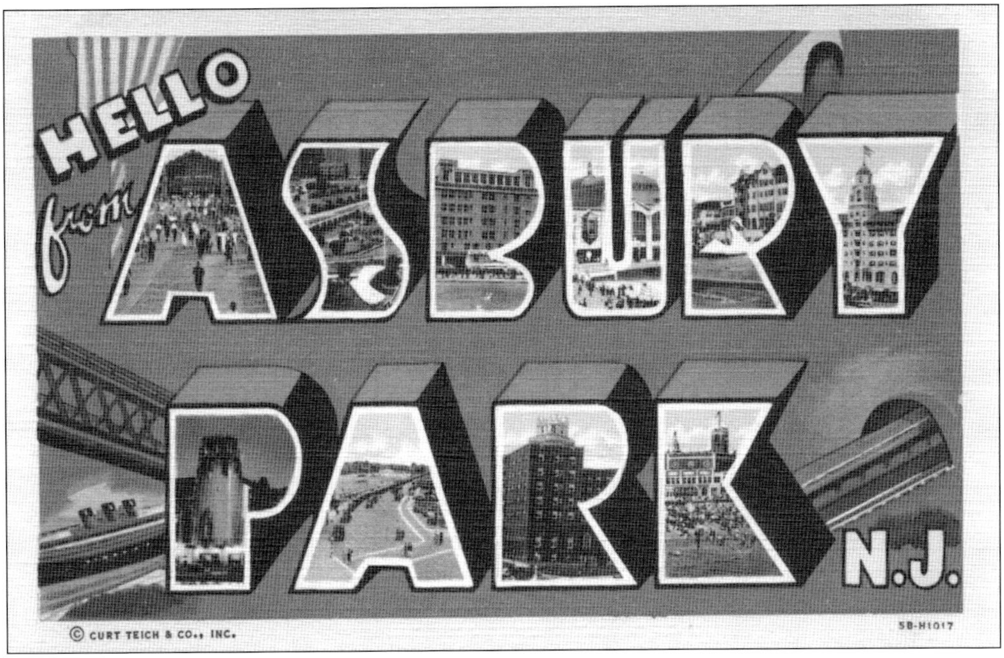


The locations shown in this postcard, which dates to 1945, include the new Casino, the Hotel Kingsley Arms, Ocean Grove's North End Hotel, the Monterey hotel, the Mayfair Theater by night, Lake Avenue, the Berkeley-Carteret hotel, and the convention hall.

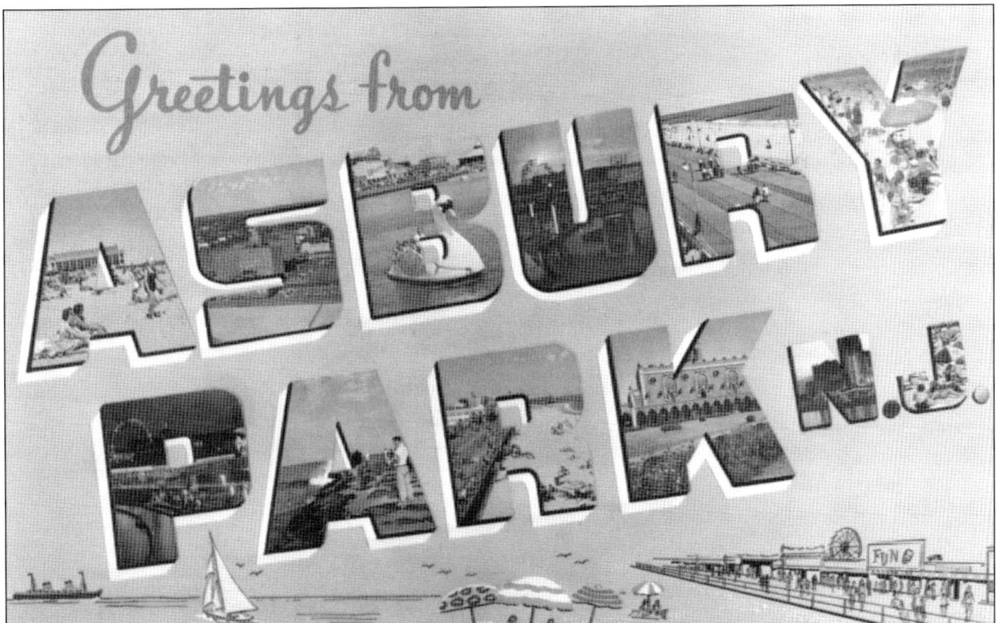


Locations shown in this card are, from left to right at the top, the convention hall, the Berkeley-Carteret hotel, swan boats on Wesley Lake, sunset over Wesley Lake, the boardwalk, and the beach; at the bottom are Palace Amusements at night, the fishing jetty, the boardwalk, the Paramount Theater, the Mayfair Theater, and the beach.

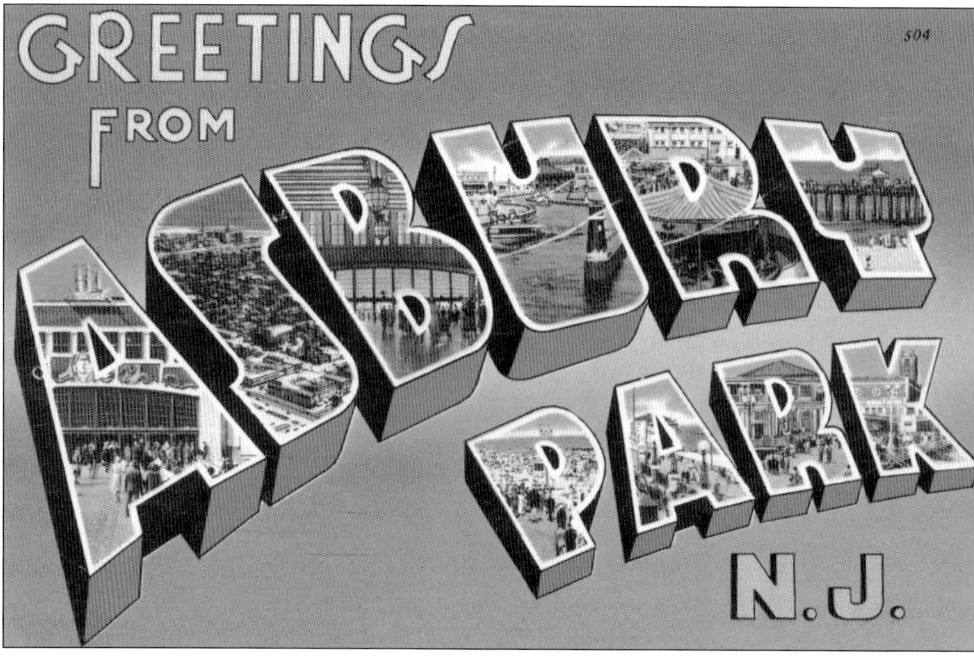


This postcard was mailed in 1962, eleven years before it would grace the cover of Bruce Springsteen's debut album *Greetings from Asbury Park* and become the most iconic image associated with the town. The locations shown here include the convention hall, Wesley Lake, the boardwalk, the beach, and the Seventh Avenue pavilion.

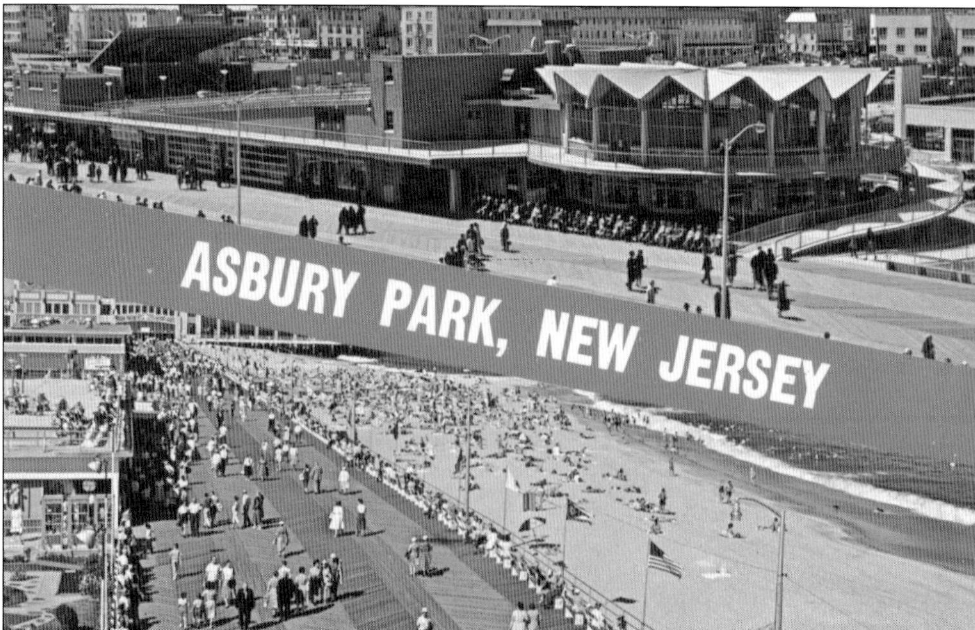


By the 1960s, split views like this one had become more common than large letter greetings. At the top, to the left, is the newly constructed Fifth Avenue pavilion topped by the Arthur Pryor band shell, which had seating for 1,400. Howard Johnson's is to the right. On the bottom is the boardwalk and beach looking north towards the convention hall.

# *Two*

# Around Town

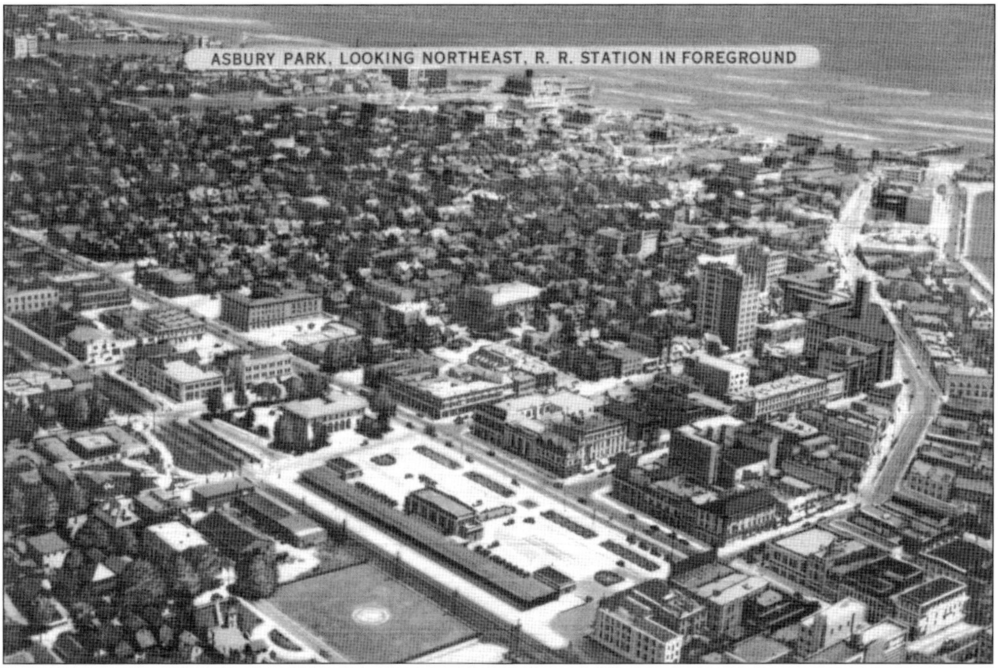


Before New Jersey's highways made it easy for day-trippers to come to town by car, visitors would arrive most often by train. Hotels like the Metropolitan offered transportation that would meet visitors as they arrived. This aerial view, postmarked 1938, shows just how convenient Asbury Park's train station (in the foreground) is to the beach, which is just over a mile away.

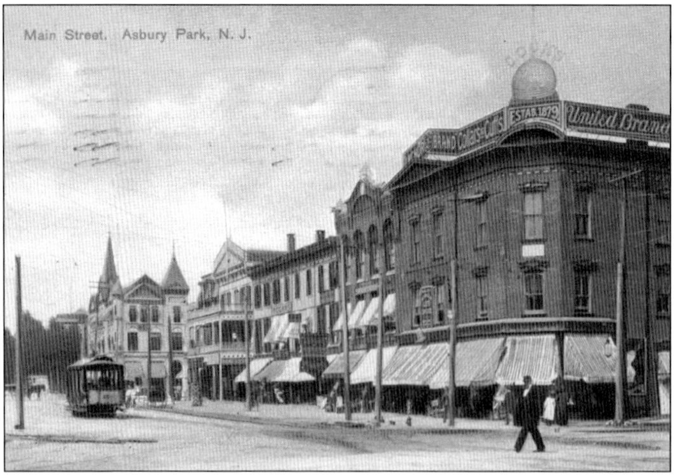


In addition to the beachfront, Asbury Park's downtown was a major draw for the better part of the 20th century. Called the "commercial center of the North Jersey coast" by the chamber of commerce, there were hundreds of stores in town by the early 1900s. This postcard, mailed in September 1911, shows some of the stores heading north along Main Street. On the right was Cook's Beehive, a three-story department store.

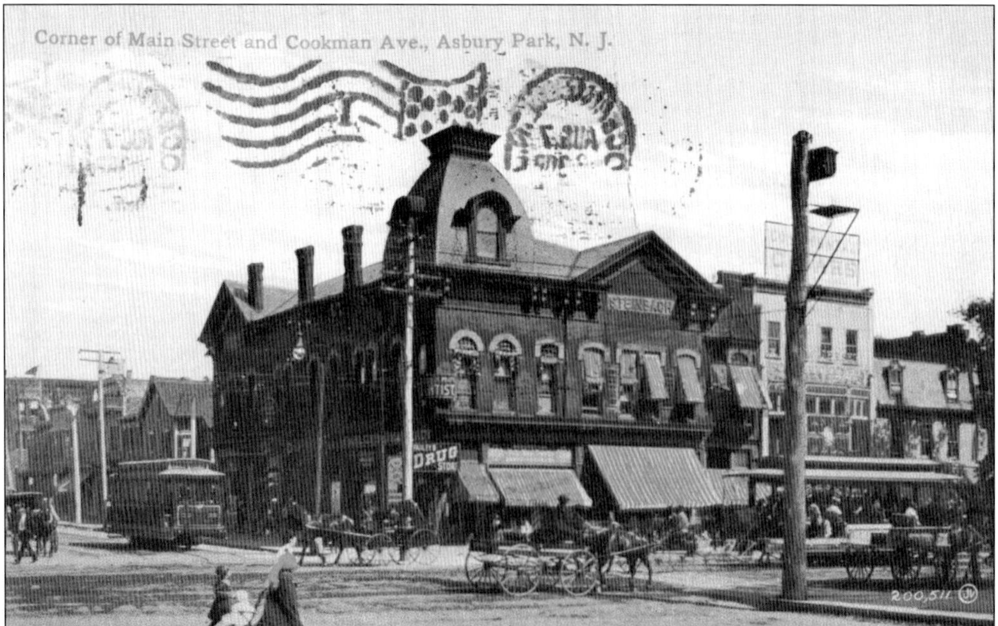


This brick building housed Henry Steinbach's Ocean Palace, a department store that sold dry goods, shoes, clothing, and housewares. Located on the corner of Main Street and Cookman Avenue opposite the train station, Steinbach's Ocean Palace was directly opposite Cook's Beehive. In December 1893, an advertisement for the store in the *Ocean Grove Times* offered a gift of silverware with every $10 to $35 worth of goods purchased.

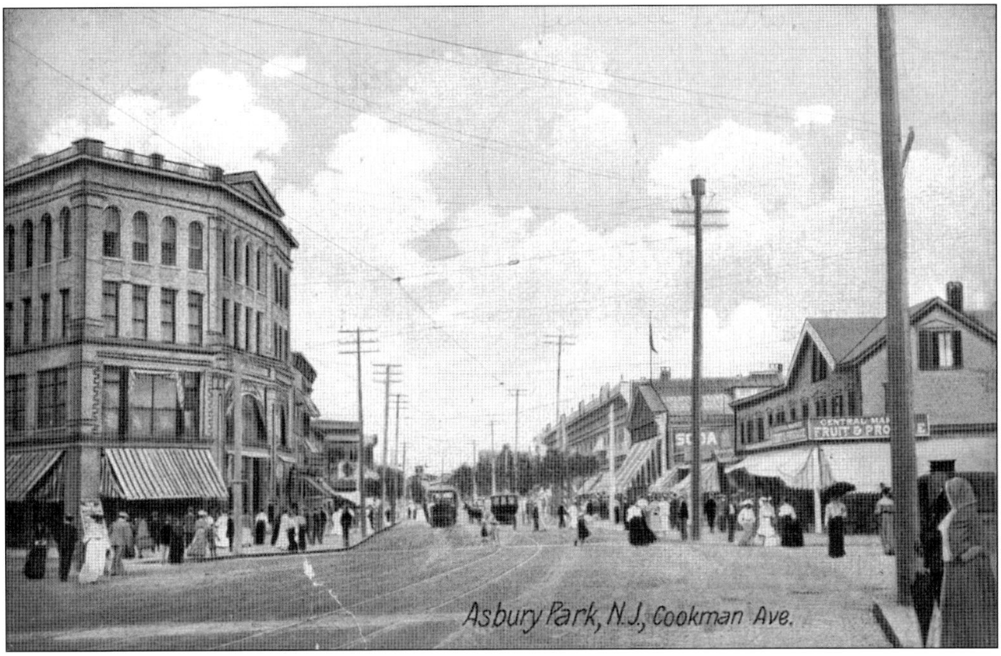


Heading east from Main Street on Cookman Avenue was the Steinbach department store (left), which was owned by Henry's brothers John and Jacob. The fruit and produce market across the street (right) would be replaced in the 1920s by the Seacoast Trust Company, and that building would later become Liggett's Drug Store.

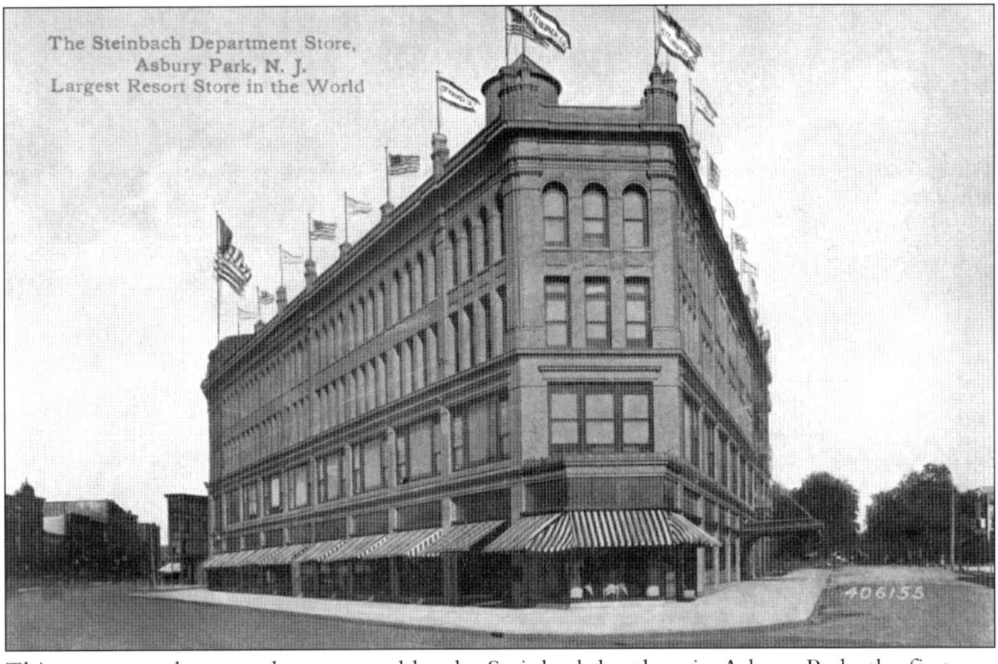


This store was the second one owned by the Steinbach brothers in Asbury Park; the first one had been built in 1876 and was located on Main Street. In 1897, the Steinbachs moved to this store, building "the world's largest resort store" on the site of what had been the Commercial Hotel. By 1912, Steinbachs had been expanded to take up an entire block.

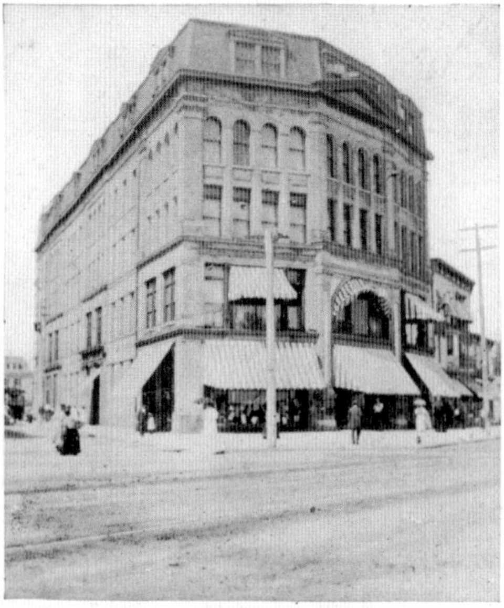

*Steinbach Company's Big Department Store, Asbury Park, N. J.*

This postcard depicts Steinbach's in 1909. After eight decades as Asbury Park's downtown anchor store, Steinbach's closed in 1979, having seen declining business as shopping centers like Monmouth Mall drew patrons elsewhere. In 1989, arson destroyed the building's fifth floor as well as a clock tower that had been added to the building in the 1920s.

Like many large department stores in the mid-20th century, Steinbach's had a restaurant, shown here decorated for Christmas. Lunch was served here daily. Today, the Steinbach building has reopened after $7 million in renovations. The ground floor houses retail and restaurant space, and the top three floors have been converted to apartments.

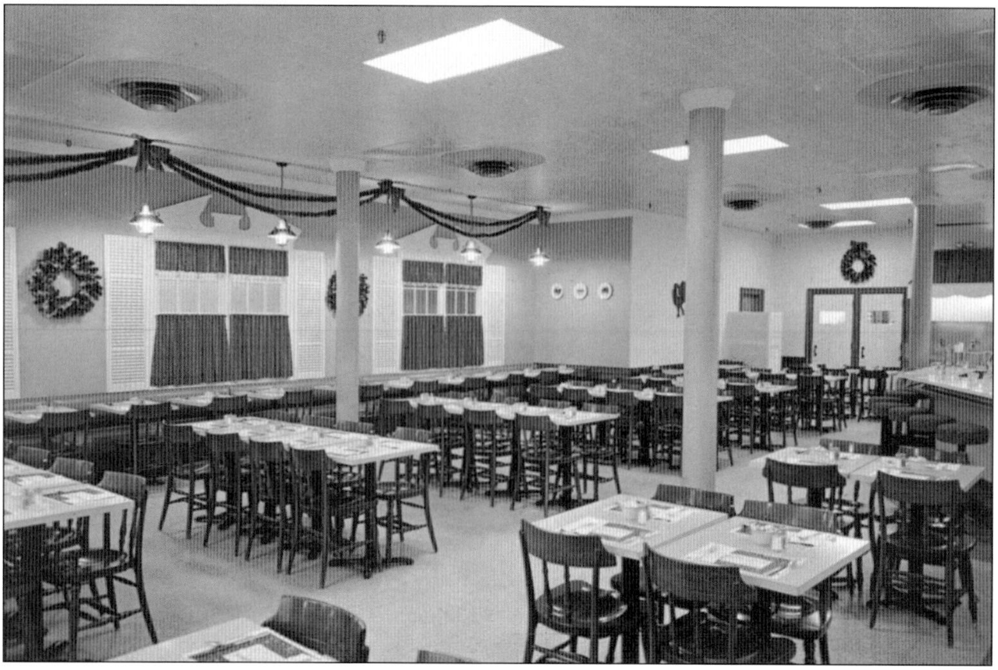

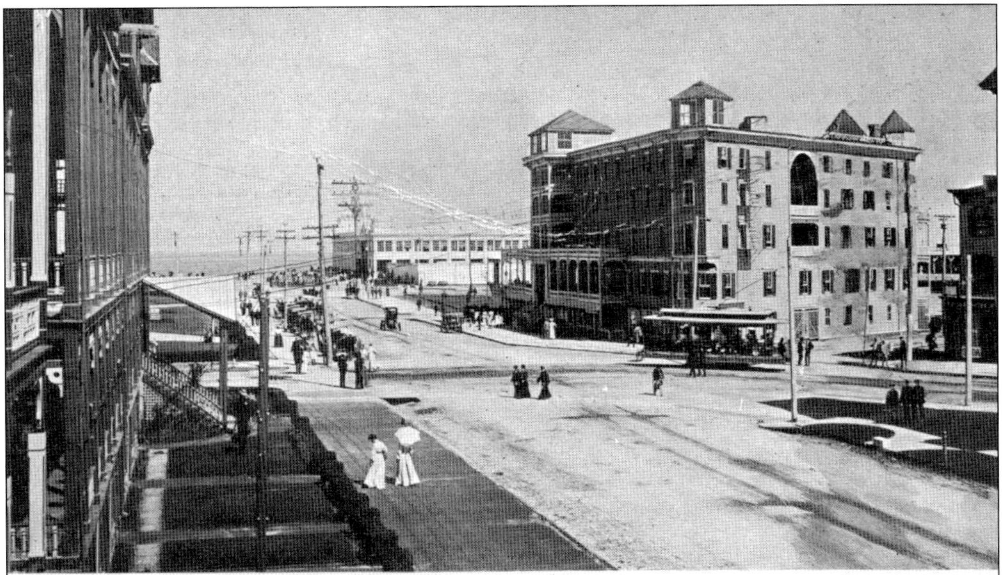

73 — Asbury Avenue—Asbury Park, N. J.

Here, ladies in Edwardian dress walk along Asbury Avenue toward the boardwalk. At center in the distance is the Casino, the West End Hotel is on the left, and on the right is the Plaza Hotel. In front of the Plaza Hotel is Asbury Park's trolley, which was part of the first electric trolley system in New Jersey.

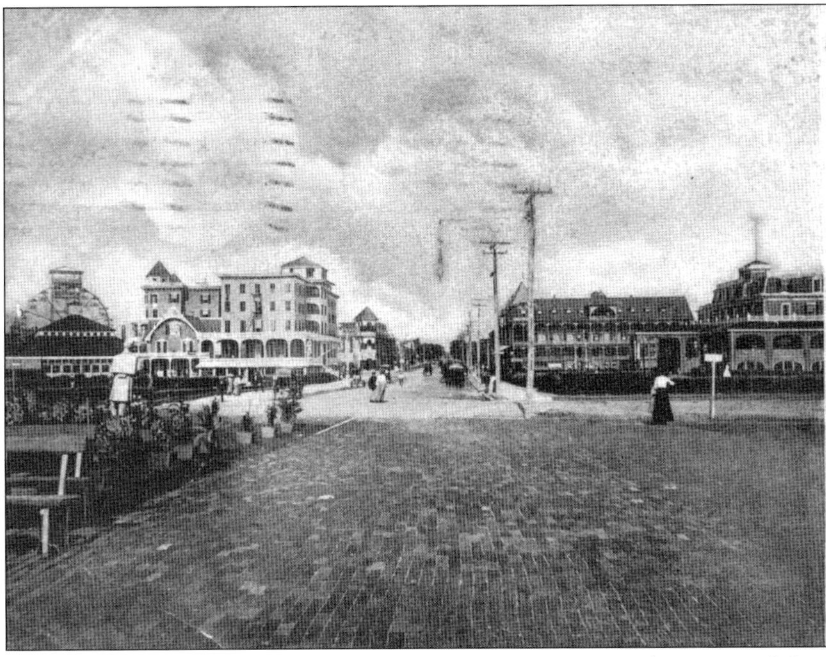

3453— At the foot of Asbury Ave., Asbury Park, N. J.

SOUVENIR POST CARD CO., NEW YORK

Looking in the direction opposite from the previous postcard, one sees Asbury Avenue facing west as it appeared in 1905. On the left is the Plaza Hotel and Palace Amusements. On the right side of the street is the Coleman House hotel and the West End Hotel. Asbury Park had 60 miles of paved sidewalk around this time, some of which is visible here.

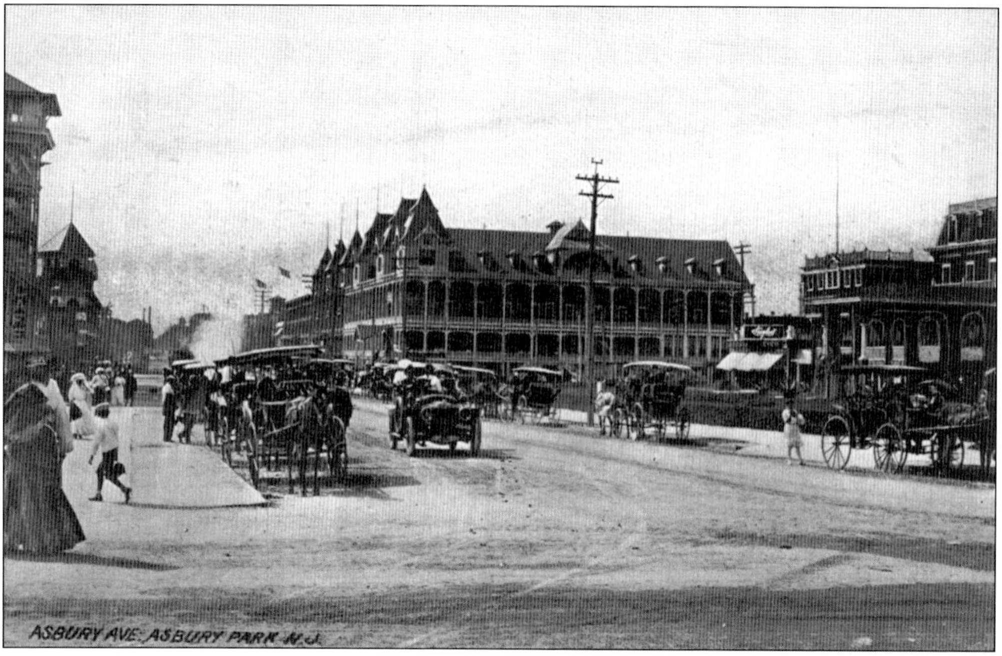


In 1909, when this card was mailed, horse-drawn carriages were still a common sight on Asbury Avenue. At center is the West End Hotel, and to the right is the Coleman House hotel.

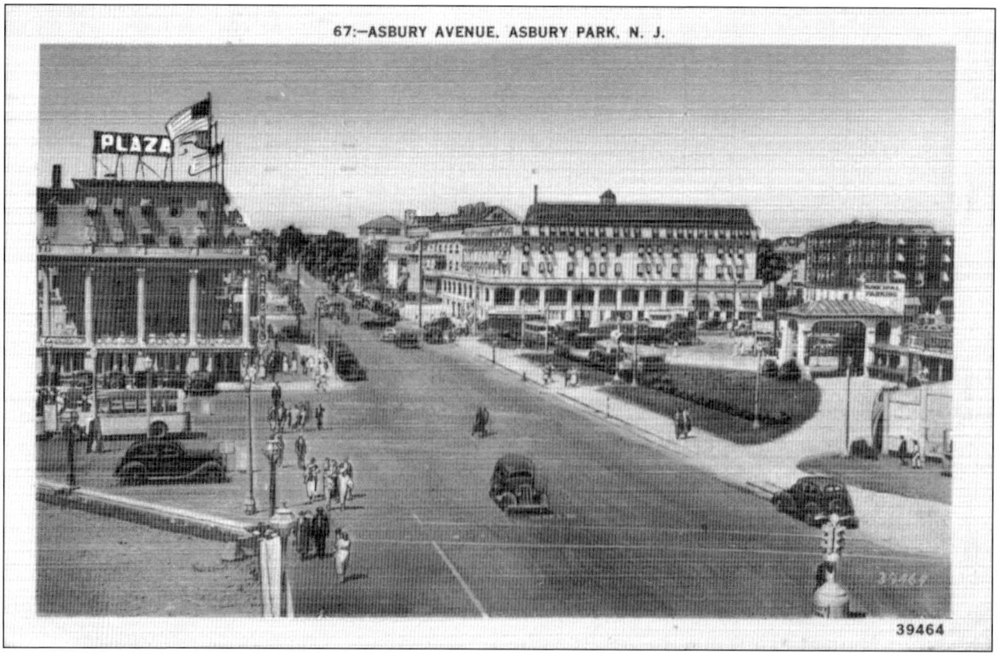


This is Asbury Avenue looking west around 1950. Motorist travel to Asbury Park had increased, and traffic signals (bottom right) now controlled the flow of traffic. The Plaza Hotel is to the left, and at center sits a renovated West End Hotel.

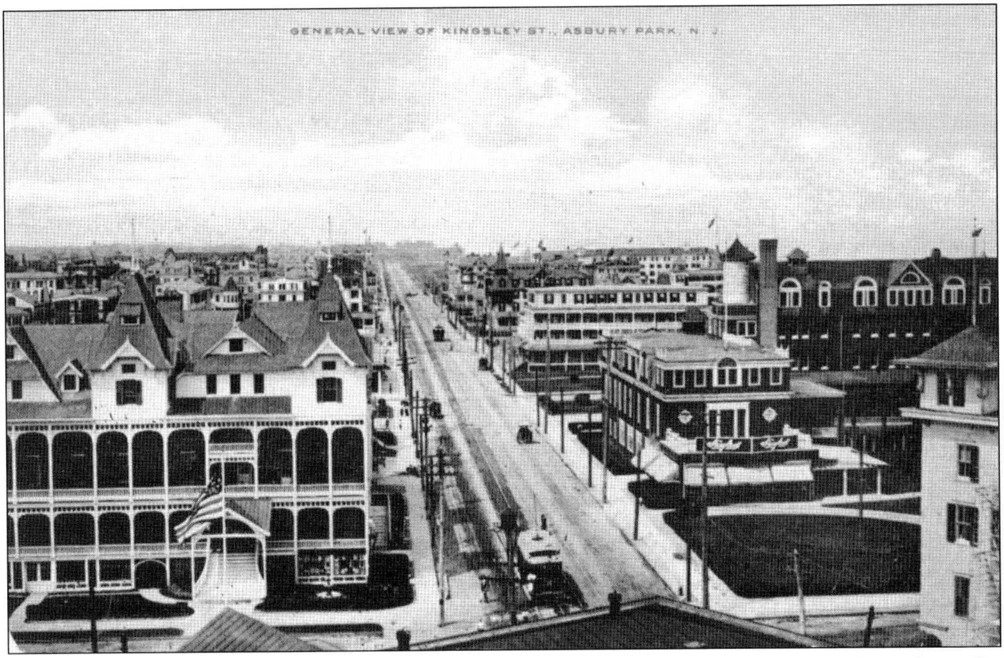


Kingsley Street is the second street inland running parallel to the boardwalk. This is how the intersection of Kingsley Street and Asbury Avenue facing north looked in 1909. The large white hotel on the left is the West End Hotel, and the Coleman Housel hotel is on the right.

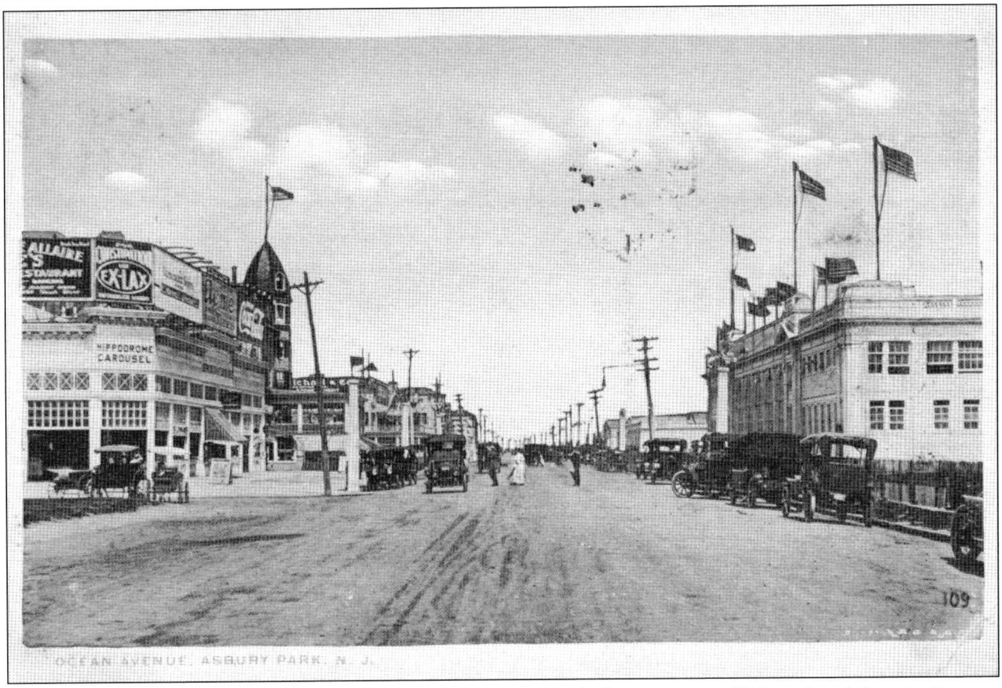


Ocean Avenue is the closest thoroughfare in Asbury Park that runs parallel to the Atlantic Ocean. On the right side are buildings along the boardwalk. The white building to the immediate right is the indoor swimming pool known as the Natatorium. The building on the left, which housed a carousel, was topped by billboard advertisements for Ex-Lax and Coca-Cola.

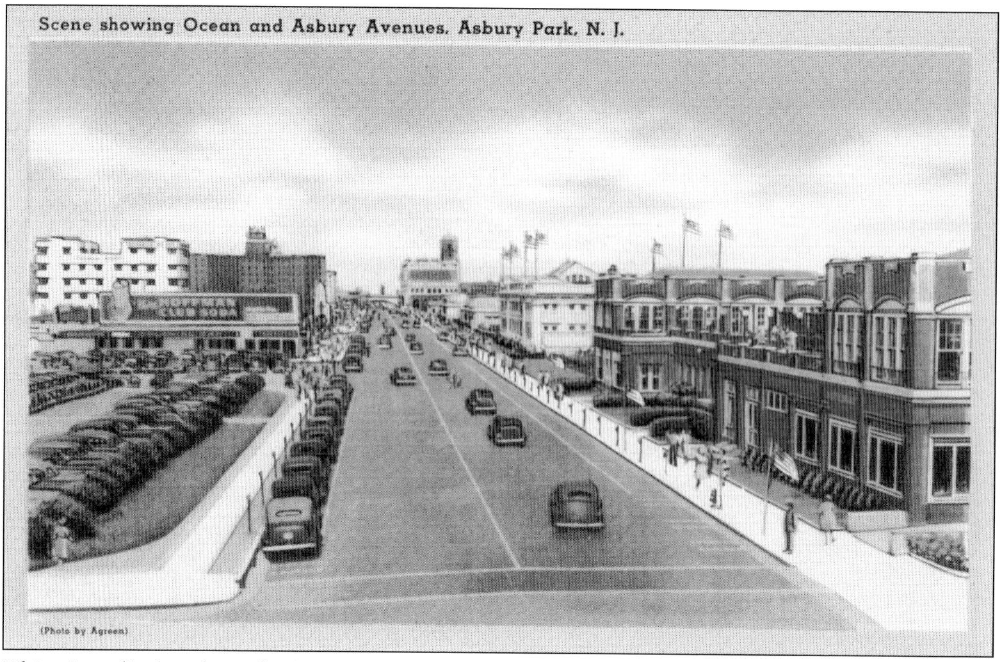


This view displays how the intersection of Ocean Avenue and Asbury Avenue appeared facing north around 1949. The boardwalk is out of view to the right. The convention hall, Berkeley-Carteret hotel, and Albion hotel can be seen in the distance.

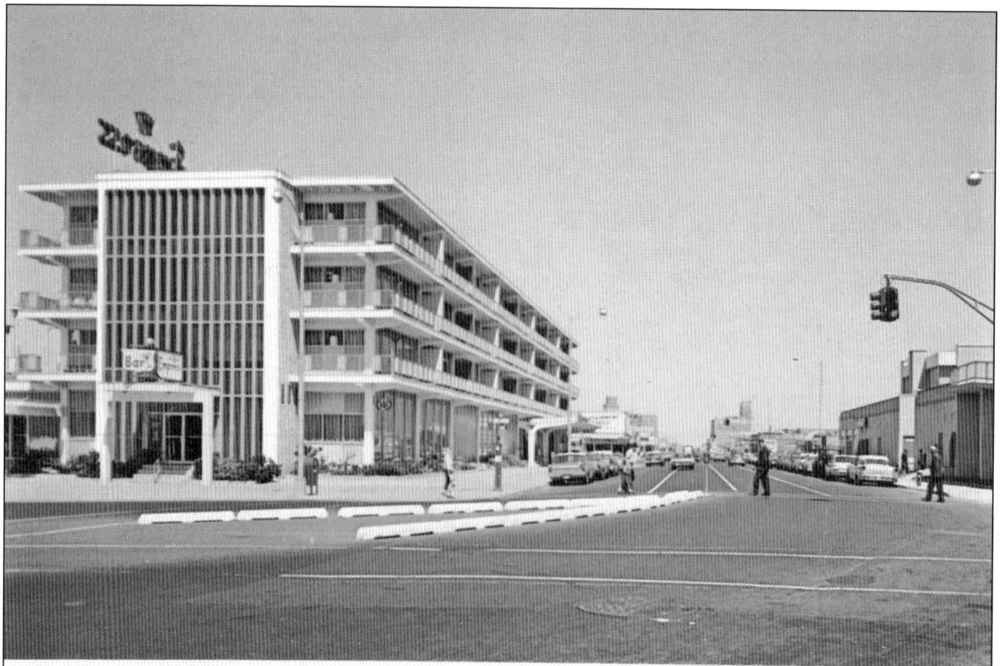


Ocean Ave. is the main thoroughfare along the beachfront

This is how the intersection of Ocean and Asbury Avenues looked in 1967. On the left, the Empress Motel has been built on the lot that previously housed the Coleman House hotel.

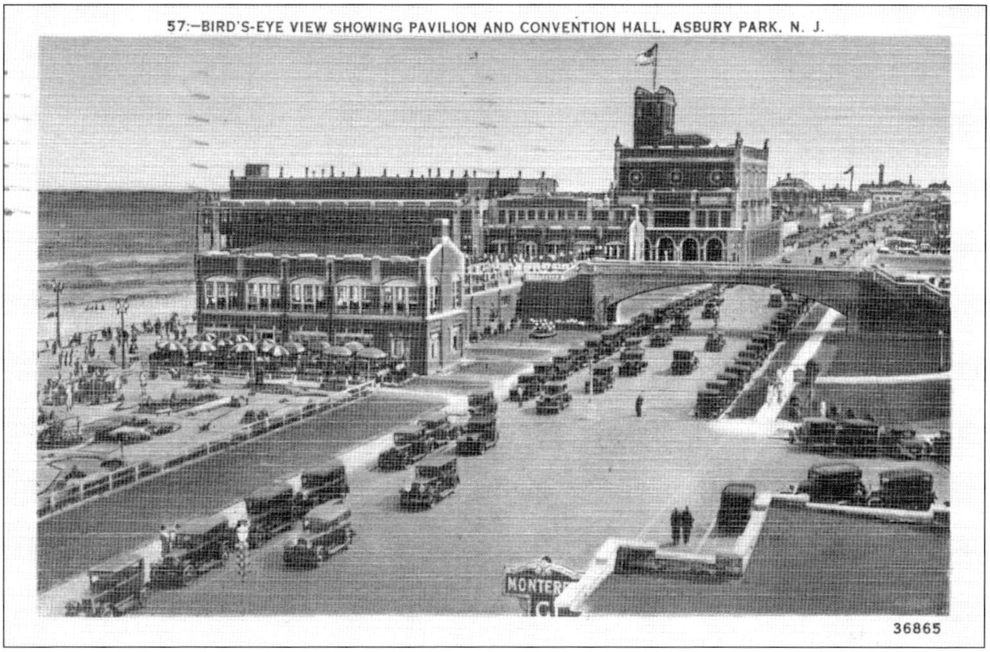


Looking south along Ocean Avenue in the opposite direction of the previous two images, one can see the footbridge that connects the Berkeley-Carteret hotel (right, out of view) to the Sunset Avenue pavilion. Beyond the pavilion is the convention hall and Paramount Theater. The Casino can be seen in the far distance.

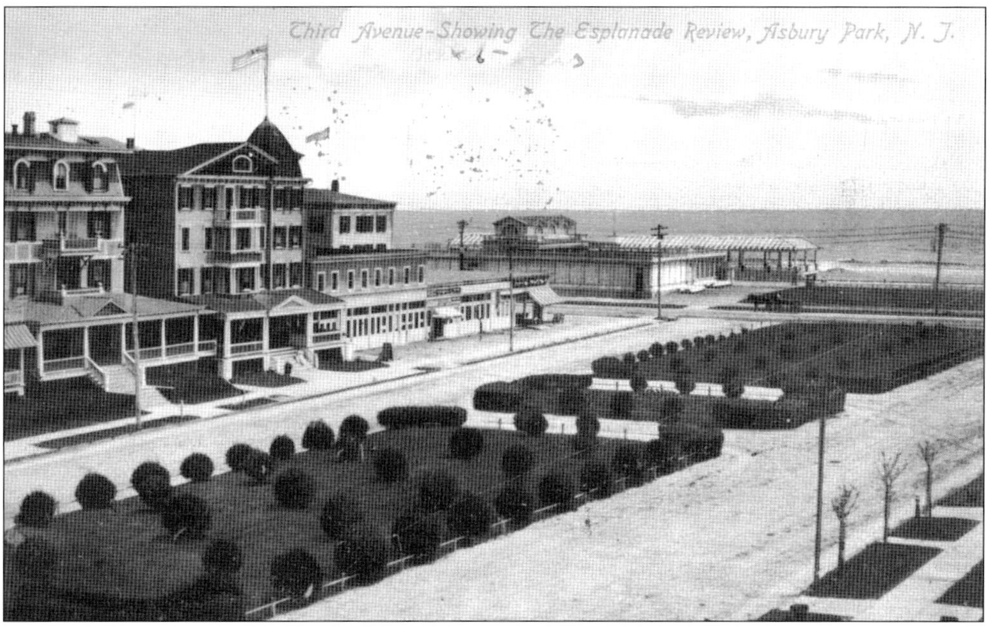


In this 1911 view of Third Avenue, the wide avenues that Founder Bradley incorporated into his plans for the city are evident. Asbury Park's streets flare out to 200 feet wide at the waterfront, which provides an expansive ocean view as one approaches the beach and allows the breeze from the Atlantic to carry as far inland as possible. Landscaped medians add to the park-like atmosphere of the beachfront.

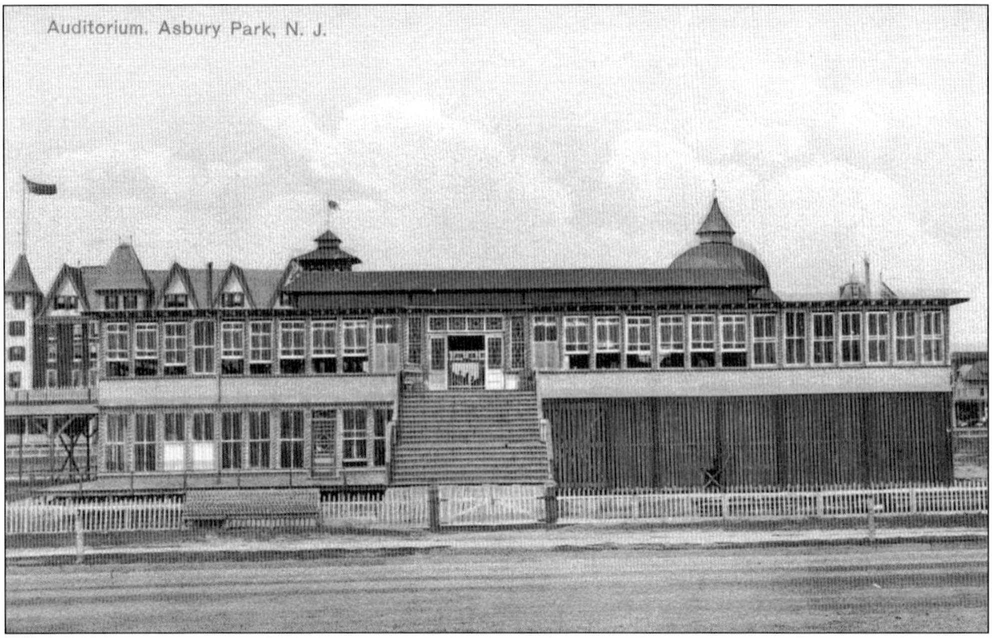


Asbury Park's 2,500-seat auditorium was located at Sunset and Ocean Avenues, on what would later be the site of the Berkeley-Carteret hotel. The auditorium was used for religious services on Sundays, but it also hosted secular diversions; musicians, jugglers, minstrel shows, and mock trials were presented to entertain visitors here.

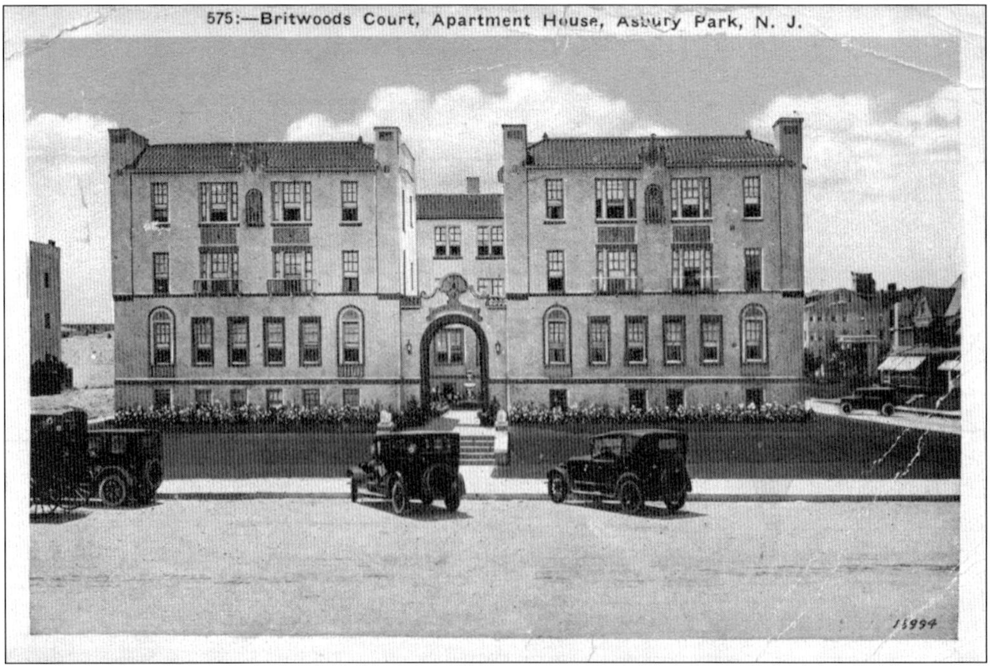


The Spanish Revival–style Britwoods Court apartment building, located two blocks from the beach on Second Avenue, was built in 1928. After sitting vacant and boarded up for years alongside the neighboring Jersey Court Apartments, it became one of the preservation successes in Asbury Park. In 2003, it was renovated into 30 condominiums.

*Three*

# Wesley Lake, Palace Amusements, and the Mayfair Theater

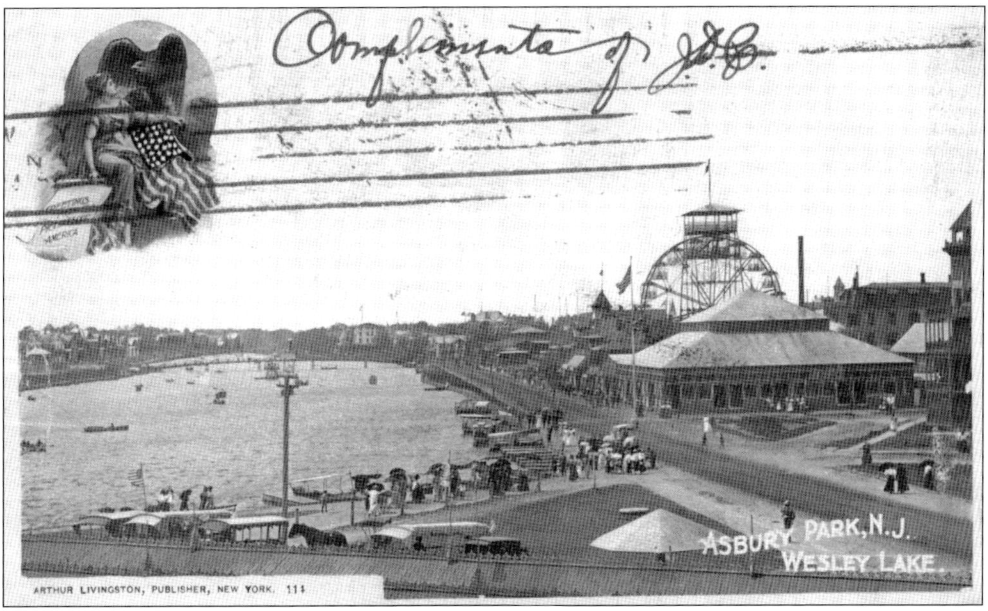


Two lakes mark the northern and southern boundaries of Asbury Park's waterfront. Deal Lake to the north separates Asbury Park from the village of Loch Arbour. Wesley Lake, shown here around 1899, is at the southernmost end of the boardwalk, where Asbury Park meets the adjacent town of Ocean Grove.

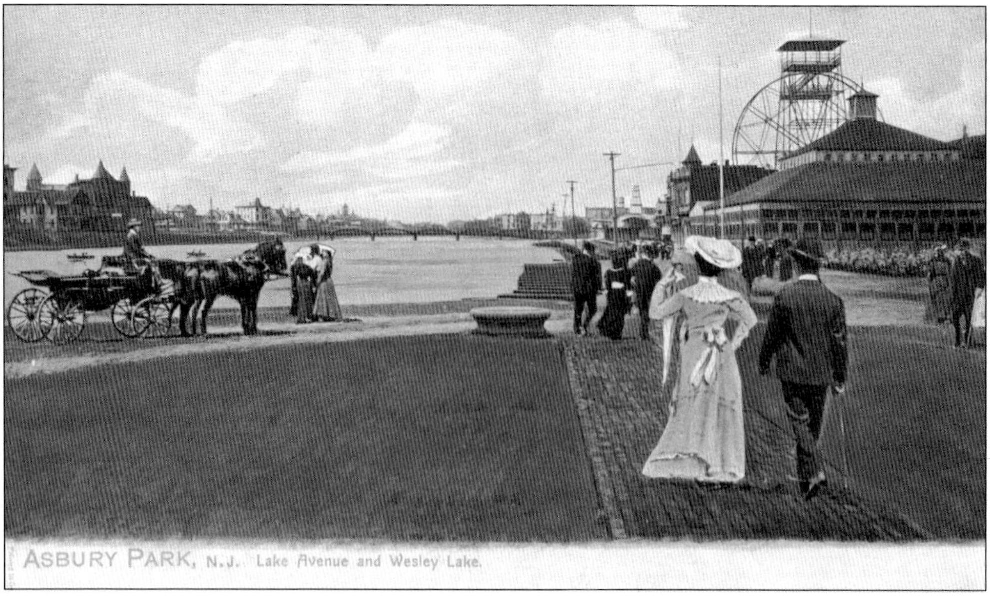


The building opposite Wesley Lake (right) was referred to on early maps as the Kingsley Street Merry-Go-Round. German immigrant Ernest Schnitzler constructed this building, which would shortly be called the Palace Merry-Go-Round, and later Palace Amusements, in 1888. Its main attraction was initially a carousel with wooden horses that were hand-carved by prolific carousel builder Charles I.D. Looff.

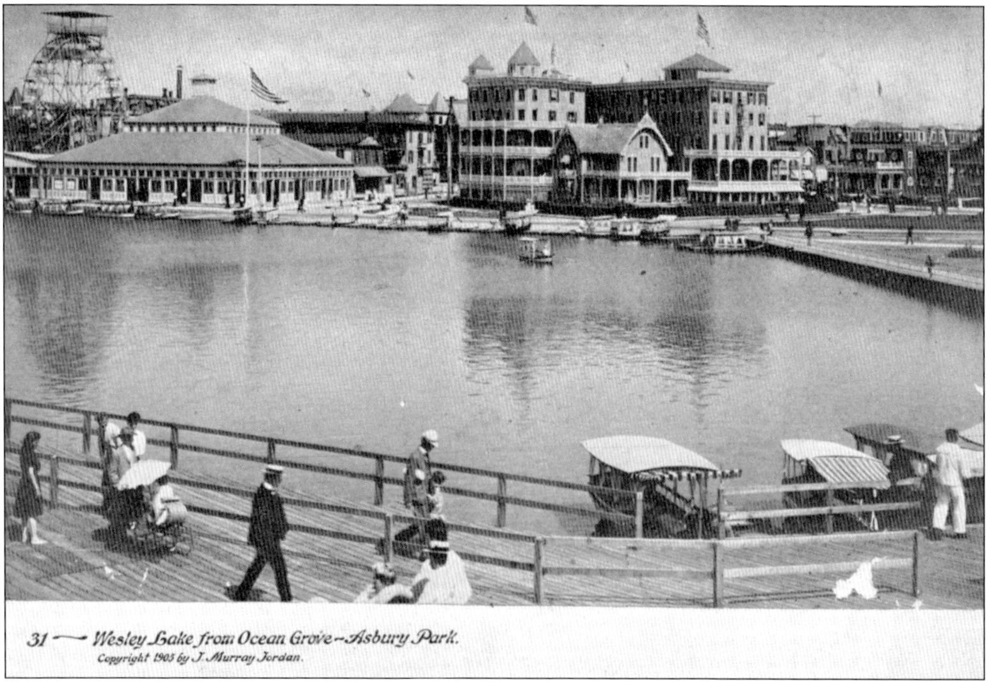


In 1895, Schnitzler added a Ferris wheel to Palace Amusements (left) at a cost of $16,000. People boarded one of the 20 cars inside the building, and were carried outside through an opening in the roof. Once outside, riders could disembark and climb a short set of stairs that led to a platform that presented a view of the Atlantic Ocean.

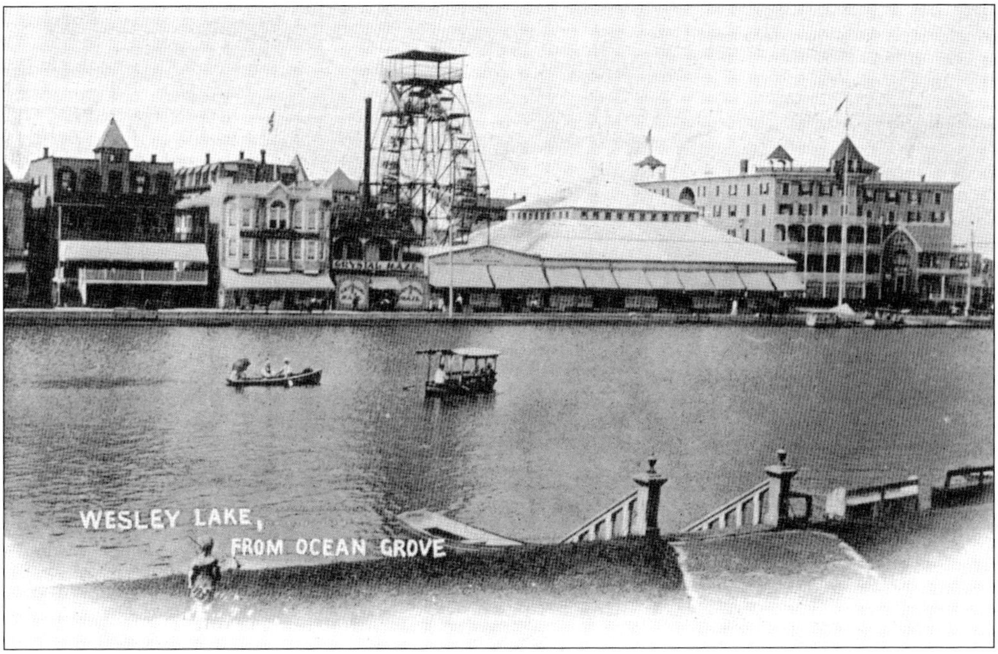


In 1903, Palace Amusements expanded again. The two-story addition (to the left of the Ferris wheel) included an attraction called the Crystal Maze on the ground floor, billed as the first hall of mirrors in New Jersey. The second story was a home for the Schnitzler family and had an entrance parlor, library, living room, dining room, kitchen, and pantry.

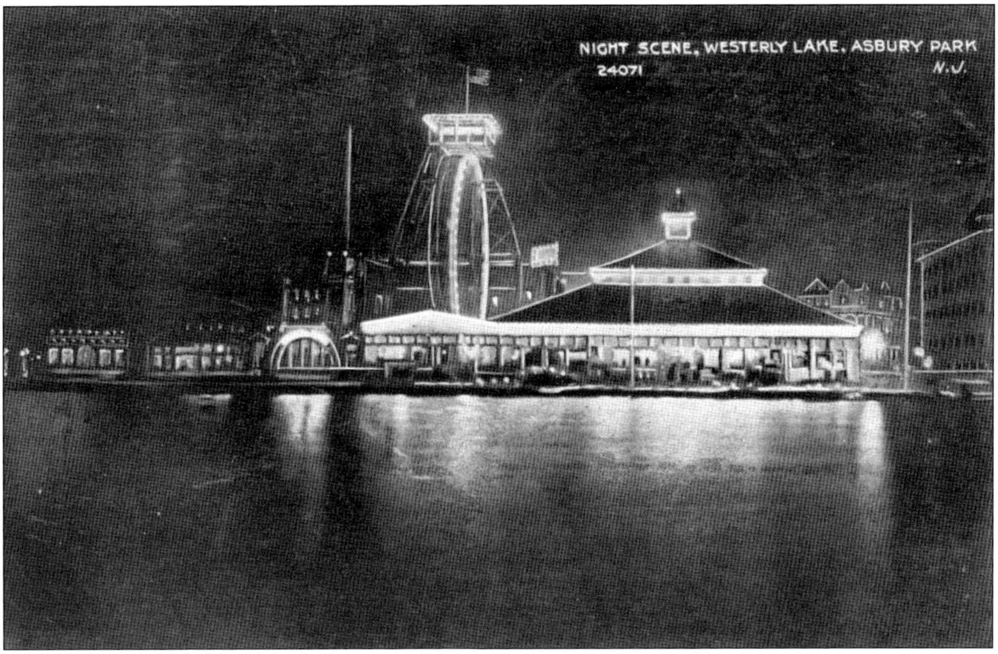


Originally, Palace Amusements' carousel ran on steam heat provided by a boiler located in the building. Before long, Ernest Schnitzler built an electric plant to power his business, making him the first private citizen in New Jersey to do so. By night, Schnitzler's two "dynamos" illuminated hundreds of incandescent lights in a rainbow of colors, as seen in this 1909 view.

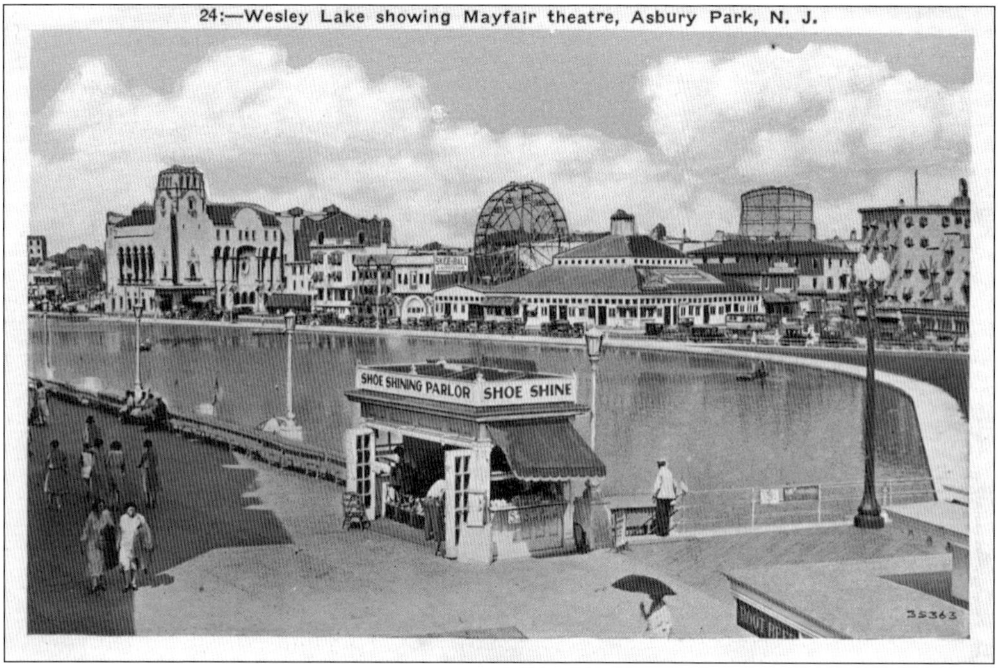


In the 1920s, when Palace Amusements was owned by August M. Williams, the viewing platform atop the Ferris wheel (at center) was removed and the number of cars reduced from 20 to 18. When the Palace's Ferris wheel stopped operating in the 1980s, it was the oldest continually operating one in the world.

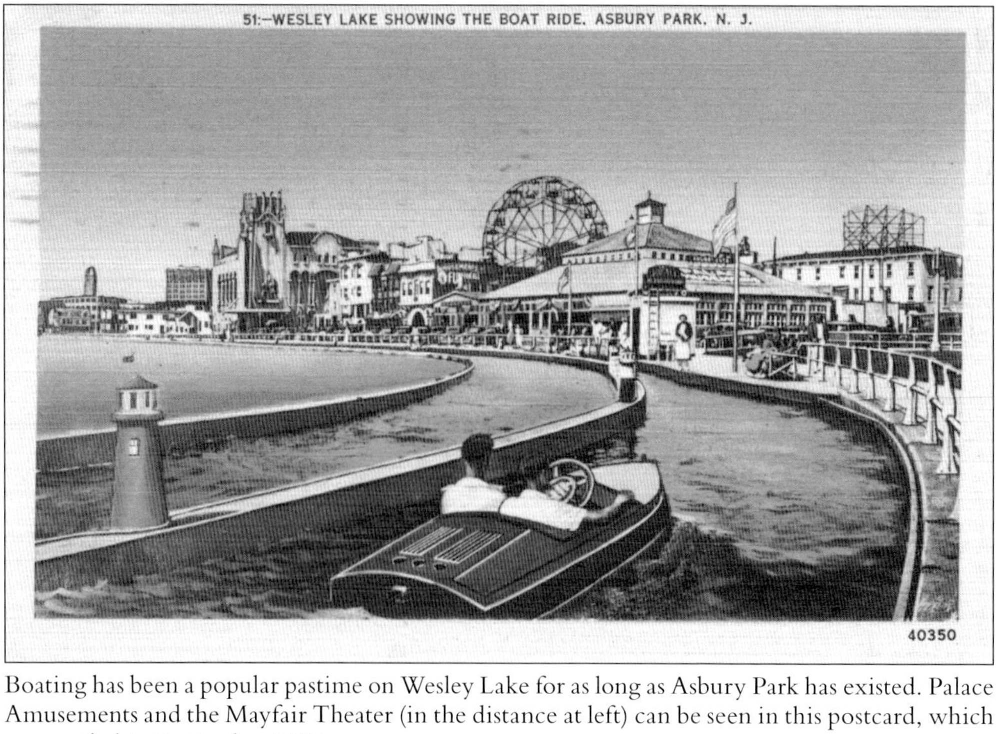


Boating has been a popular pastime on Wesley Lake for as long as Asbury Park has existed. Palace Amusements and the Mayfair Theater (in the distance at left) can be seen in this postcard, which was mailed in September 1939.

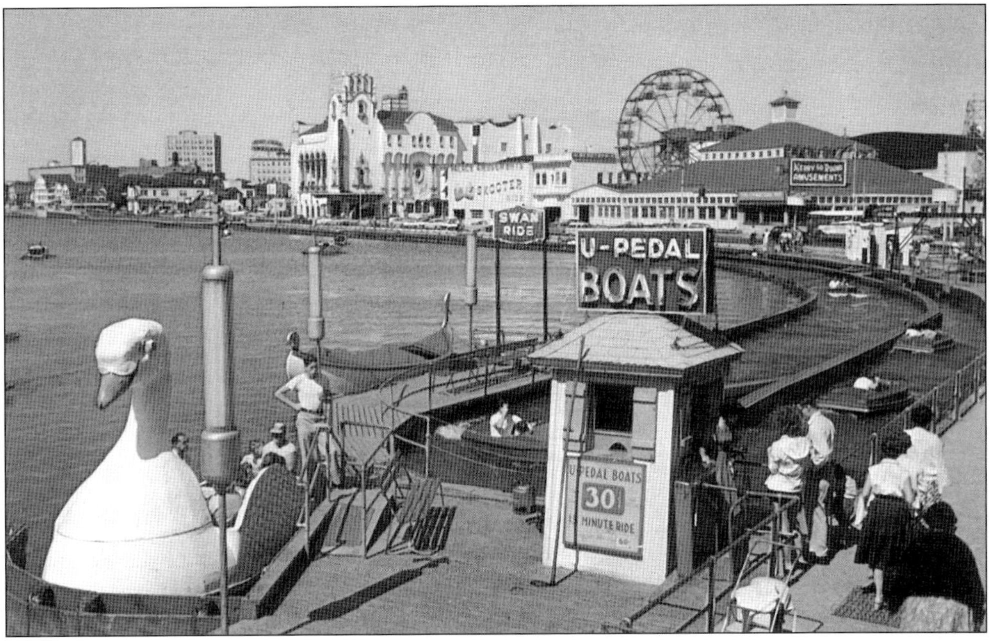


In 1956, Palace Amusements was owned by Edward Lange and Zimel Resnick, who expanded the building a final time. Along Lake Avenue, the Ocean Spray Hotel was demolished to make way for the bumper-cars area, seen to the left of the Ferris wheel. On the opposite side of the original carousel house (to the right, out of view), the section that housed the funhouse was added. Graphic designer Leslie "Worth" Thomas painted all of the images that were added at the time of the 1956 expansion, including the girls in bumper cars and lettering seen here.

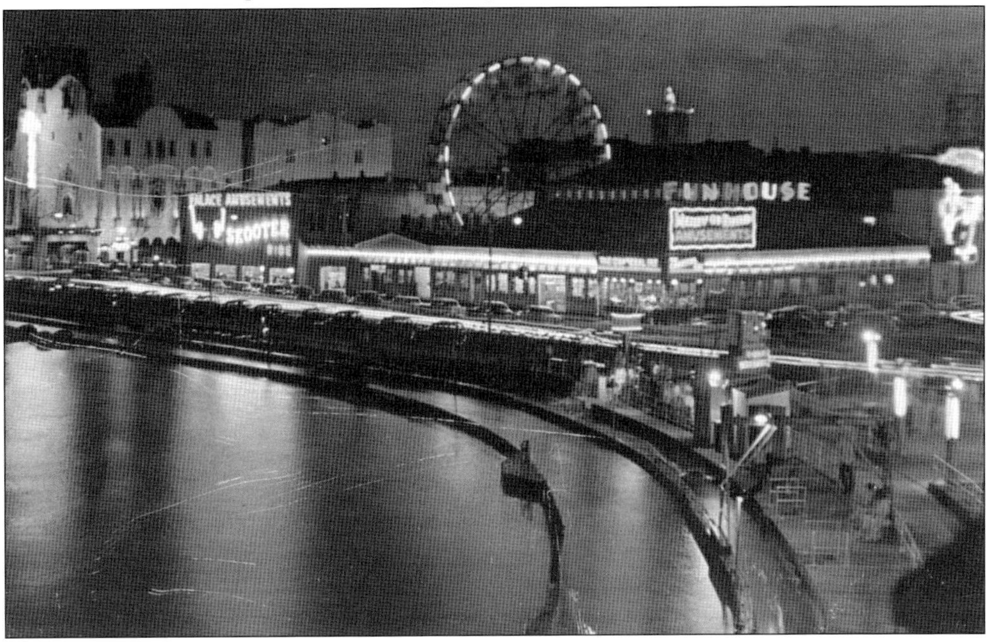


Neon lights are reflected in the water of Wesley Lake in this 1957 view. Palace Amusements' Charcoal Pit snack stand, which sold hamburgers, hot dogs, french fries, pizza, and popcorn, can be seen on the right at the corner of Lake Avenue and Kingsley Street.

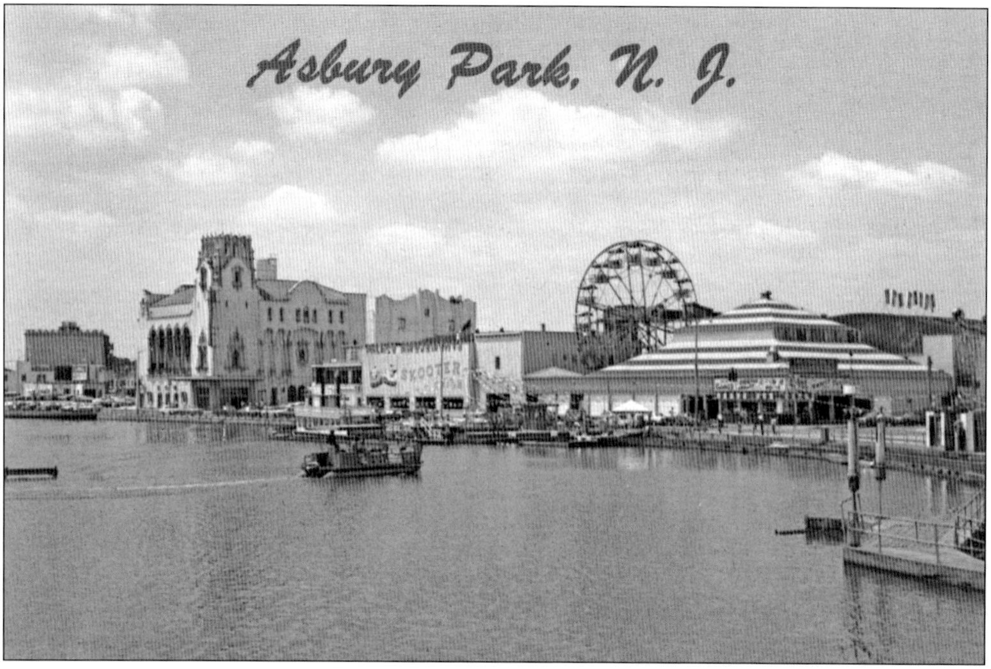


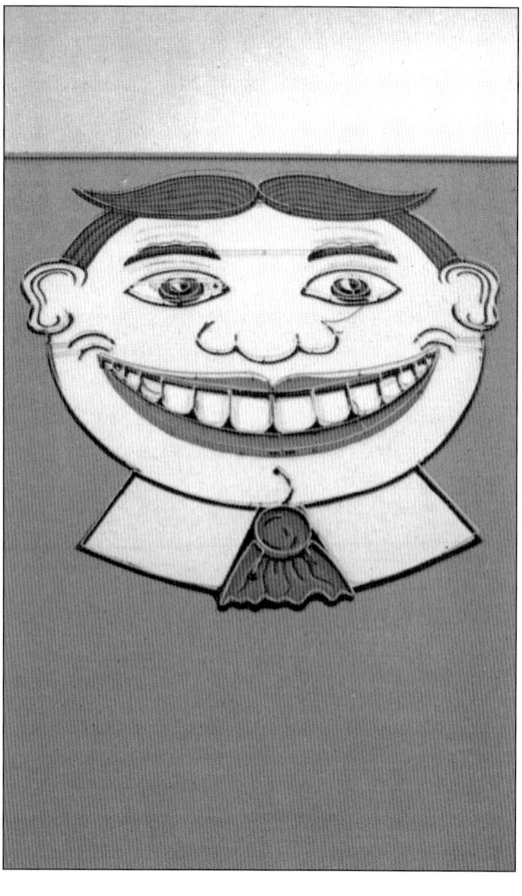

In later years, the roof of Palace Amusements' carousel house was painted in red and white stripes. Palace Amusements closed on November 27, 1988, and in the years following, no effort was made to maintain the site. In 2000, owing in large part to the still-standing square Victorian pavilion portion of the building, Palace Amusements was listed in the National Register of Historic Places. Despite this, in June 2004, the Palace was demolished. The land where it stood is now a parking lot.

Tillie is the collective name for two nearly identical smiling faces that were painted on the side of Palace Amusements that faced Kingsley Street at the time of the 1956 expansion. Shown here around 1975, Tillie was most likely modeled after the "Steeplechase funny face," a caricature of the brother of George Cornelious Tilyou, the founder of Steeplechase Park.

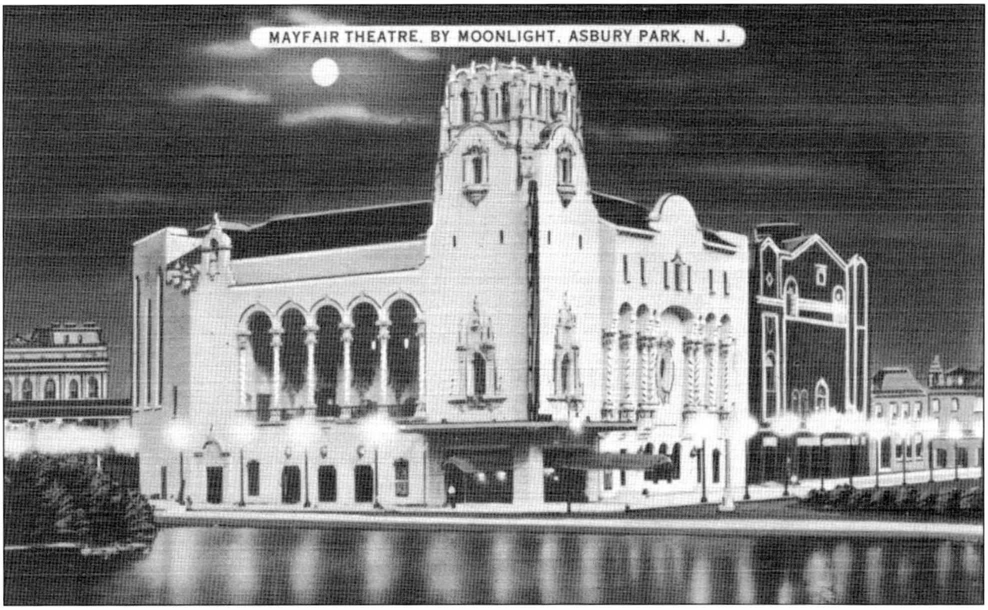


The 2,000-seat Mayfair Theatre was cinema magnate Walter Reade's fourth theater in Asbury Park when it opened in 1927. Designed by architect Thomas Lamb, this tan-colored stucco building had an elaborately decorated exterior with hand-carved terra-cotta sculptural embellishments. Inside, the Mayfair had lavish details such as marble stairs, bronze doors, silk tapestries, and wrought-iron light fixtures. The dark-colored building to the right of the Mayfair Theatre is the St. James, another of Walter Reade's theaters.

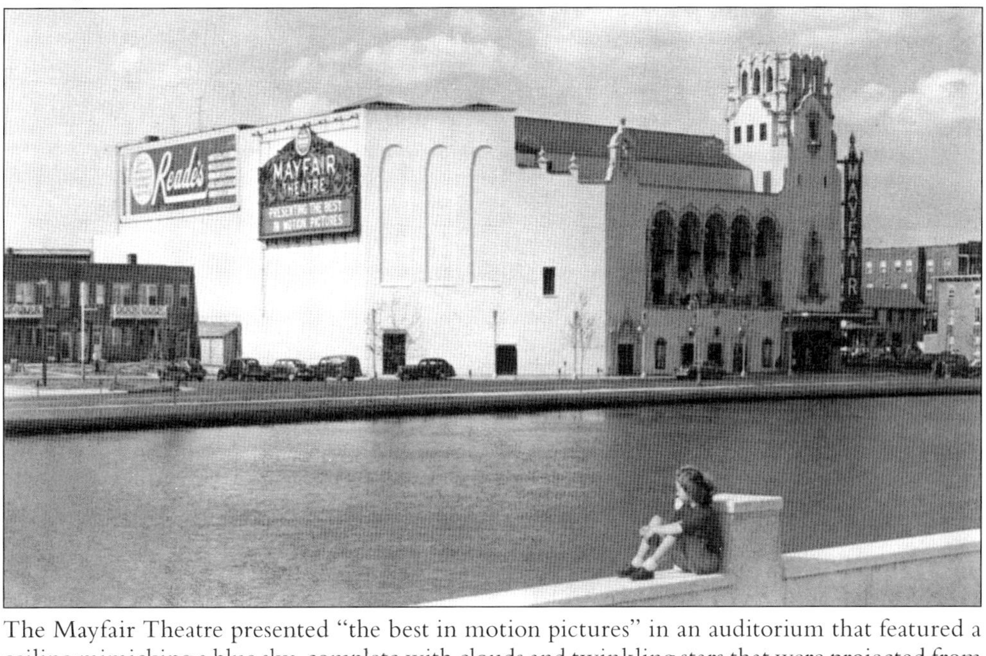


The Mayfair Theatre presented "the best in motion pictures" in an auditorium that featured a ceiling mimicking a blue sky, complete with clouds and twinkling stars that were projected from below. Movie palaces like the Mayfair Theatre fell out of favor in the 1960s, when multiple-screen theaters rose in popularity. The Mayfair and adjacent St. James Theatre fell to the wrecking ball in December 1974, shortly after closing.

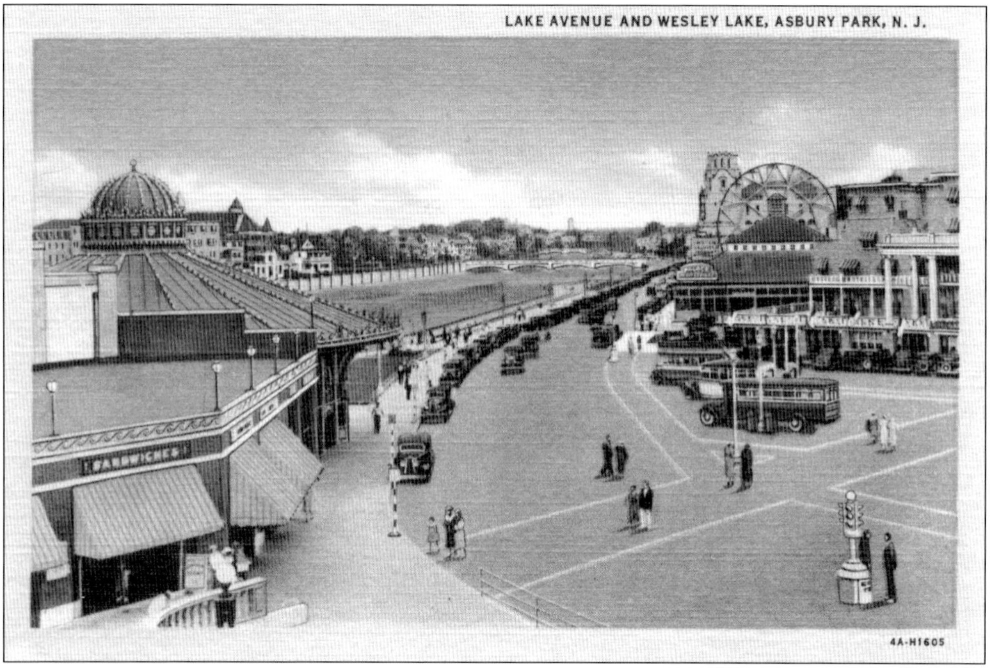


Looking toward Palace Amusements and the Mayfair Theatre along Lake Avenue, the Casino's dome-topped carousel house is to the left, and the Plaza Hotel is to the right. The Heck Street and Emory Street Bridges, which connect Asbury Park to Ocean Grove across Wesley Lake, can be seen in the distance.

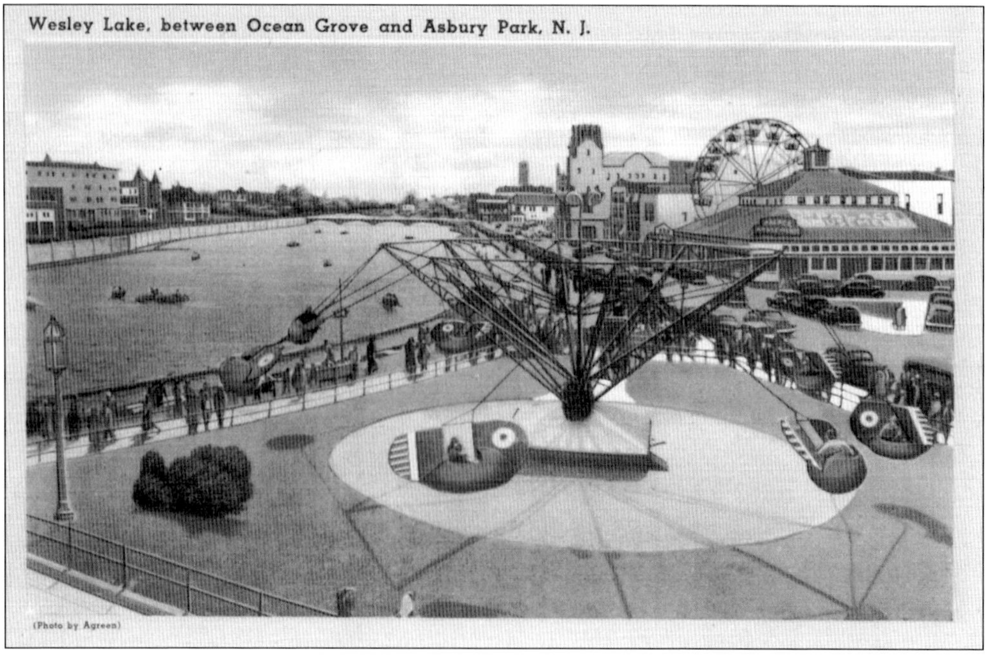


Across Lake Avenue from Palace Amusements, a swing ride occupies the area next to the Casino's carousel house.

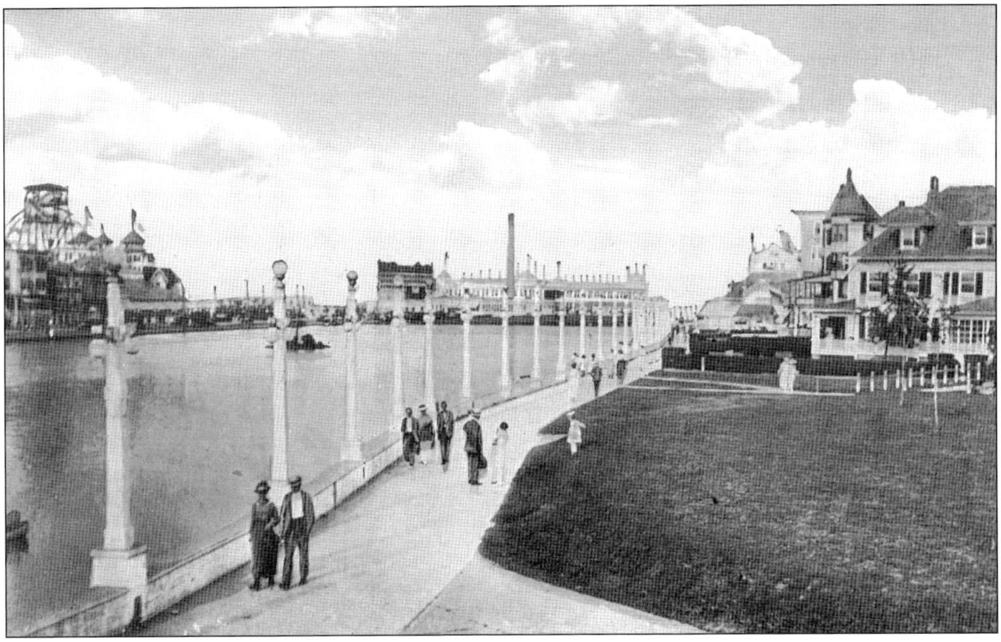

This early 1920s postcard features the view across Wesley Lake toward Asbury Park from Ocean Grove. Palace Amusements is at the far left. At the center in the distance is the original wood-frame Casino, which would be destroyed by fire in 1928.

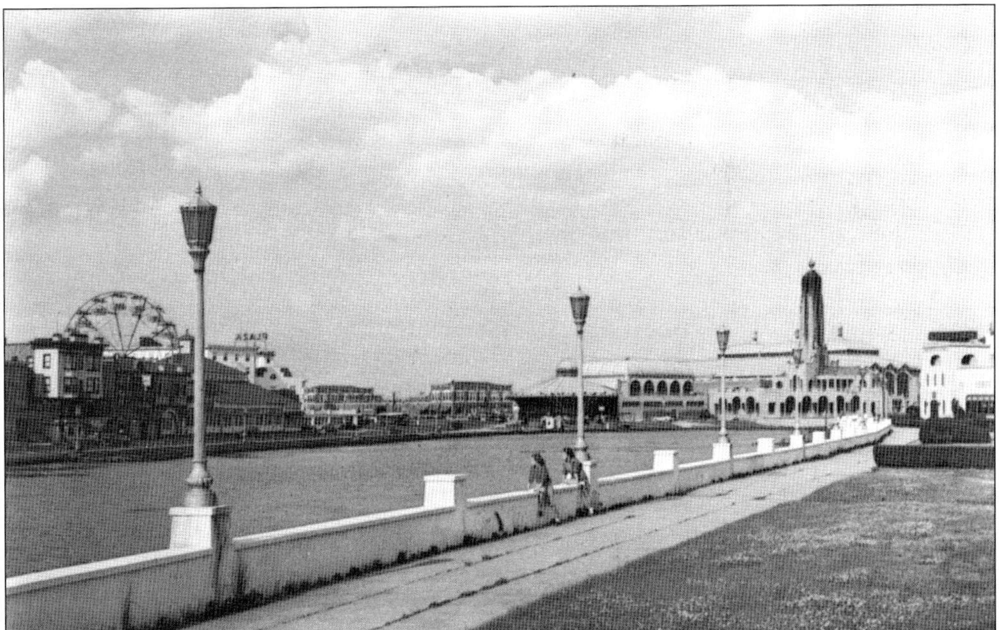


In this later view of the same area as the previous image, the observation tower of Palace Amusements' Ferris wheel (left) has been removed. The original rectangular Casino has been replaced by the later Beaux-Arts Casino (center right), which opened in 1929.

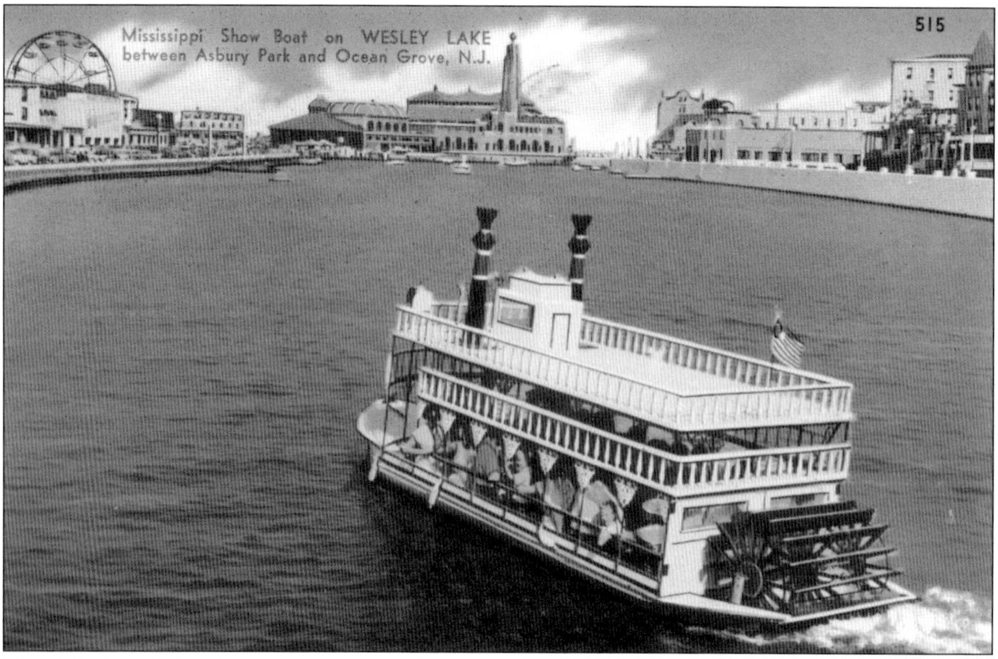


The *Mississippi* showboat transports visitors across Wesley Lake in this postcard dated August 10, 1965.

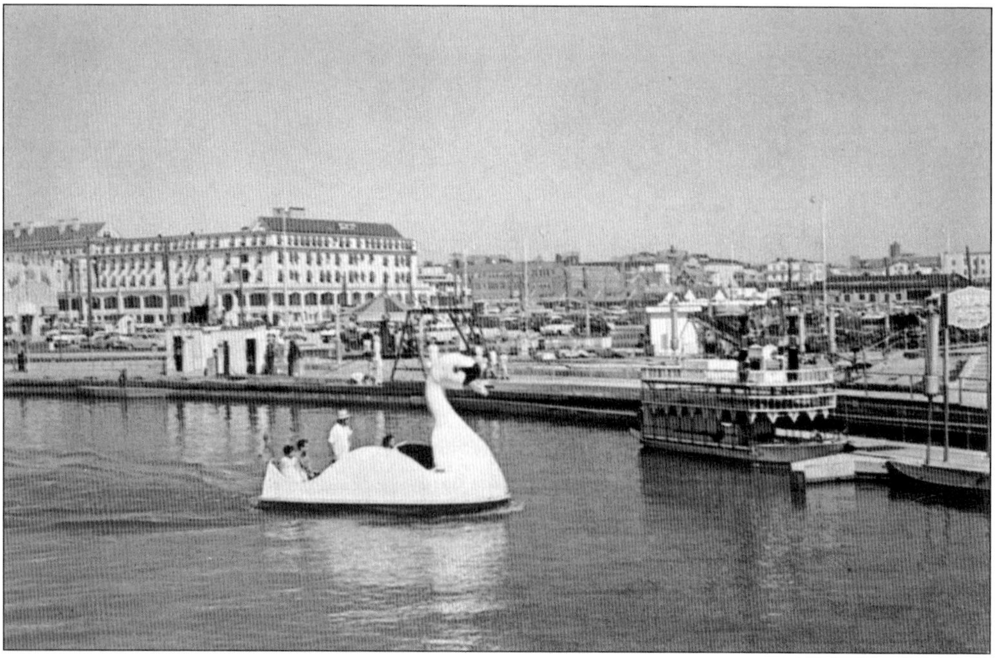

In this view, both a swan boat and the *Mississippi* showboat on Wesley Lake are shown. The white building on the left in the background is the West End Hotel.

# *Four*

# Passing the Time

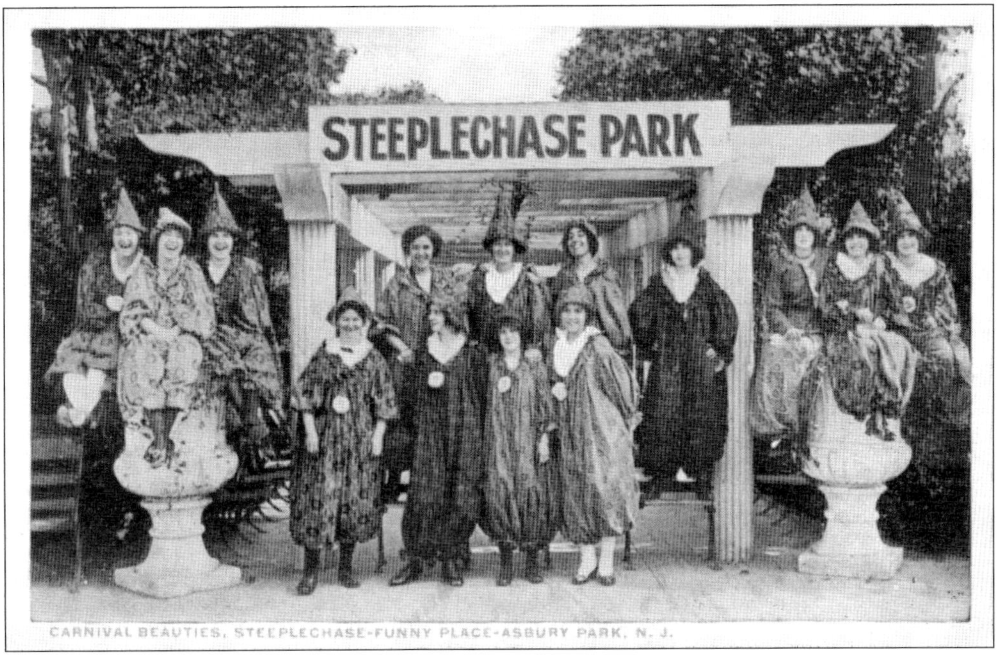


Though Coney Island is most associated with Steeplechase Park, in the early 1900s, San Francisco, Atlantic City, and Asbury Park all had their own Steeplechase Parks. Founder George Tilyou opened his establishment on Ocean Avenue in 1913 in direct competition with Ernest Schnitzler's Palace Amusements. This postcard is captioned "Carnival Beauties, Steeplechase-Funny Place-Asbury Park, NJ," though this same image was used for postcards advertising multiple locations of Steeplechase Park.

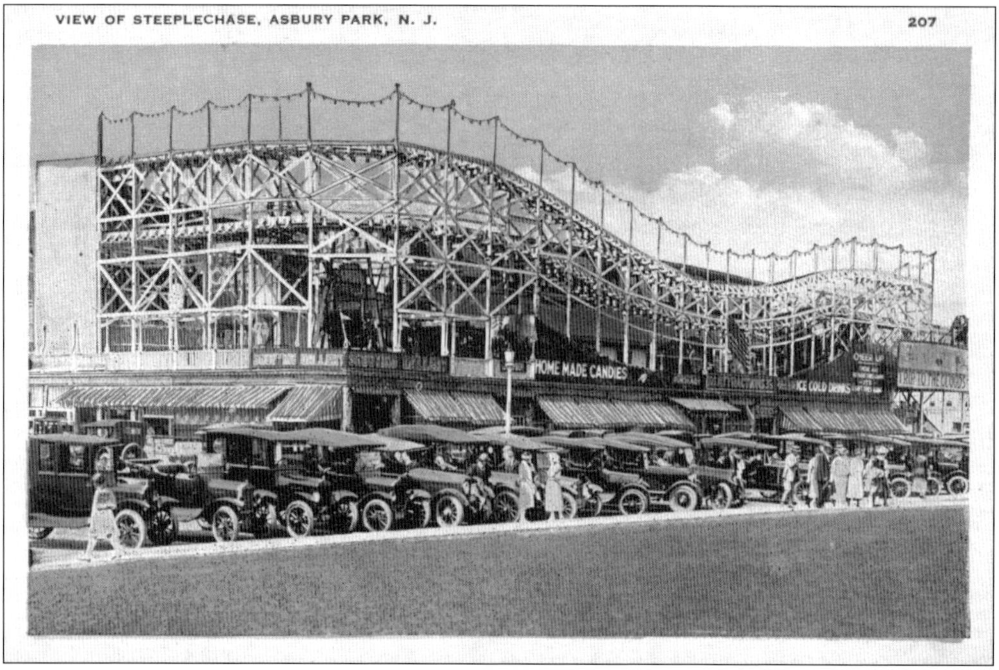


When Steeplechase Park opened, patrons could enjoy more than 50 attractions. The marquee amusement was a gravity-driven roller coaster–like ride, where people "raced" parallel mechanical horses as they traveled along a hilly track. George Tilyou continuously created new rides, and by 1919, the number of attractions at Asbury Park's Steeplechase Park had grown to 100.

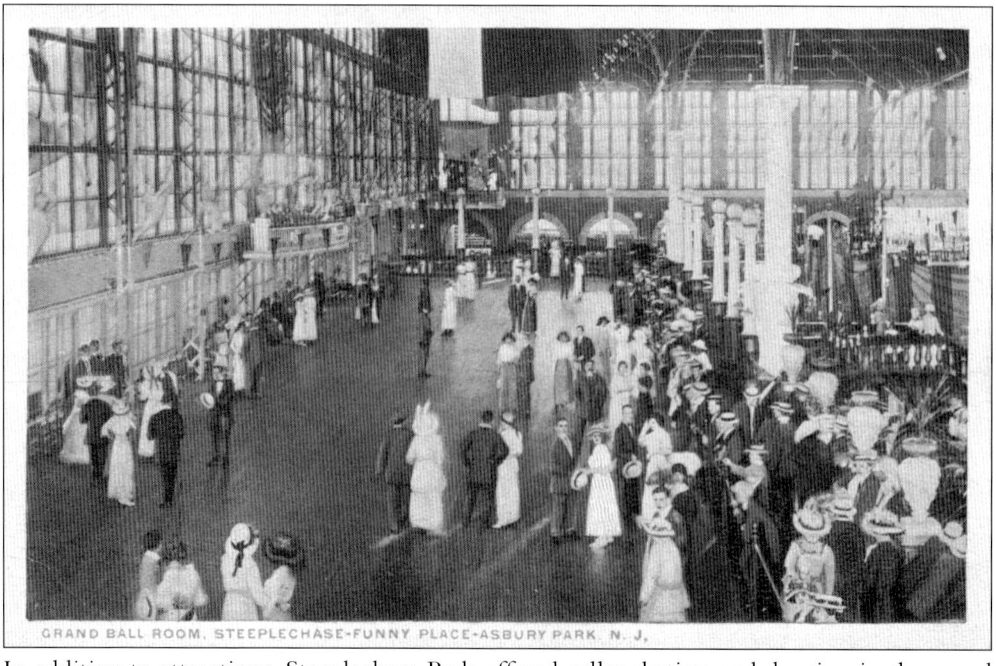


In addition to attractions, Steeplechase Park offered roller skating and dancing in the grand ballroom, shown here.

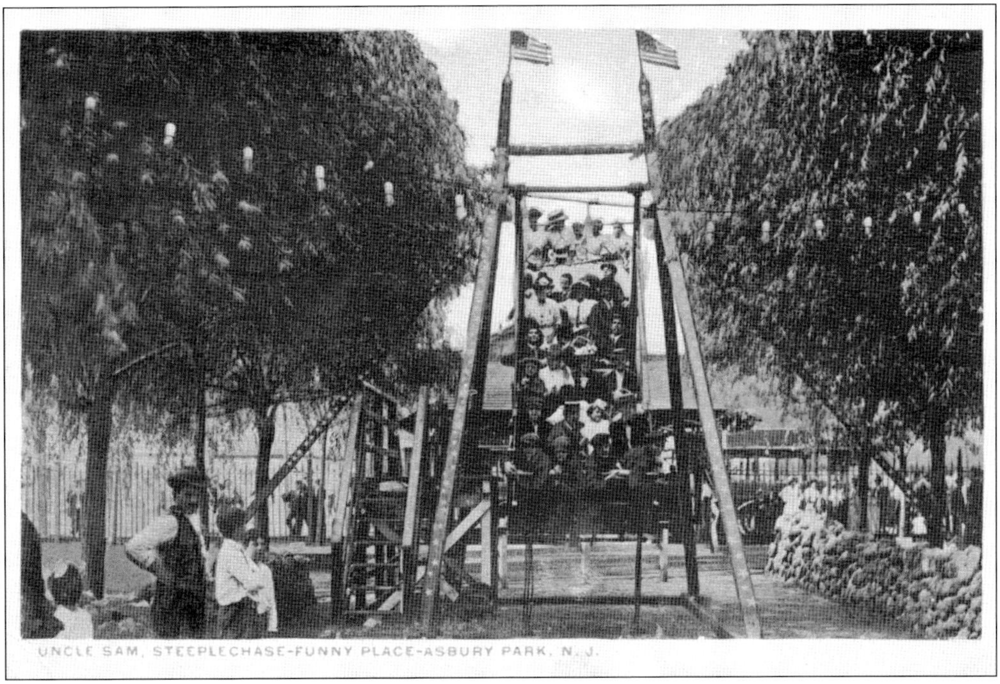


This large gondola swing, called the Uncle Sam, could accommodate 24 riders at a time, in six rows of four.

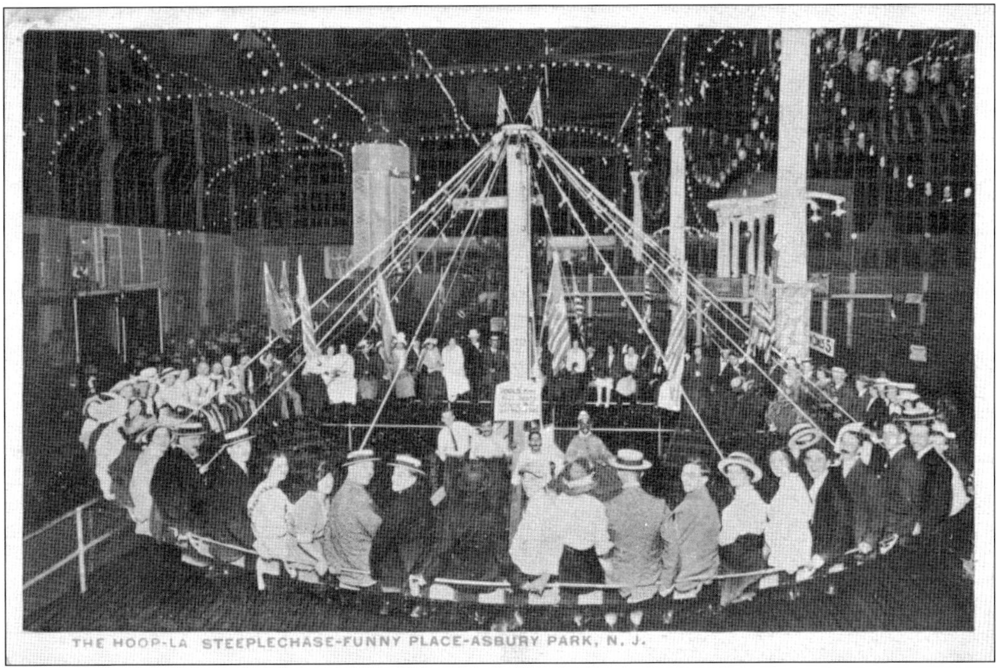


The Hoop-La, also called the Wedding Ring or Razzle Dazzle, was a large circular wooden swing that held up to 70 people. Ride attendants would push the swing back and forth like a seesaw. In 1940, a fire destroyed Steeplechase Park and the nearby Albion hotel; the park would not be rebuilt.

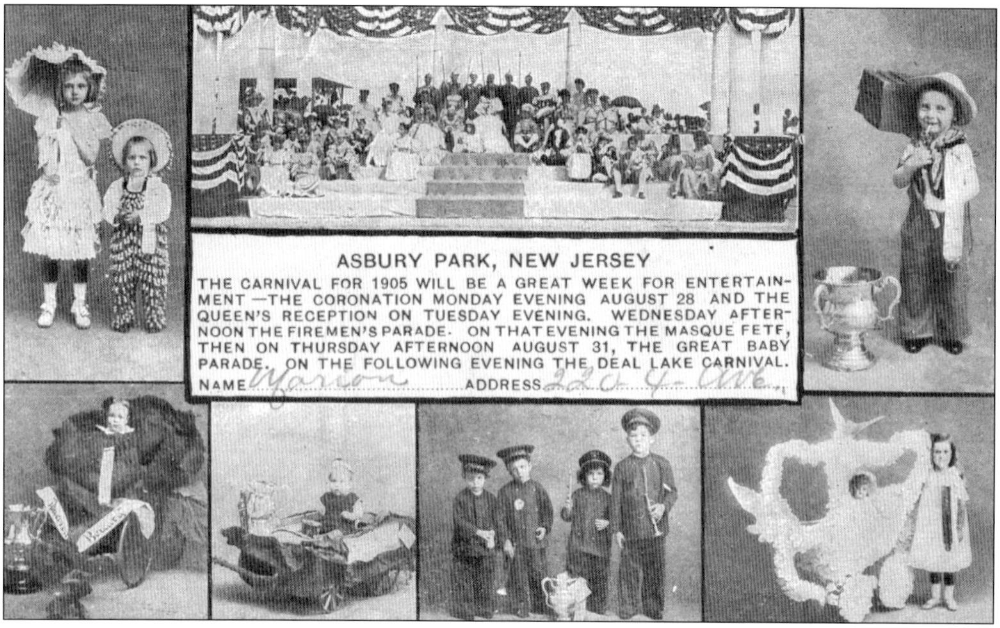


In 1890, Founder Bradley began an annual tradition when he led a parade of about 200 children in decorated carriages along Ocean Avenue. By the time this card was mailed in 1905, the baby parade had become the centerpiece of a multi-day carnival that included elements from Shakespeare's *A Midsummer Night's Dream*.

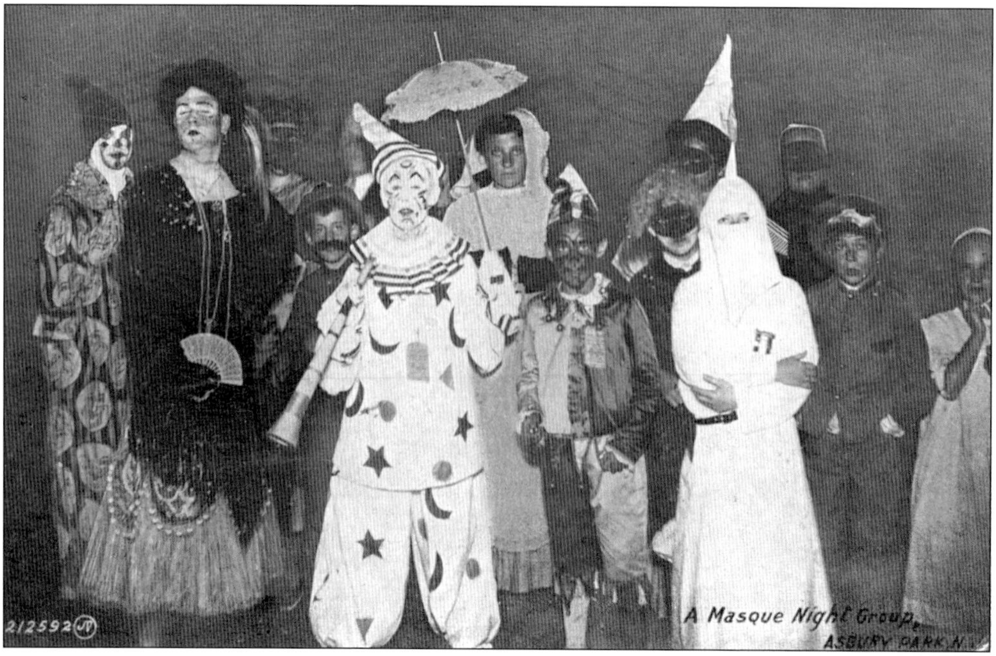


In 1904, the *Philadelphia Record* reported that 7,000 masqueraders like those in this group participated in the annual carnival's festivities.

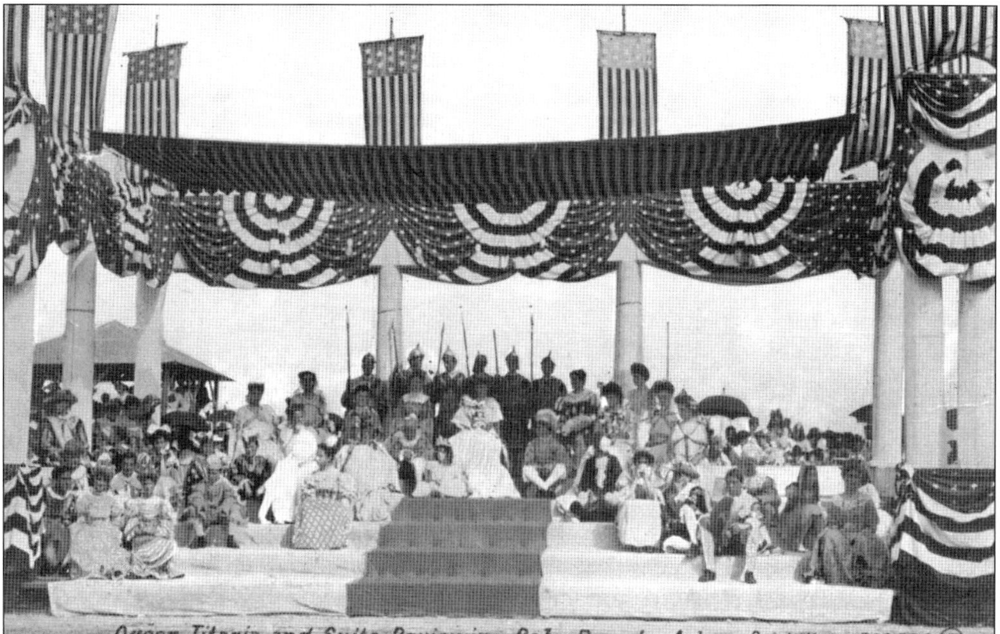

Queen Titania and Suite Reviewing Baby Parade, Asbury Park N.J. 212590

On the first night of the carnival, a young woman would play the role of queen of the fairies, crowned Queen Titania. Her royal court included local young men and women playing Lord Chamberlain, maids of honor, gentlemen in waiting, a court jester, and crown and scepter bearers. Queen Titania's responsibilities involved receiving guests at a celebratory ball and holding court during the baby parade, as seen here.

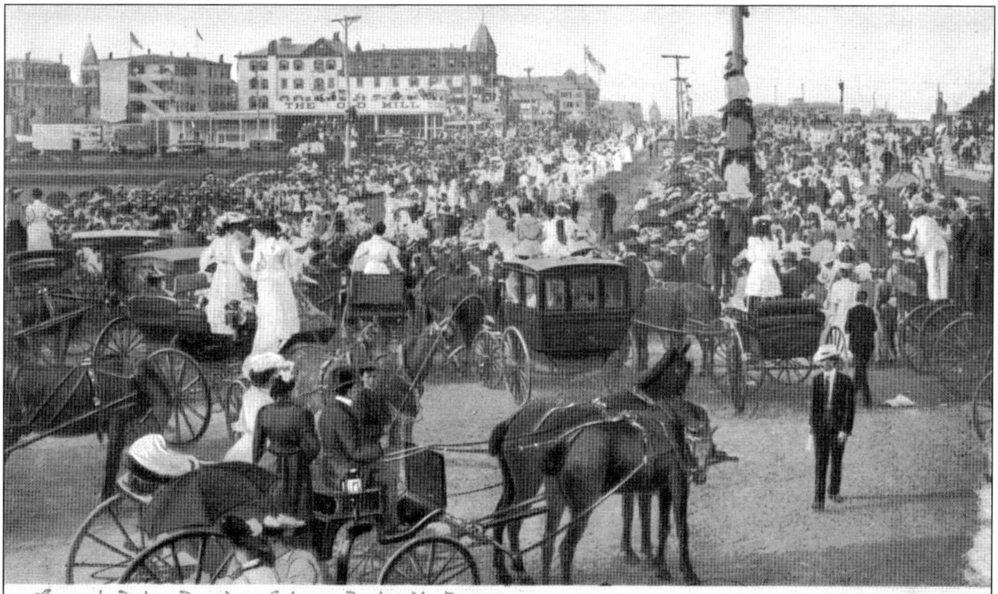


Annual Baby Parade, Asbury Park. N. J.

The annual carnival was such a grand spectacle that it attracted national interest. In 1911, the *New York Times* called it the "Annual Mardi Gras." Theodore Roosevelt came to Asbury Park to view the baby parade, as did Woodrow Wilson, both as governor of New Jersey and as president of the United States.

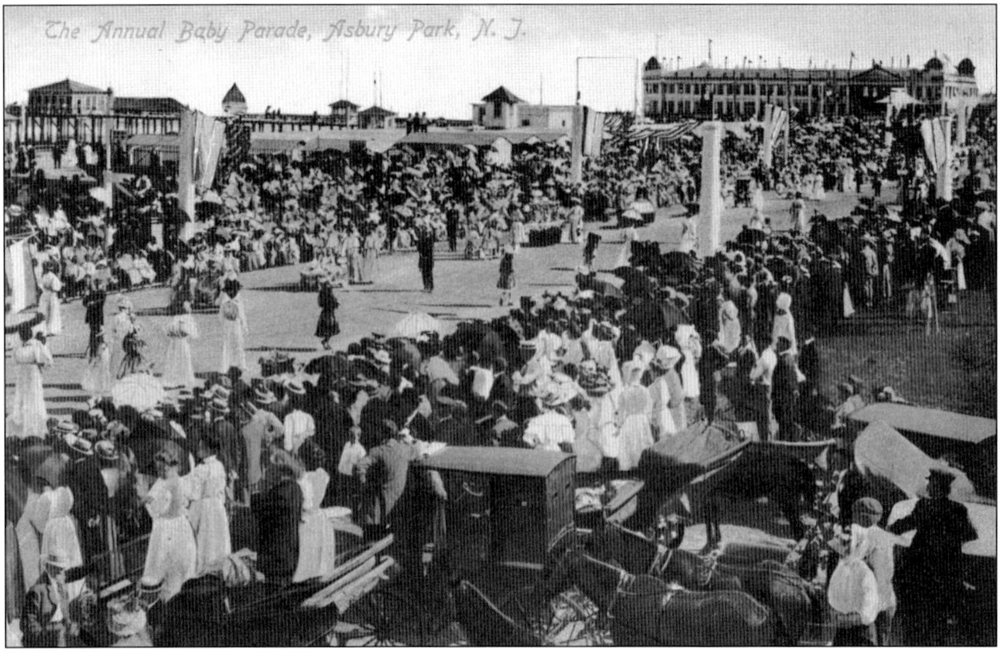


Looking south along Ocean Avenue toward the Casino, crowds are gathered for the baby parade. By 1901, participation grew to over 500 entrants. Thomas Edison filmed the parade in 1904, recording costumed children riding floats, and mothers pushing intricately ornamented baby carriages.

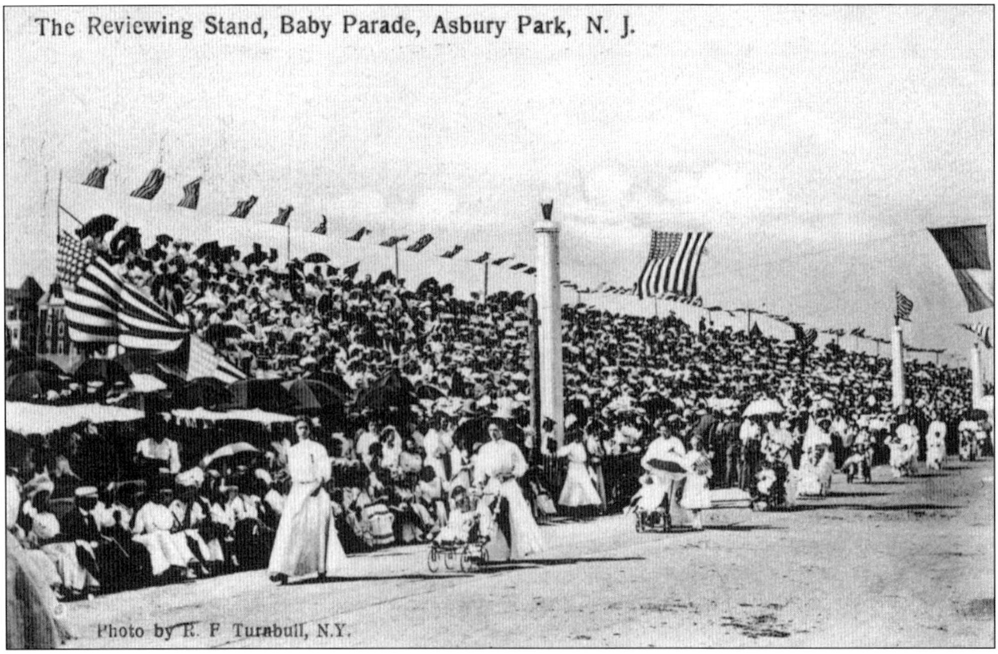


The attendance for the baby parade was so great that temporary viewing stands like the ones pictured here around 1907 were erected, and additional trains were added to the regular service to bring spectators to town. Souvenir programs sold during the carnival featured advertisements for local businesses such as Day's Ice Cream Garden and Steinbach's Department Store, as well as for national brands like Borden's and Nestle.

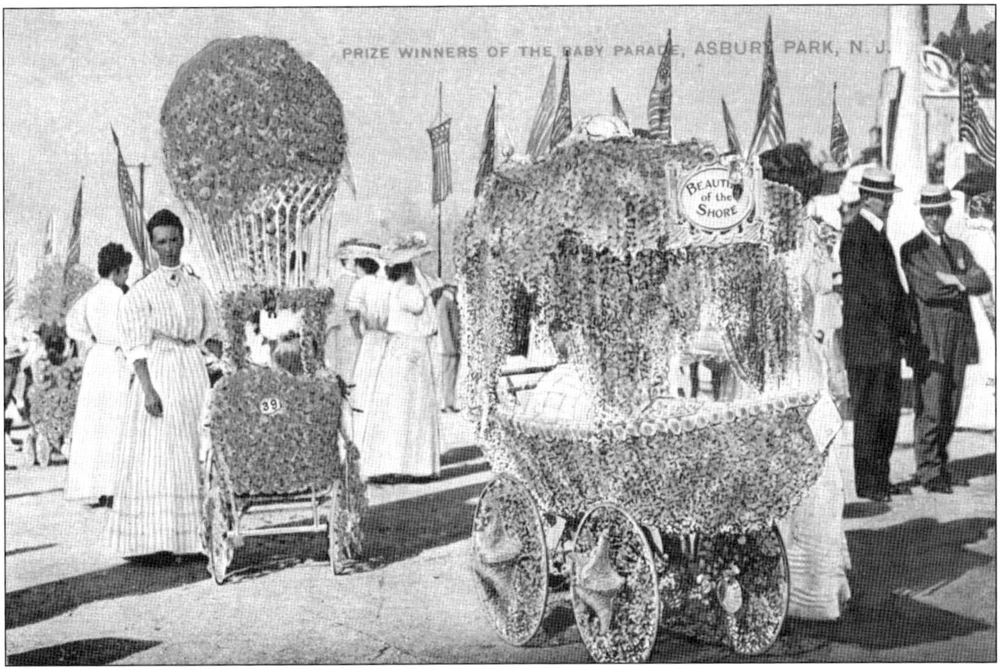


Mothers adorned their baby carriages with decorations such as shells and flowers in the hopes of receiving a prize. While all participants received souvenirs like a box of candy, winners could receive valuable prizes: a gold wrist watch, wardrobe trunk, imported tea set, silver candelabra, or even a pony.

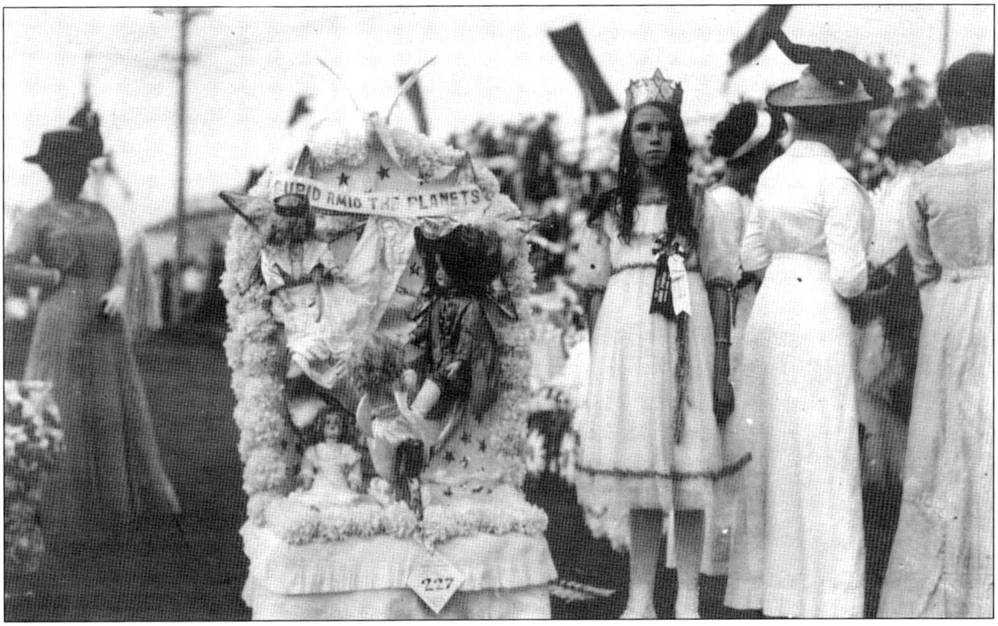


A prize winner at the 1912 baby parade poses with her winning carriage, which represents Cupid among the planets.

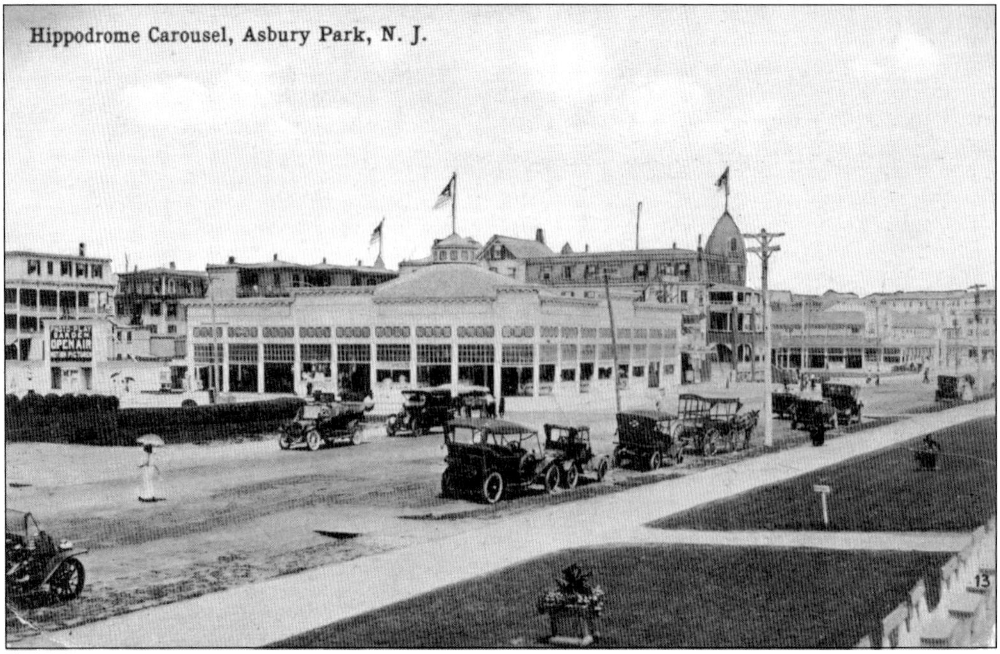


The Hippodrome Carousel, named after the Greek word for a horse racing stadium, was located on Ocean Avenue in the early 20th century.

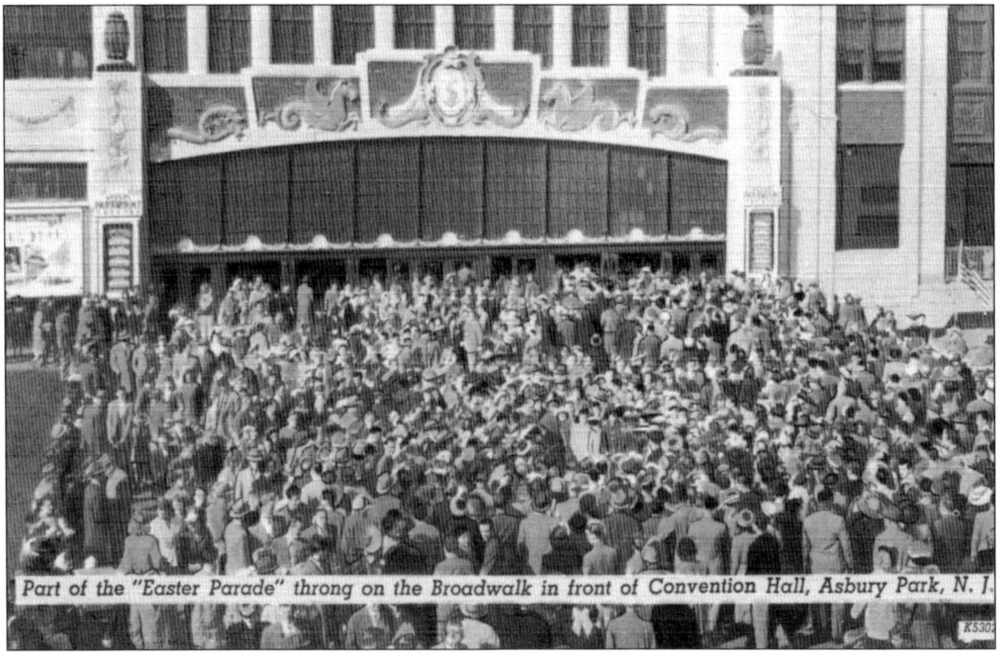


The annual Easter parade on the boardwalk is seen here in front of Asbury Park's convention hall. Each year, orchids were presented to the 100 best-dressed women aged 16 to 60. In 1936, seven women and one child were hurt when a 50-foot section of the boardwalk they were standing on collapsed while they were waiting for the winners of the orchids to be announced.

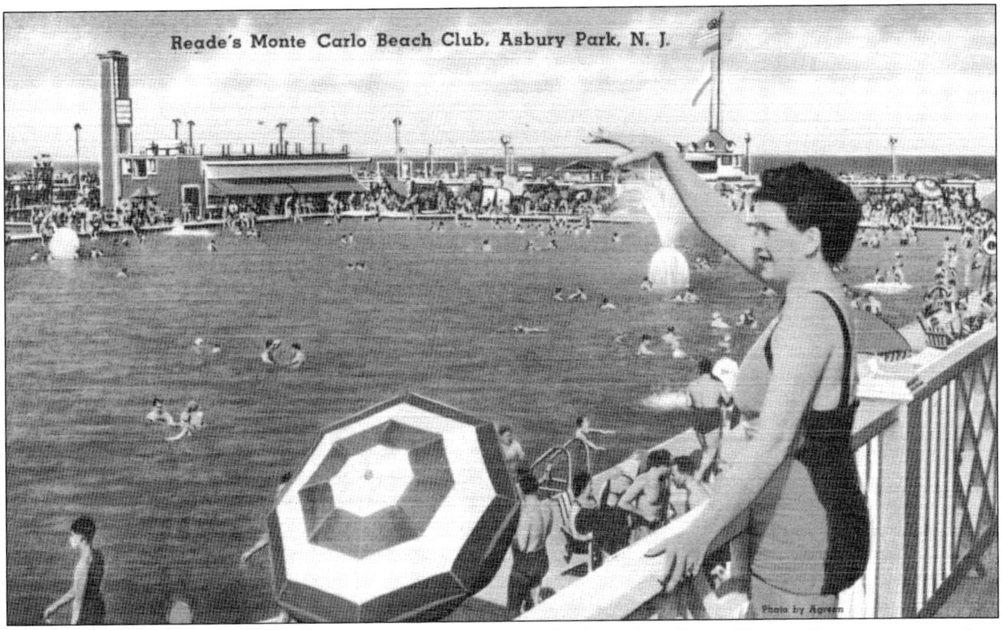


Reade's Monte Carlo Beach Club, located opposite the boardwalk on Ocean Avenue, opened in June 1942. With a capacity of 1.3 million gallons, it was billed as the world's largest saltwater pool. Nearby accommodations such as the Kingsley Arms and the Cavalier Motel offered admittance to the Monte Carlo Beach Club with a stay. For those who were paying, in 1949, admission was 75¢ for a weekday and $1 on Saturday and Sunday.

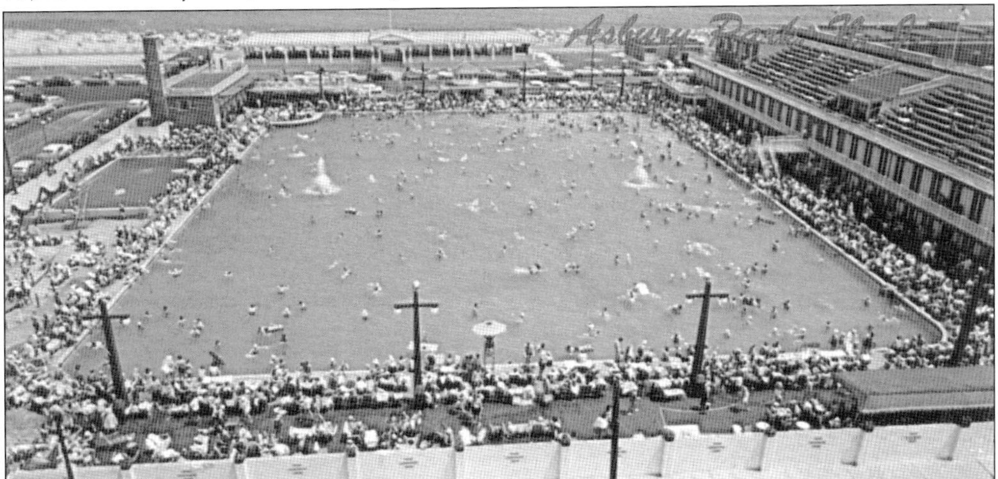

On the north side of the Monte Carlo's big pool there was a nine-and-a-half-foot-deep athletic pool for diving (above left), as well as a baby pool. The beach club had cabanas and lockers that could be rented for the day or for the season, and a tunnel under Ocean Avenue led directly to the beach. In 1974, the Asbury Tower senior apartment complex was built on the site of the Monte Carlo Beach Club.

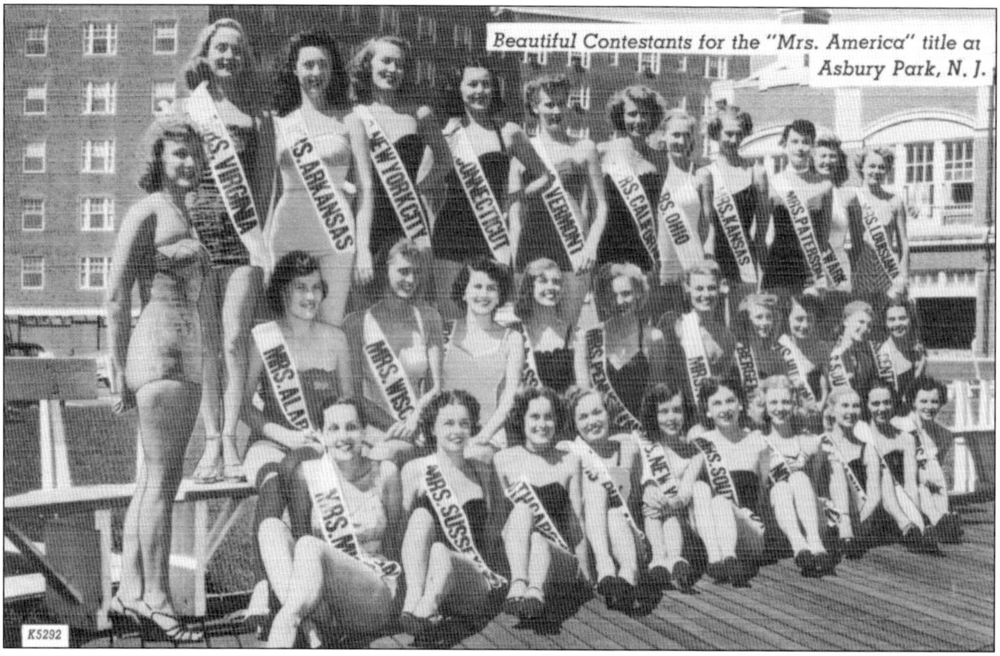


The Mrs. America competition, a more wholesome counterpart to Atlantic City's Miss America pageant, was held in Asbury Park from 1948 to 1954. Here, contestants pose on the boardwalk near the Sunset Avenue pavilion. In addition to appearance, participants were judged on their proficiency in areas of home economics such as cooking, cleaning, sewing, and crocheting.

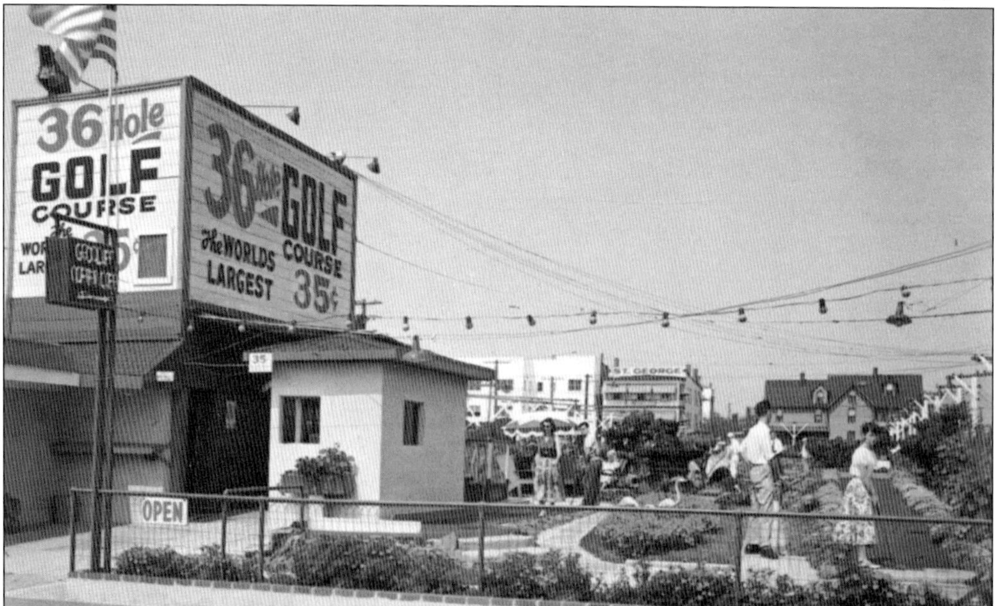


Miniature golf was a popular way to pass the time in the mid-20th century, so much so that there were four separate places to play in Asbury Park. This 36-hole mini-golf course, located across from the boardwalk at Fourth Avenue between Ocean Avenue and Kingsley Street, called itself the world's largest.

*Five*

# The Old and New Casino

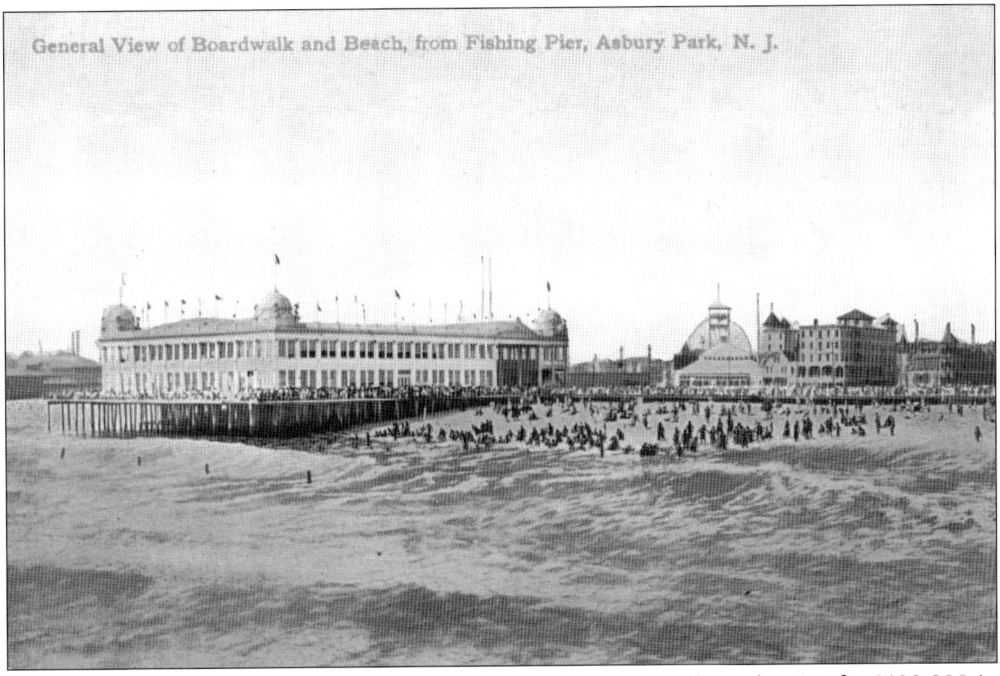


When Founder Bradley handed over ownership of the boardwalk to the city for $100,000 in 1903, an existing wooden waterfront pavilion at Asbury Avenue was replaced with the more contemporary pavilion called the Casino, shown here extending over the beach. Designed by Asbury Park architects William C. and Arthur F. Cottrell, the Casino cost the city $50,000 to build.

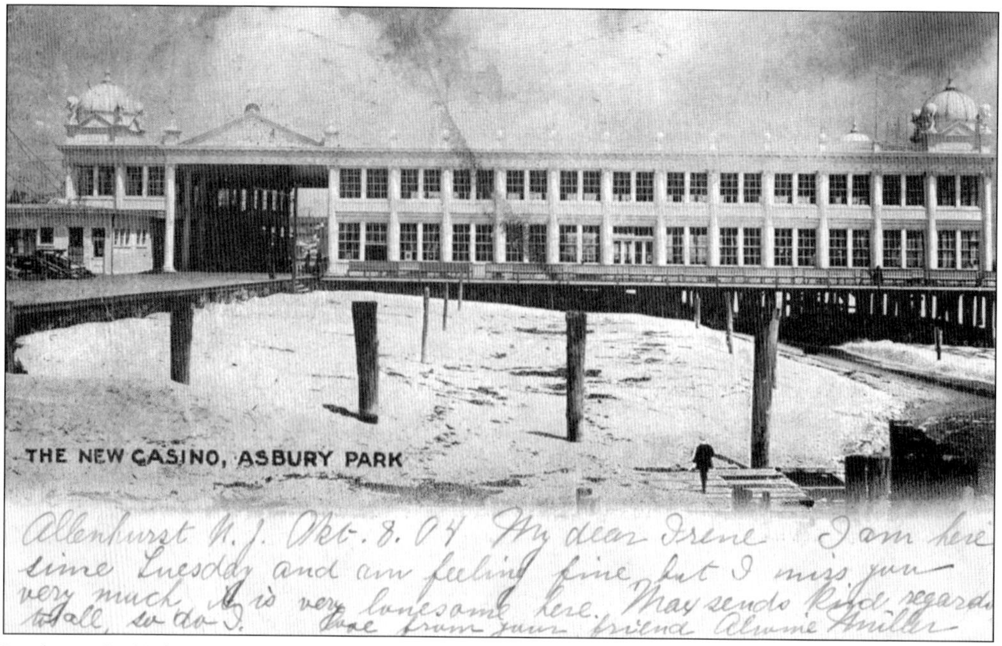


In the early 20th century, the term "casino" referred to a building that was used as a gathering place for entertainment such as dancing or musical and theatrical performances. There was no gambling in Asbury Park's Casino; referring to places for gambling as "casinos" did not become common in America until the late 20th century.

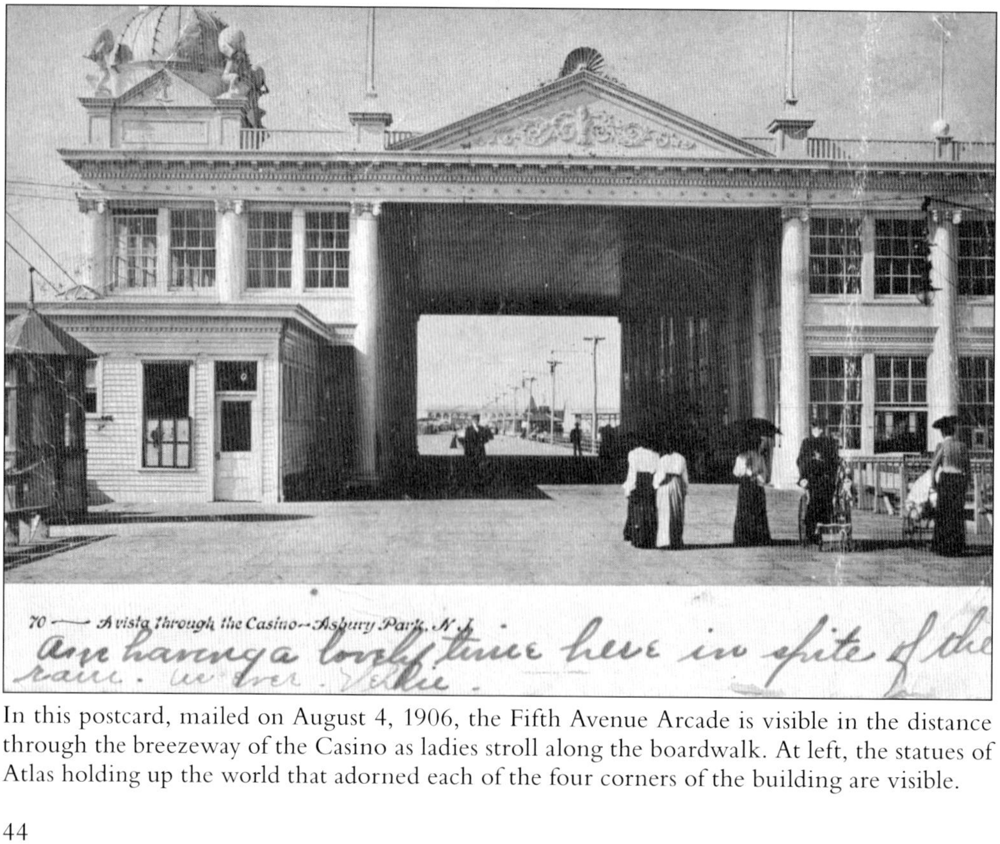


In this postcard, mailed on August 4, 1906, the Fifth Avenue Arcade is visible in the distance through the breezeway of the Casino as ladies stroll along the boardwalk. At left, the statues of Atlas holding up the world that adorned each of the four corners of the building are visible.

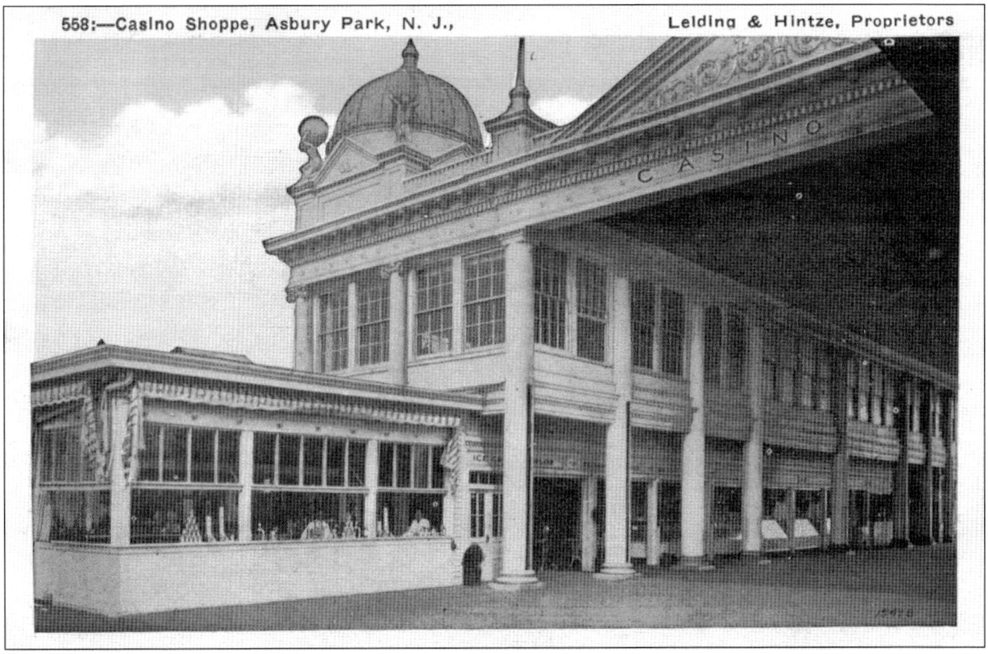


This postcard served as an advertisement and mail-order form for Leiding and Hintze's Casino Candy Shop. By filling out the back of the card with one's address, a pound of assorted saltwater taffy would be sent to one's home, and the postman would collect 50¢ upon delivery.

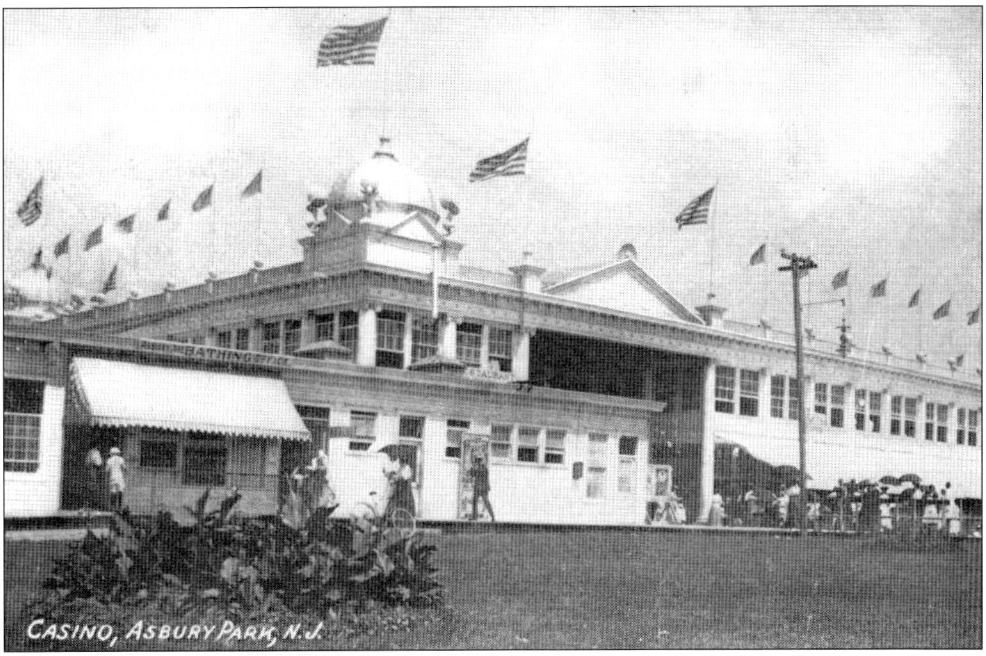


Facing northeast, on the left is the Asbury Avenue bathing office. Also seen here is the Casino's restaurant, which served waffles and sandwiches and was advertised as having the most reasonable prices of any restaurant on the boardwalk.

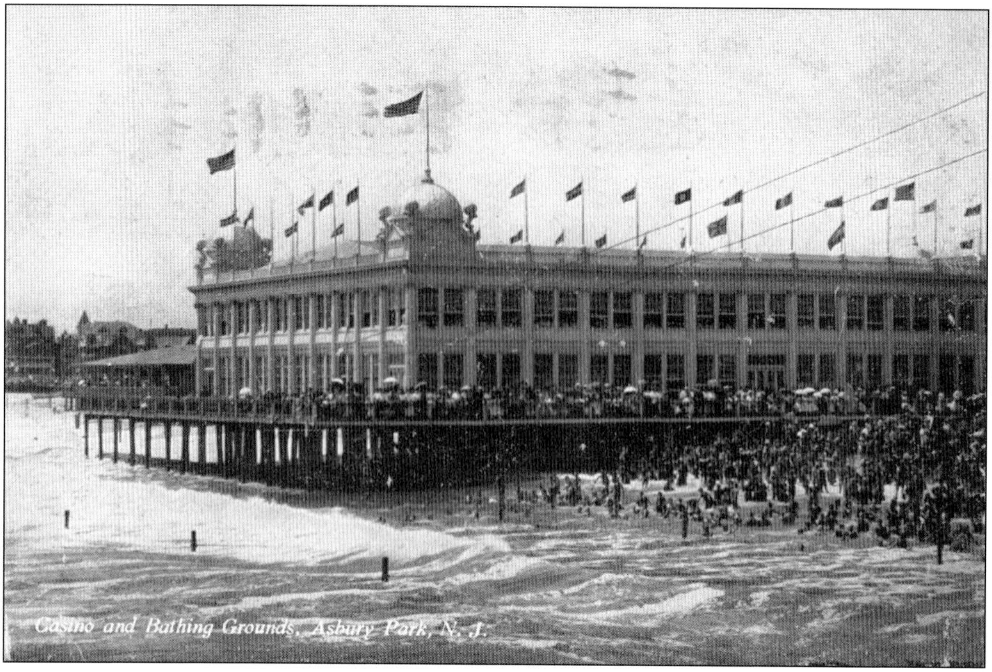


In the summer of 1927, the Casino hosted lectures by author Elsie Audrey Hille, who was a representative of Bernarr MacFadden, an early advocate of health and nutrition. Lecture subjects included "Self-expressions vital for women," "Constipation," "Disease and its fad," and "Proper care of [a] woman's body and its life force."

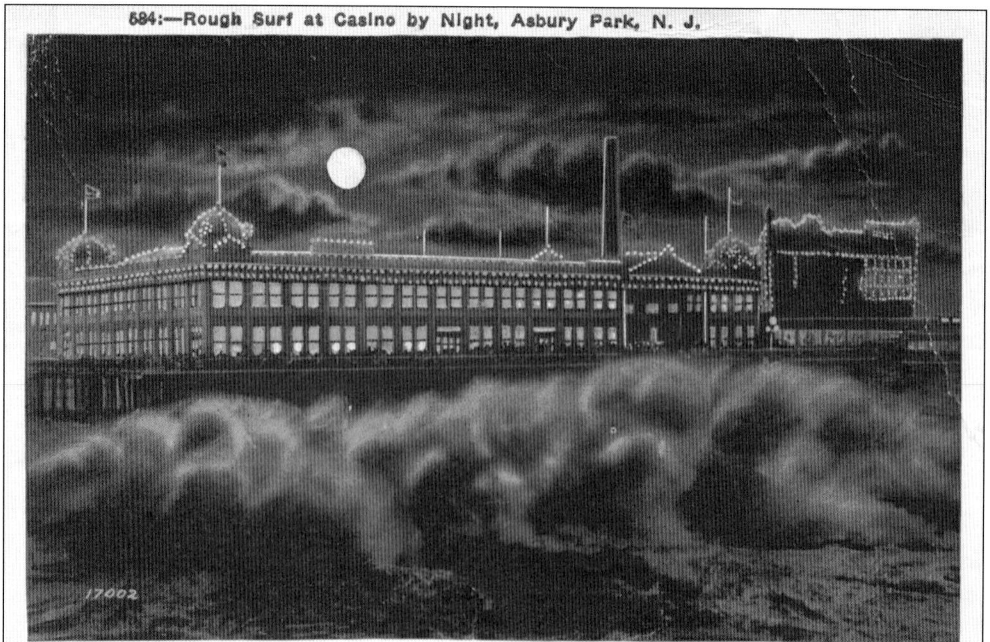


By night, 3,000 incandescent lights illuminated the Casino. Dancing was available each weekday during the summer, with music provided multiple times a day by the 35-piece Casino Dance Orchestra directed by Lorin Patterson. Soloists performed each Sunday evening.

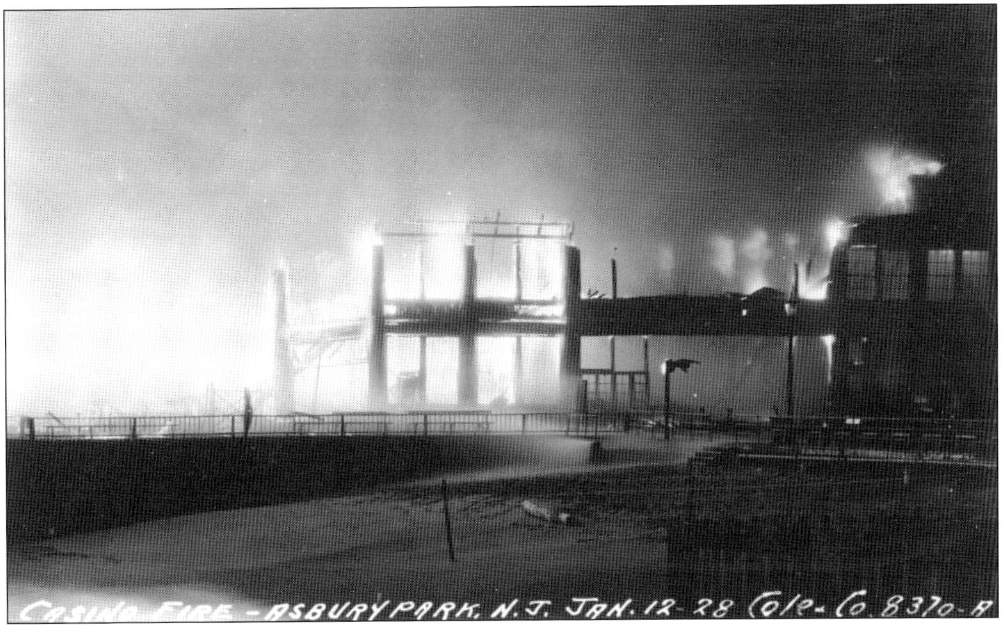


The Casino was consumed by fire on the night of January 12, 1928. Four months later, in May 1928, work began on a new Casino. This new $1.5-million building was part of an ambitious $5-million waterfront redevelopment program that also included a new convention hall, theater, heating plant, and pavilions at Asbury and Sunset Avenues.

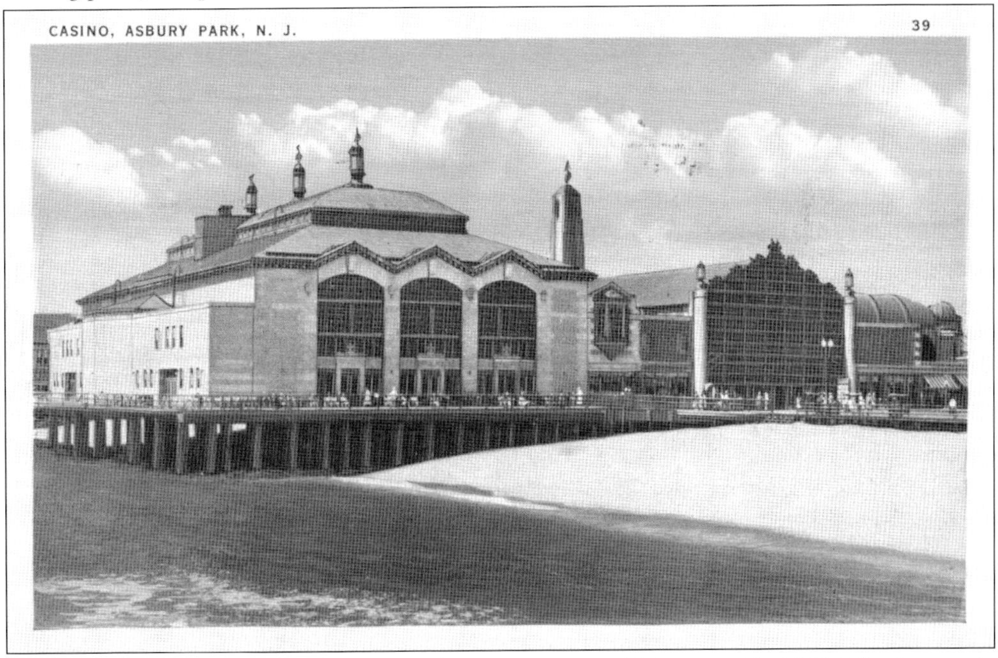


This postcard, mailed in July 1937, shows the new Casino, which opened in 1929. Like the wood-frame building it replaced, this Casino extended out over the beach to the ocean. Along with the other buildings constructed along the boardwalk at this time, the Casino was designed by prominent New York architect Whitney Warren of Warren and Wetmore, the firm responsible for Manhattan's Grand Central Terminal.

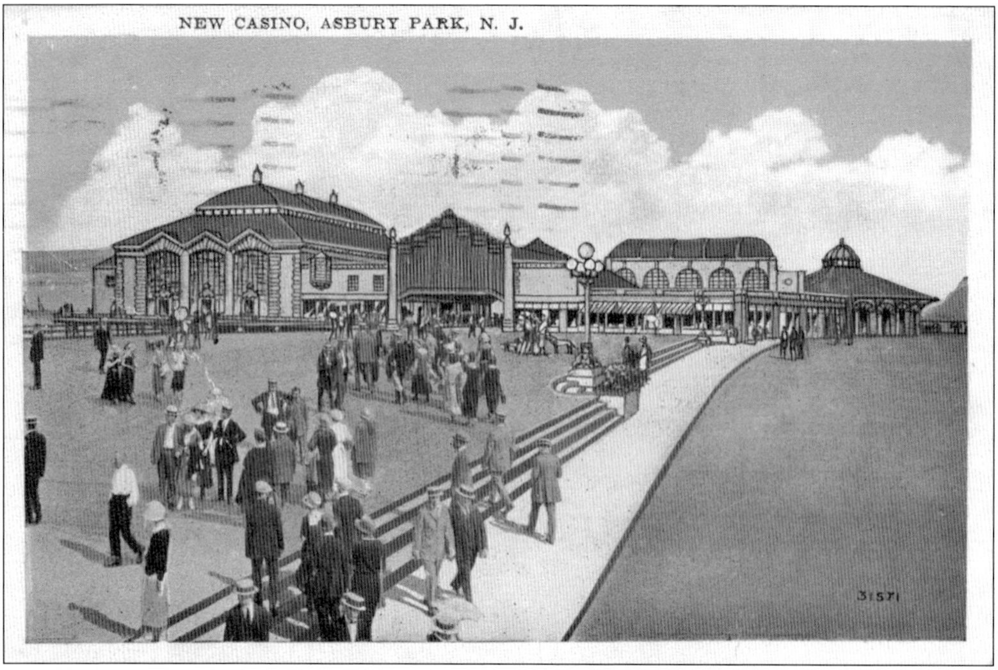


Warren's Casino looked quite different from the large rectangular structure it replaced. At the far left was a large two-story skating arena. An arcade extended over the boardwalk, which allowed patrons to continue through the building to the other side. The area to the west of the walkway (at right) housed rides and concessions, and the circular portion of the building at far right is a carousel house.

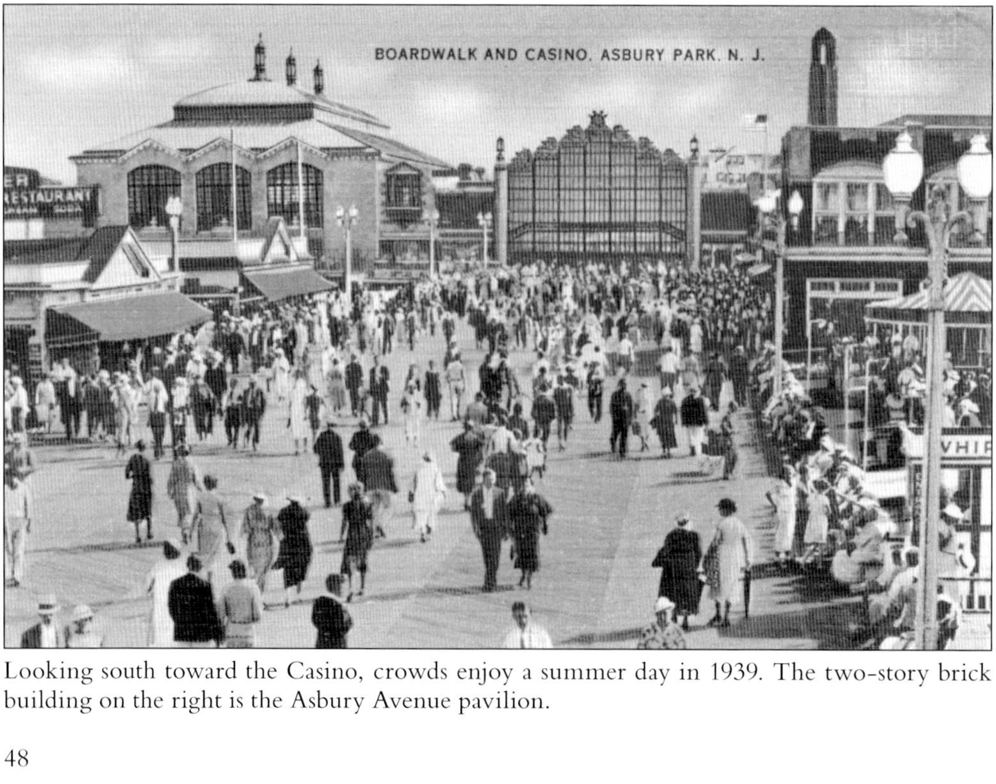


Looking south toward the Casino, crowds enjoy a summer day in 1939. The two-story brick building on the right is the Asbury Avenue pavilion.

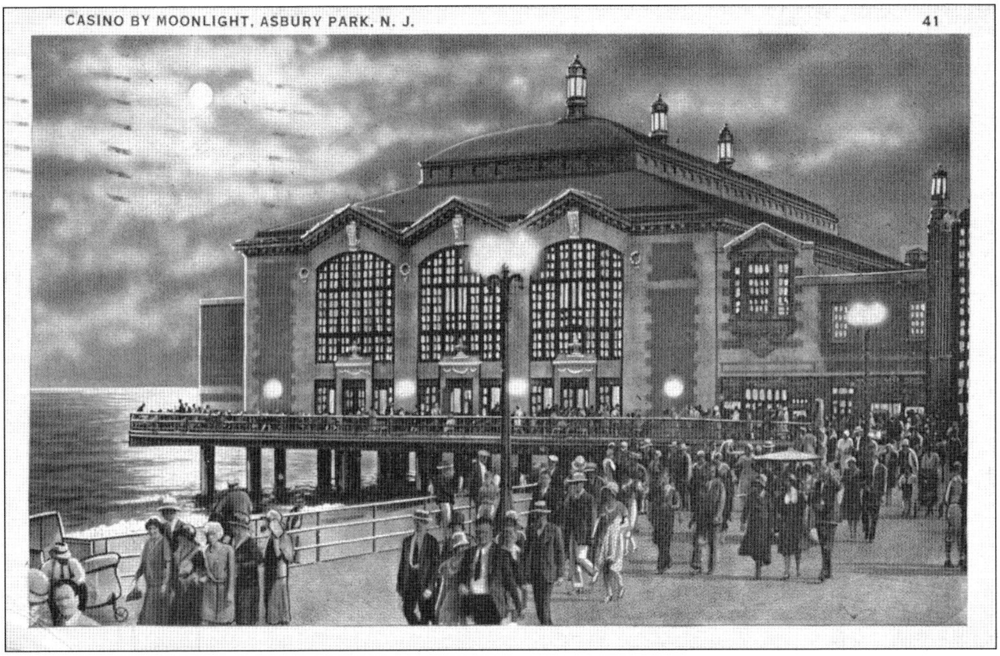


The skating rink portion of the Casino is shown here at night. The arena was open for roller skating until 3:00 a.m. during the summer in the 1940s. From May to October, ice skating took place here.

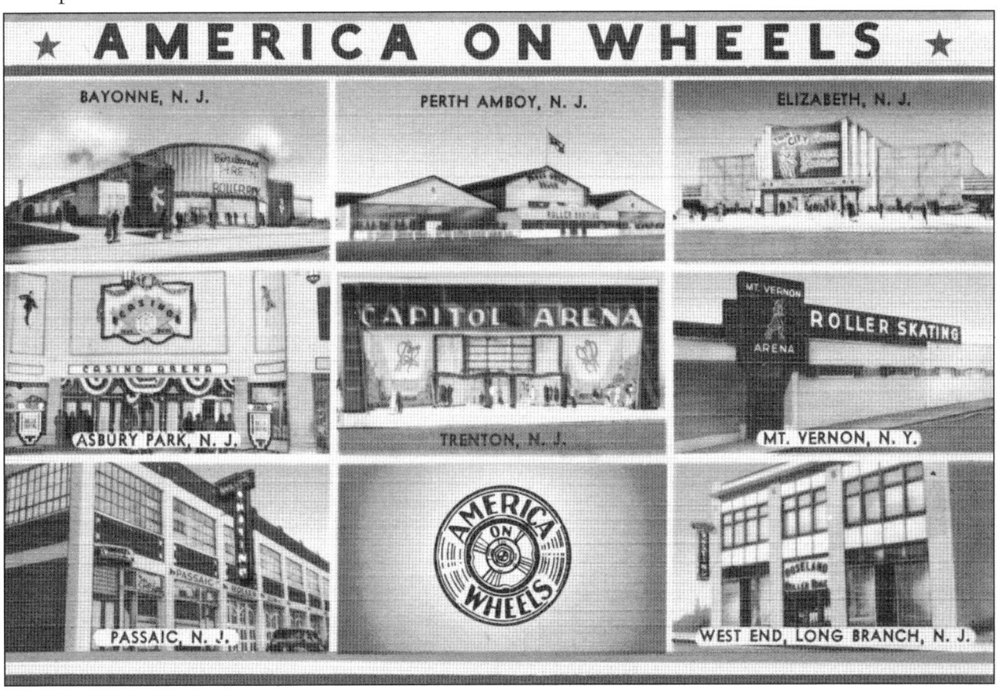


In the 1940s, the skating arena at Asbury Park's Casino was operated by the America on Wheels chain of roller rinks. The company advertised the Asbury Park location as "skating to the rhythm of the Atlantic surf." The entrance to the Casino's skating arena, which was located inside the arcade that spanned the boardwalk, can be seen at center left.

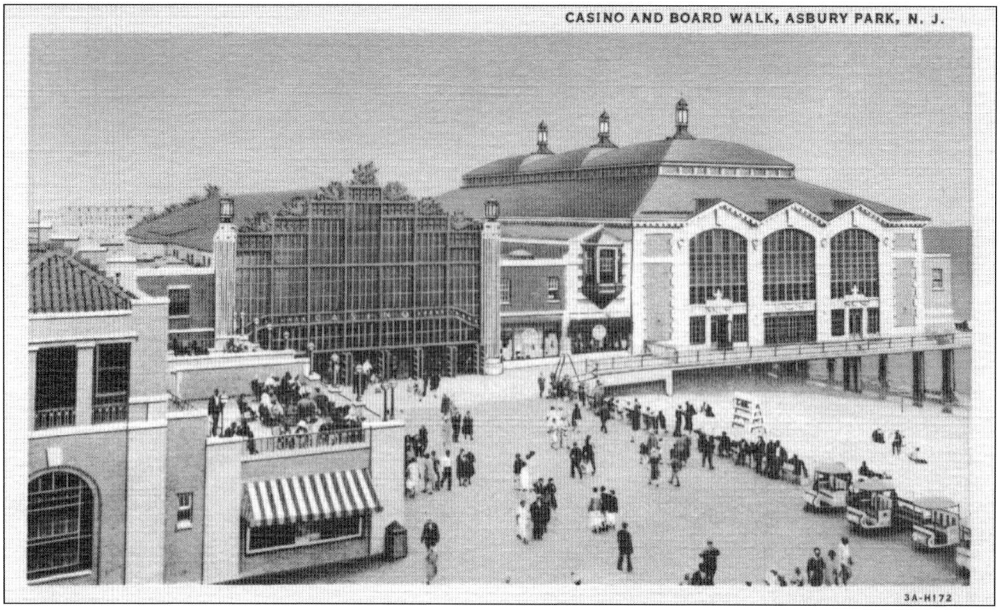


This is the view from Ocean Grove, looking north toward the Casino. The building on the left is a heating plant, which provided steam heat to the buildings on the waterfront via a concrete tunnel below the boardwalk. The heating plant also housed concessions and had a solarium on the second floor for enjoying views of the Atlantic Ocean.

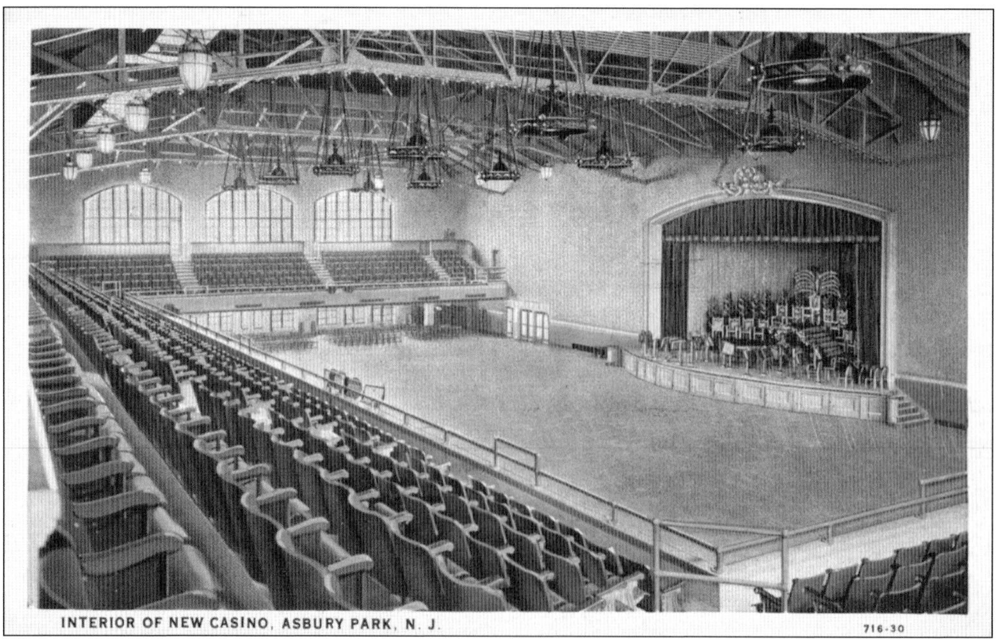


The interior of the Casino's skating rink is shown here around 1931. In the 1970s, this stage hosted bands such as Blue Öyster Cult, Aerosmith, and ZZ Top. In the 1980s, this portion of the Casino was closed after an improperly installed roof and damage from Hurricane Gloria combined to cause plaster to fall from the ceiling. By 2003, most of the roof had fallen away, but the ornate light fixtures seen here still hung from the ceiling's steel frame. In 2006, having been deemed too damaged to save, the arena portion of the Casino was demolished.

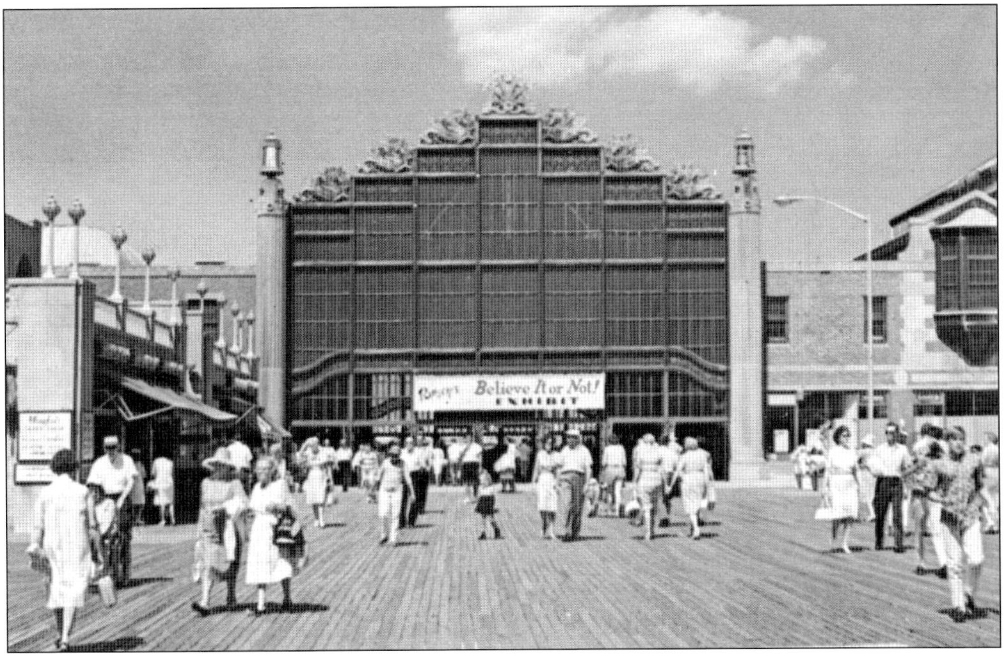

A sudden thunderstorm in September 1987 brought winds that blew down the doors below the Casino arcade's wall of windows. Also damaged were decorative elements like the copper lanterns and winged seahorses seen here; several of them were twisted and warped, and quite a few fell or needed to be removed. Both sides of the arcade were boarded up at this time, and it would remain closed to the public until 2005.

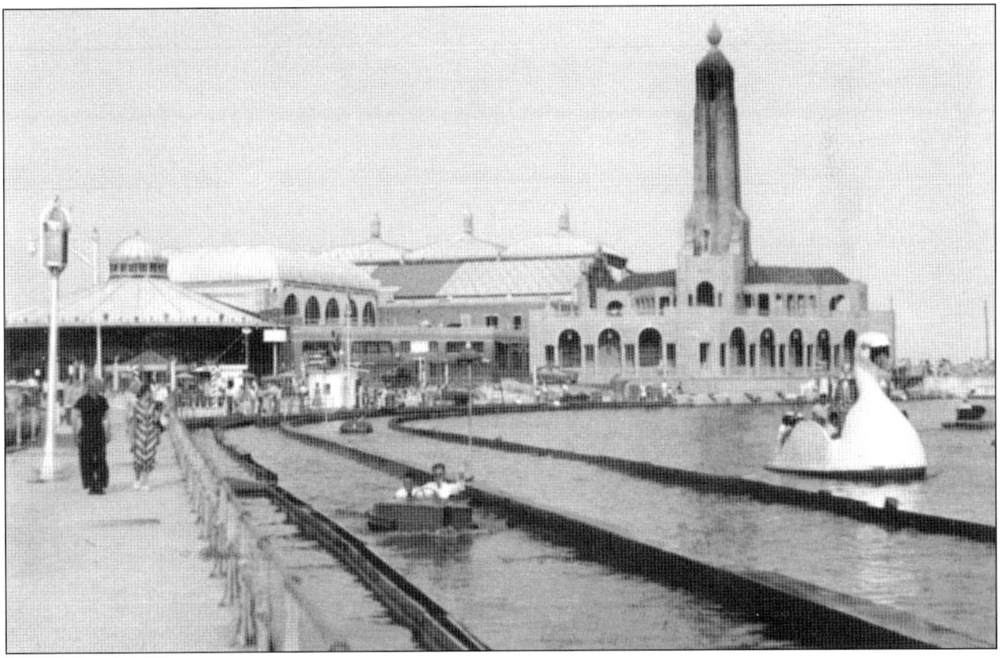

Looking east toward the ocean, this 1953 view shows the Casino with boaters on Wesley Lake in the foreground. The heating plant (next to the Casino at right) was constructed with an attention to detail and an eye toward design that is now rare in utility buildings.

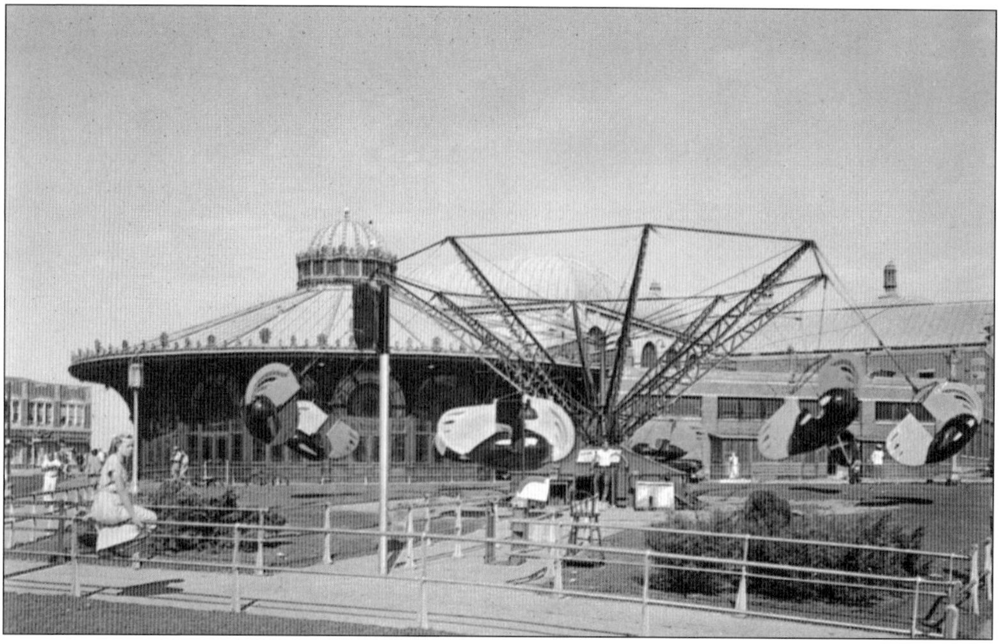

The Casino's circular domed carousel house can be seen behind the swing ride in this image. The building has distinctive patinated copper windows featuring circular medallions bearing the face of the Roman god Mercury.

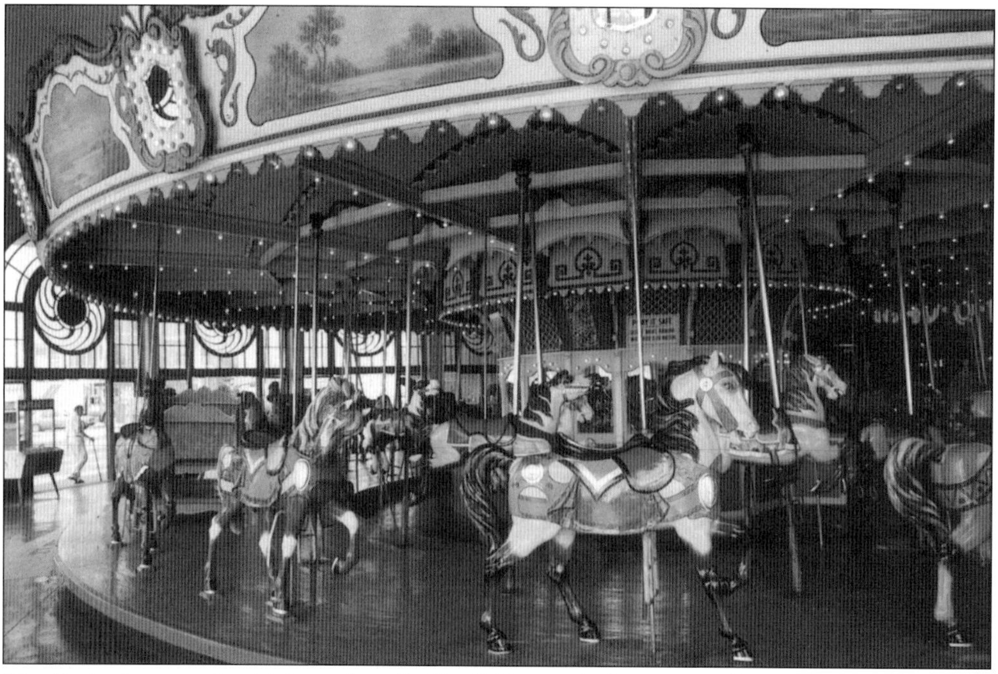

The Casino's carousel, which was installed in 1932, was the last carousel built by the Philadelphia Toboggan Company. Behind the carousel on the right, a portion of the sign for a dark ride called the Mad-O-Rama can be seen. The Casino also had attractions that included a funhouse and bumper cars and games like pinball, Skee-ball, and video poker. Instead of money, players won tickets or tokens, which were traded in for prizes.

# *Six*

# The Fifth Avenue Arcade and Convention Hall

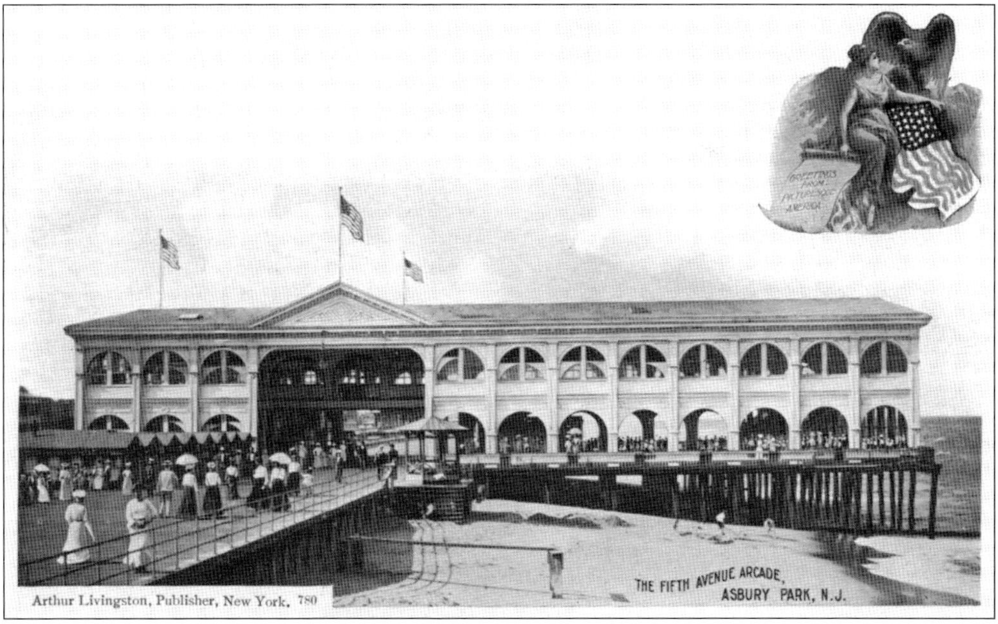


At the time the city of Asbury Park gained control of the boardwalk, an existing band shell was replaced with the building seen here, the Fifth Avenue Arcade. For over 20 years, trombone virtuoso Arthur Pryor led concerts every afternoon and evening here during the summer. Inside the building was a raised circular platform where Pryor's band would perform compositions by Tchaikovsky, Wagner, Mendelssohn, and Beethoven, and of course, melodies composed by Pryor himself.

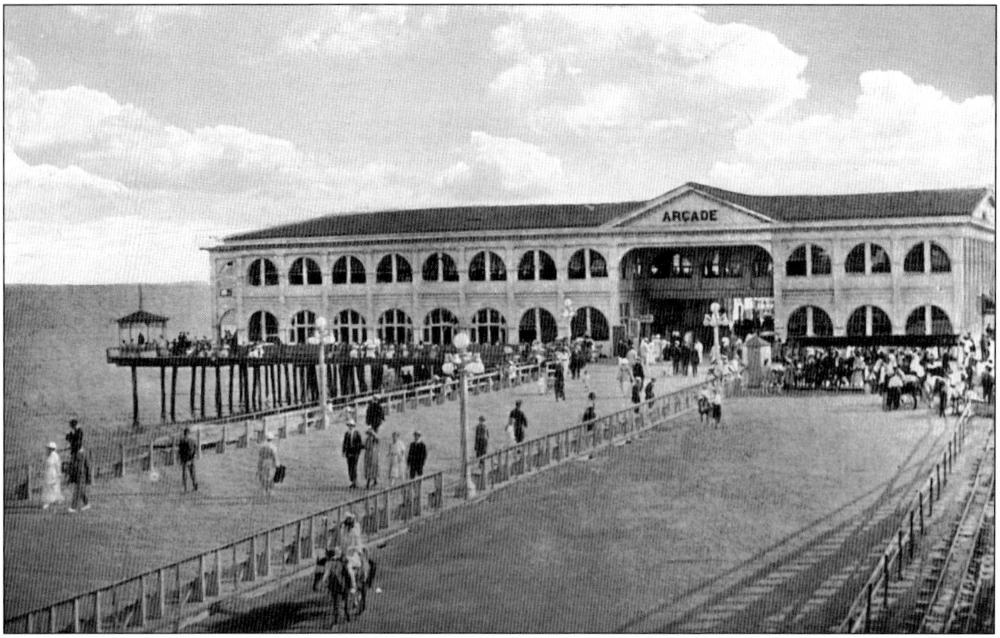


Like the original Casino at Asbury Avenue, the Fifth Avenue Arcade was designed by Asbury Park architects William and Arthur Cottrell, whose offices were located downtown on Mattison Avenue in the Appleby building. Also similar to the Casino farther south on the boardwalk, the Fifth Avenue Arcade extended out over the ocean and had large windows that could be opened or closed depending on the weather. This image features the Fifth Avenue Arcade looking south from the boardwalk at Sunset Avenue. On the right next to the arcade is a track for pony rides.

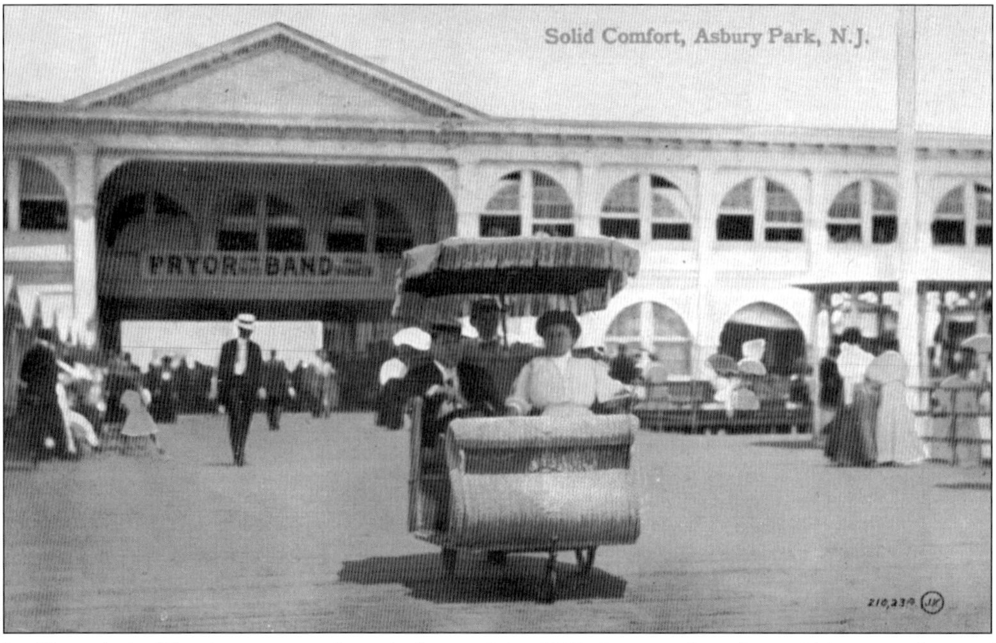


Rolling chairs like the one seen here in front of the Fifth Avenue Arcade could be rented out of three separate stations on the boardwalk. In the 1940s, the cost for an hour of "solid comfort" was $1.

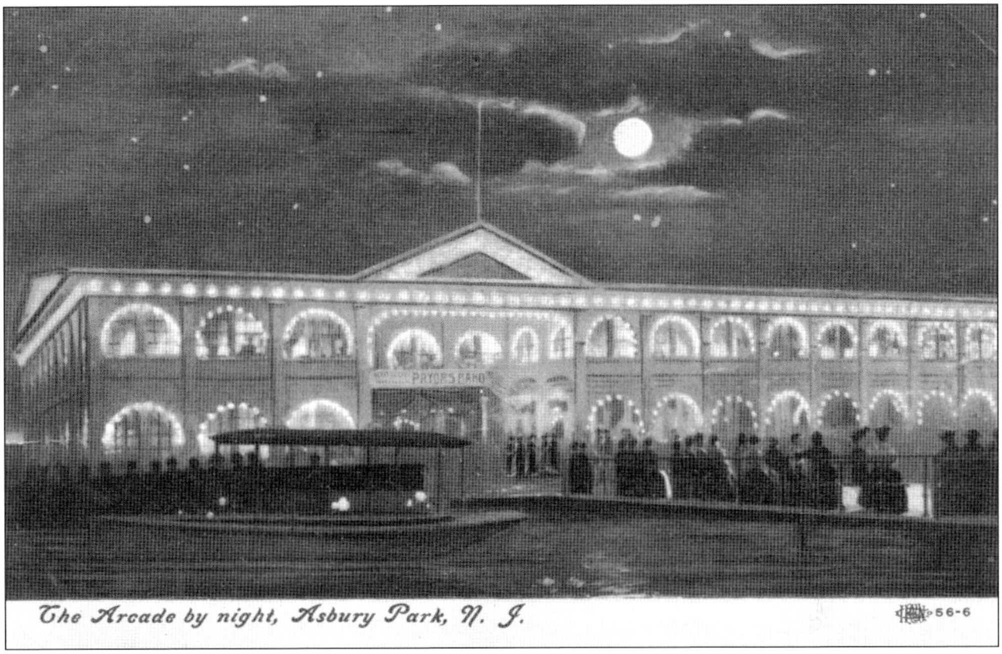


The two-story Fifth Avenue Arcade had a seating capacity of 5,000. The 3,500 lamps that lined the building and its windows were powered by a dedicated plant that also supplied electricity to the boardwalk and Casino.

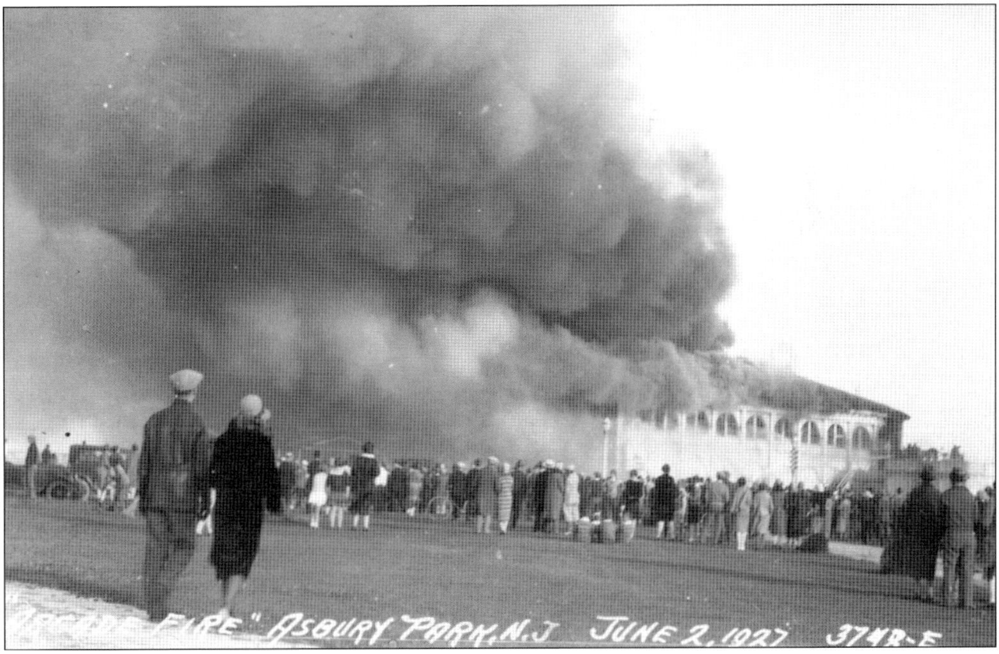


On June 2, 1927, the Fifth Avenue Arcade was destroyed by a mysterious fire. This made way for a convention hall, which is something local businessmen had argued was necessary for more than a decade. They reasoned that in order for Asbury Park to stay competitive with other cities, specifically Atlantic City, an exhibition space that could hold at least 6,000 people was needed.

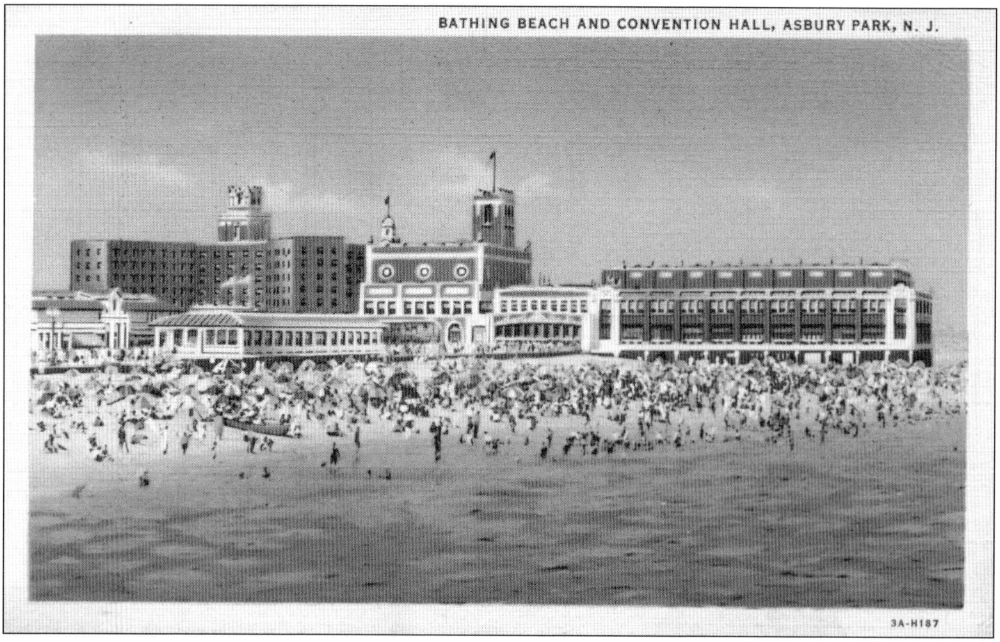


Like its contemporary, the Casino at the southern end of the boardwalk, the building that replaced the Fifth Avenue Arcade was designed by Warren and Wetmore. Located just north of the previous structure, this new complex, commonly referred to as the convention hall, included the Paramount Theater on the western side of the boardwalk and an exhibition space (the convention hall proper) that extends over the beach to the east. The two buildings are joined by an arcade that allowed visitors to pass through to the other side of the boardwalk.

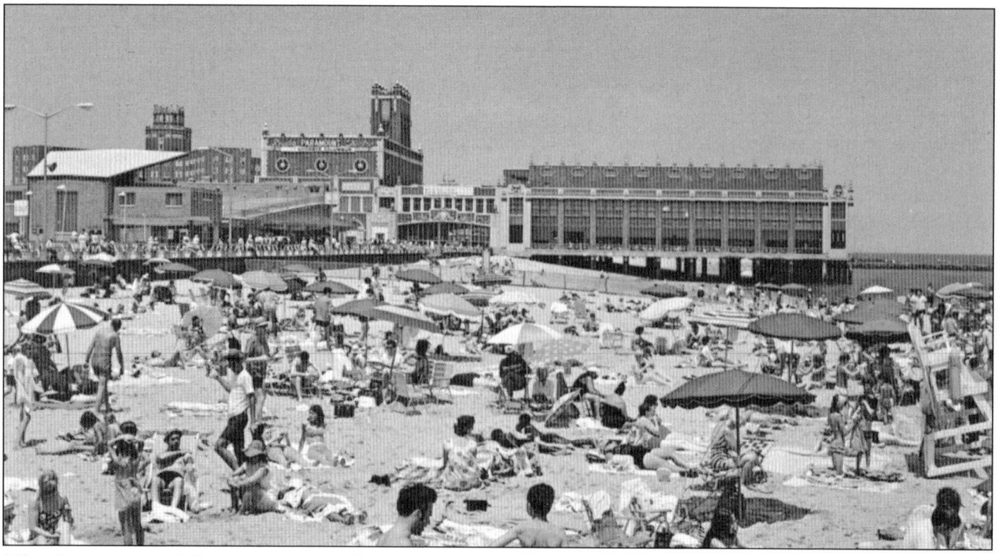

The Paramount Theater was Walter Reade's fifth theater in Asbury Park. Reade originally expressed concern that five theaters may be too many for the city, but he reconsidered once he was given the contract to book movies there. The theater's grand opening in July 1930 featured appearances by Ed Wynn, Nancy Carroll, Ginger Rogers, and all four Marx brothers. In addition to movies, the Paramount Theater's stage also hosted live performances, which is what it is primarily used for today.

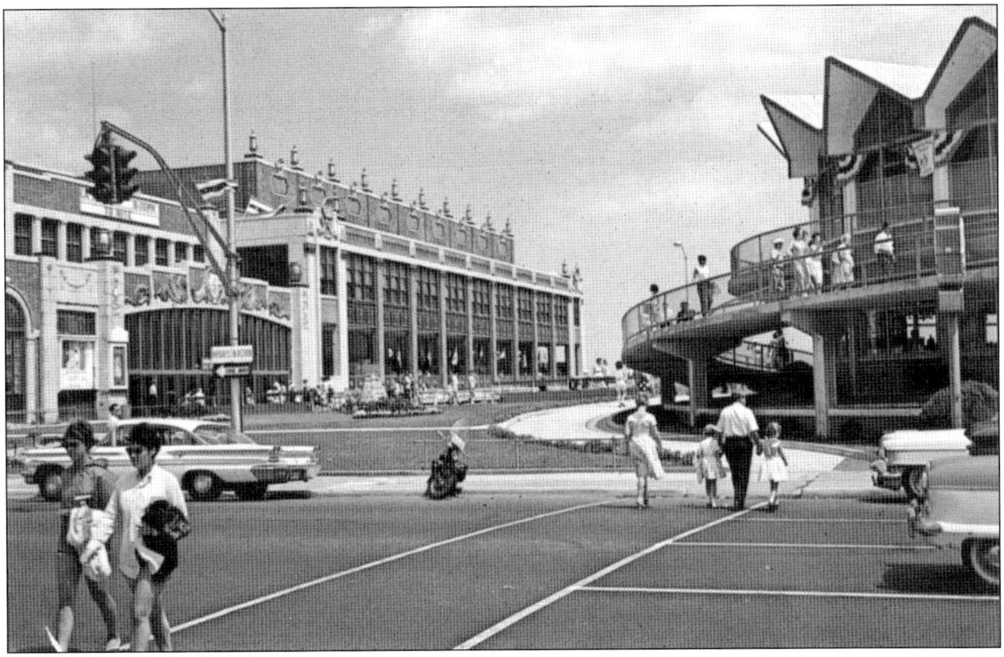

This is the view of the convention hall facing east from across Ocean Avenue. The Wonder Bar would be directly behind the photographer. The building on the right surrounded by the circular ramp is Howard Johnson's restaurant.

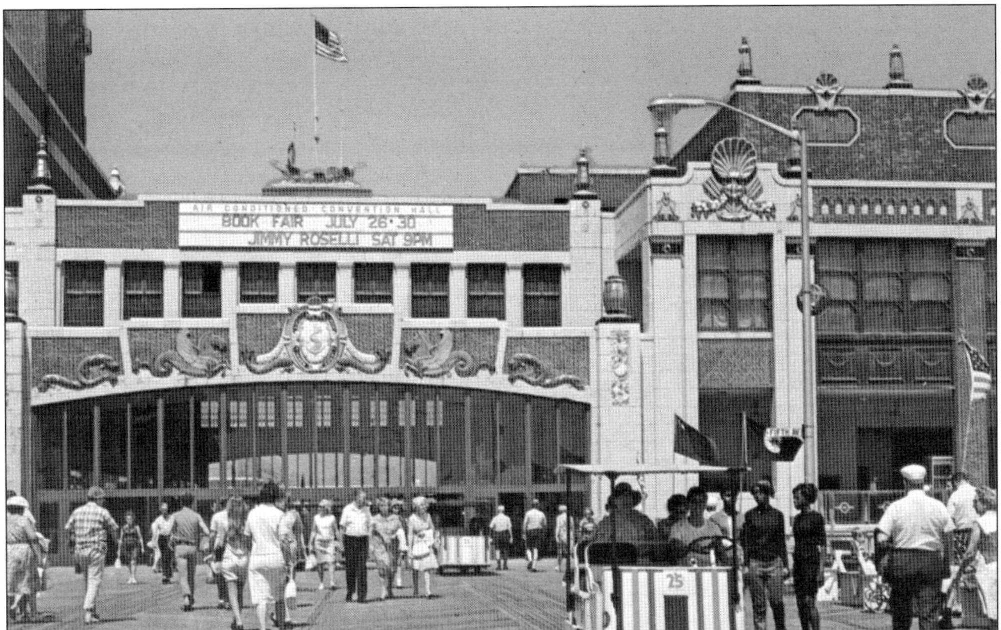


The entrance to the convention hall's arcade can be seen here. The building's exterior is decorated with patterned brick and copper panels, as well as nautical terra-cotta sculptural elements, including seashells, sea serpents, ships, anchors, and winged seahorses. In 2007, these decorative details underwent an extensive restoration after years of damage due to exposure to the salt air.

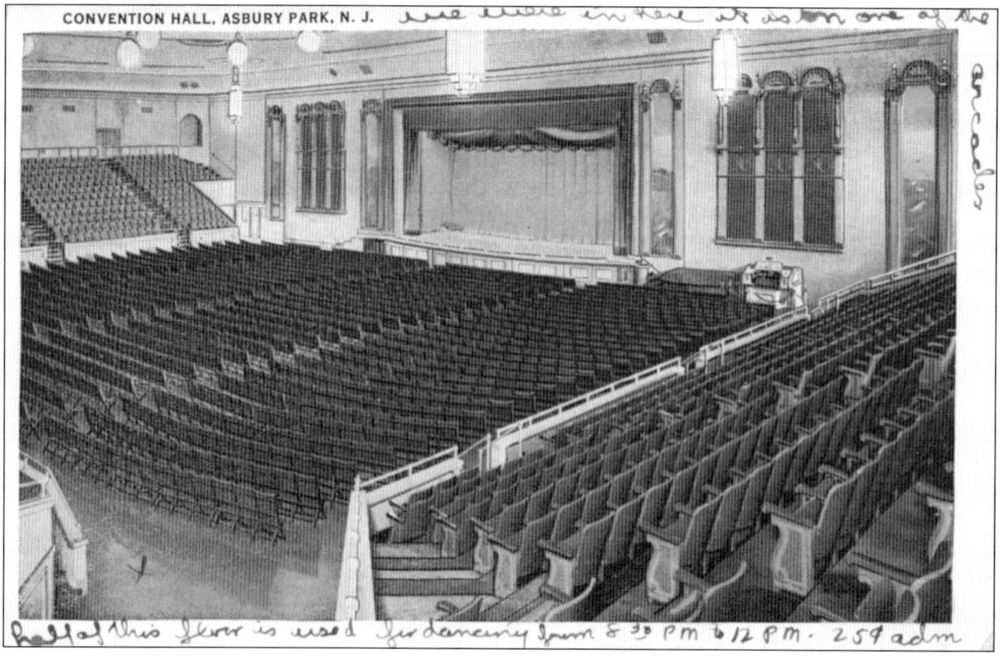


Over the years, the convention hall has hosted concerts by Frank Sinatra, the Who, Led Zeppelin, the Doors, KISS, and of course, Bon Jovi and Bruce Springsteen. The convention hall fell out of favor as a concert venue once the much larger Garden State Arts Center (now the PNC Bank Arts Center) opened in 1968.

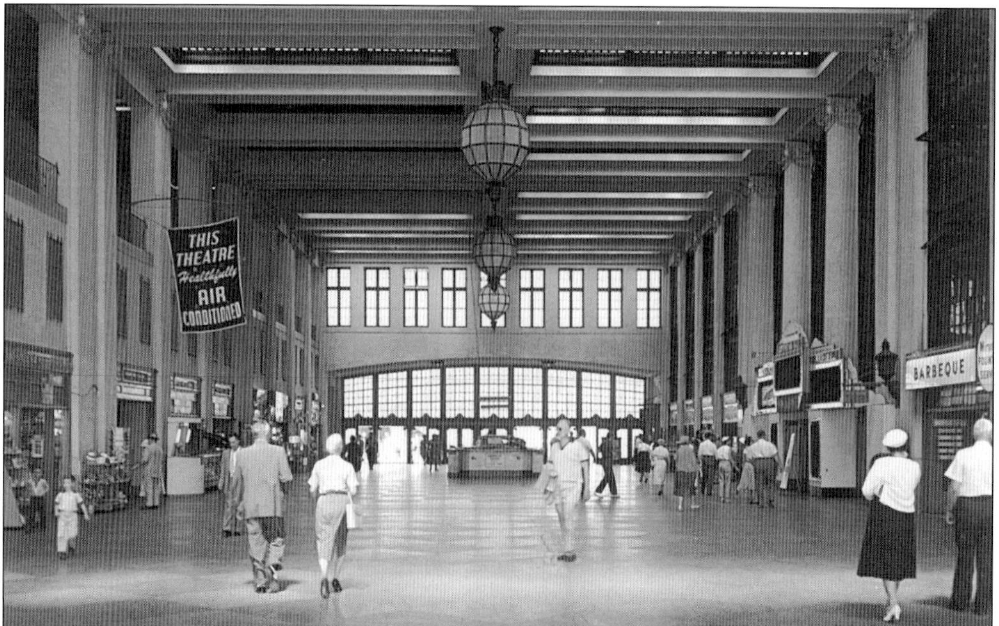


The interior of the convention hall's arcade still looks much as it does in this postcard, with shops and refreshment stands lining the sides of the building. On the right is the entrance to the convention hall, and the Paramount Theater's entrance is to the left.

# *Seven*

# The *Morro Castle* Disaster

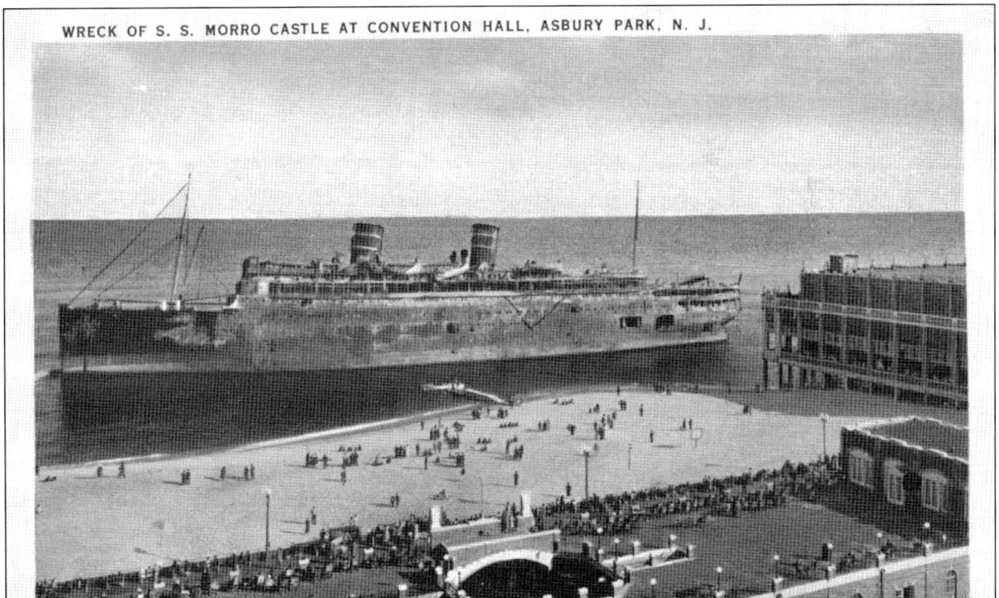


In September 1934, the luxury liner *Morro Castle* was headed to New York, carrying vacationers returning from a trip to Havana, Cuba. The last night at sea for the *Morro Castle* ended in one of the worst maritime disasters in US history, and the ship itself became an unlikely tourist attraction when it came to rest in the shallow water just 100 yards from Asbury Park's convention hall.

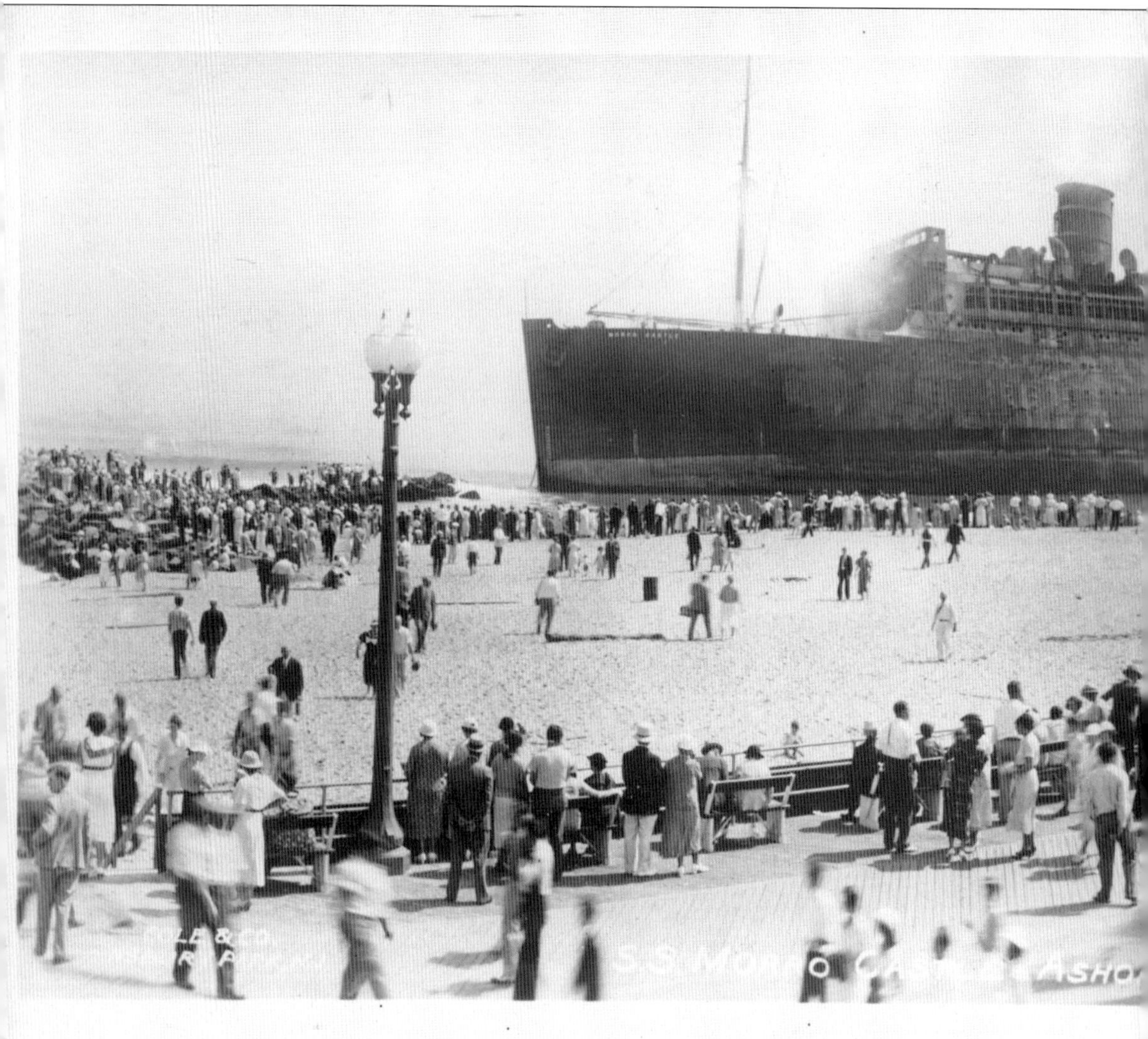

On September 7, 1934, a nor'easter was brewing, and the *Morro Castle* was moving swiftly to arrive home ahead of it. Around 8:00 p.m., diners were greeted by the terrible news that the ship's captain, Robert Wilmott, had died. The cause was reportedly a heart attack brought on by indigestion. With Captain Wilmott dead, first officer William Warms became acting captain, and he set about guiding the ship safely to port. A few hours later, around 2:50 a.m., the new captain would have to contend with an even greater challenge—a fire was discovered aboard the

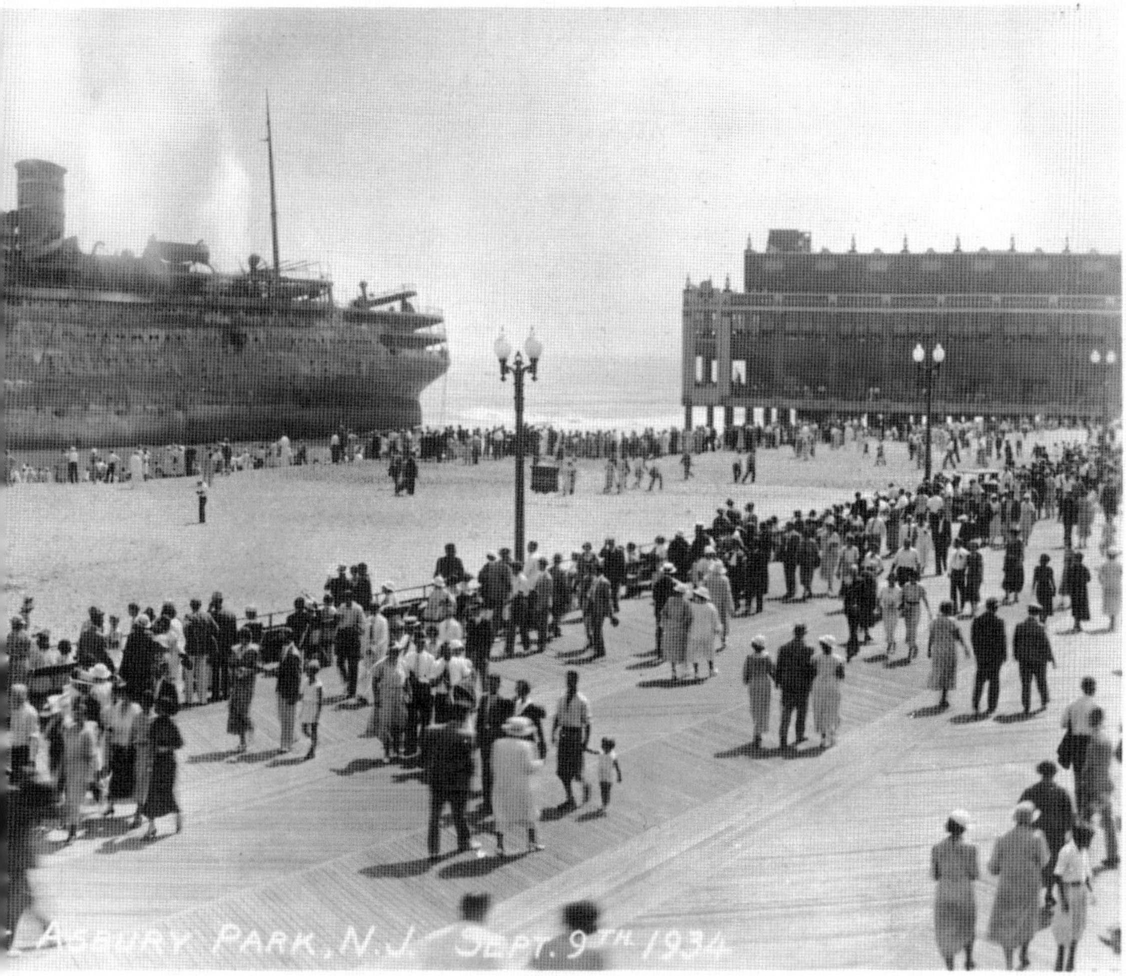


ship. The fire spread quickly, fanned by stiff winds and fed by the ship's wooden appointments covered in layers of flammable lacquer. Just one SOS was sent before the electrical lines were destroyed, and soon the fire burned through the ship's hydraulic lines, rendering it unable to steer. By 4:00 a.m., nearly the entire ship was engulfed in flames. The Coast Guard cutter *Tampa* attempted to tow the *Morro Castle* to port, but she became stranded as well. Ultimately, the *Morro Castle* drifted along the shore, beaching at Asbury Park.

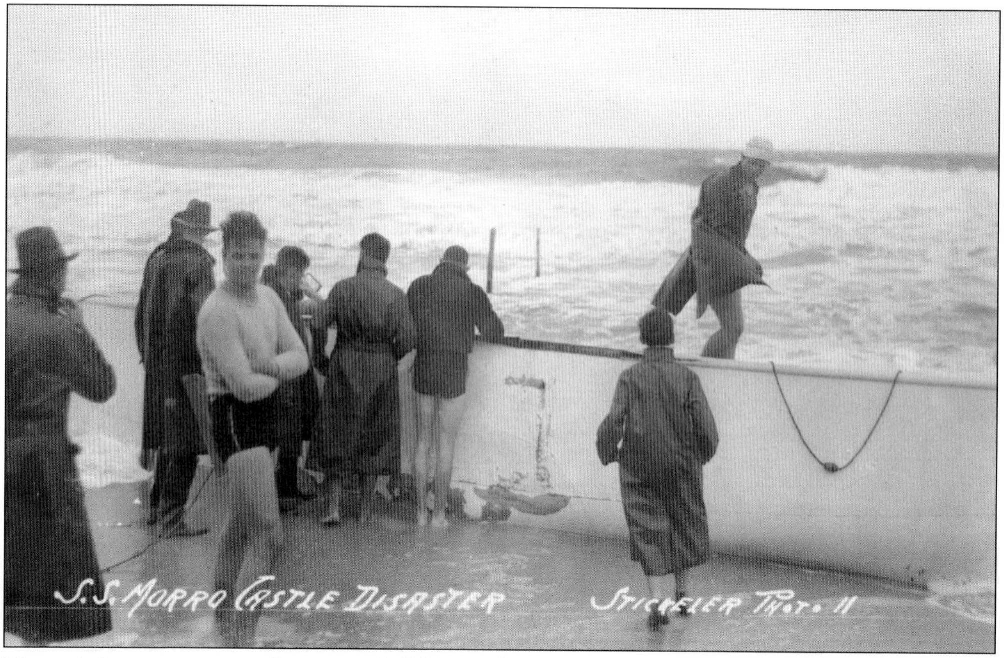


Though there were more than enough lifeboats for everyone on board the *Morro Castle*, only half were launched. There had been no lifeboat drills, so passengers and even some of the crew were not prepared to evacuate. To make matters worse, some of the lifeboats had been shellacked in place. This is one of the lifeboats as it landed at Spring Lake.

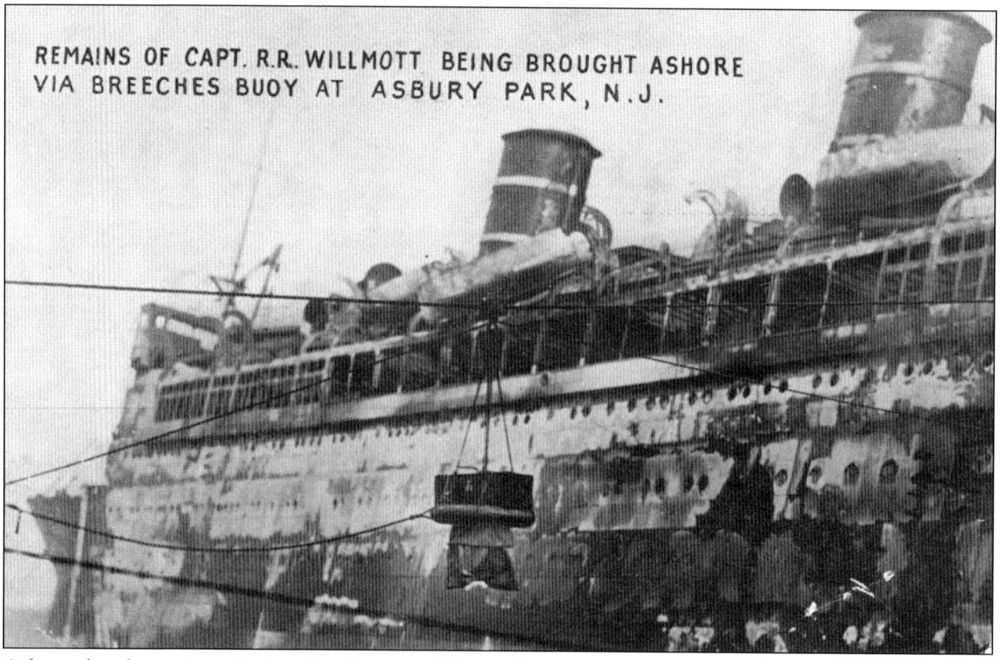


A breeches buoy is a device that is typically used to rescue passengers from disabled ships. A small cannon called a Lyle gun shoots a line to or from the ship, and a life preserver or harness attached to the line ferries people to safety. Here though, the breeches buoy is used to bring the remains of Captain Wilmott to shore.

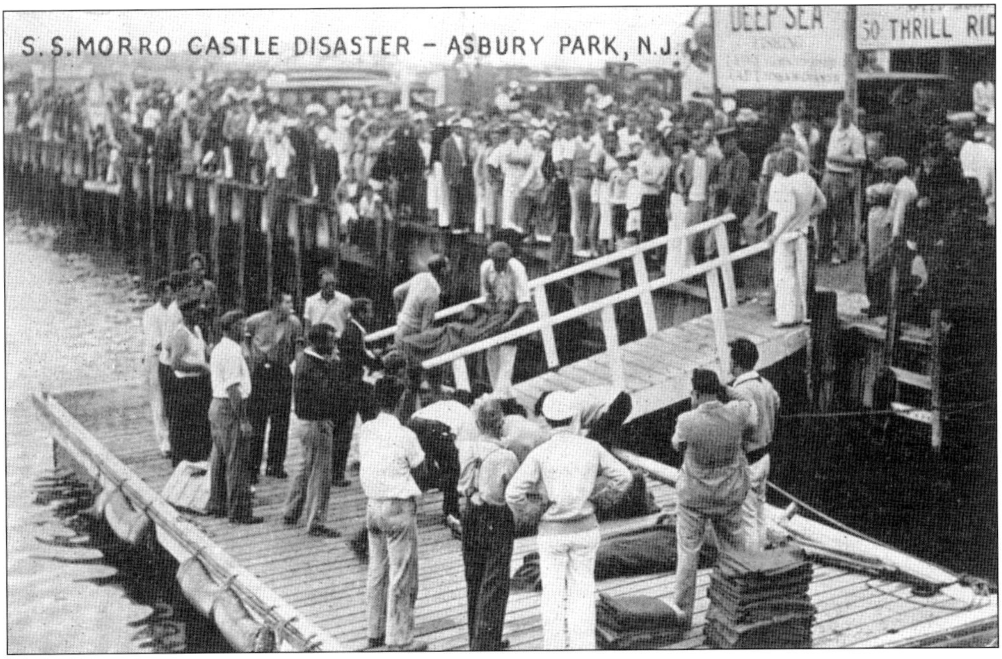


When the fire spread, the intense heat left many of the passengers with no choice but to jump overboard. Despite the storm, individuals up and down the Jersey Shore volunteered to help rescue survivors and recover victims, some of whom are seen here on a dock on the Manasquan River. A makeshift morgue was set up at Sea Girt to handle some of the 134 victims.

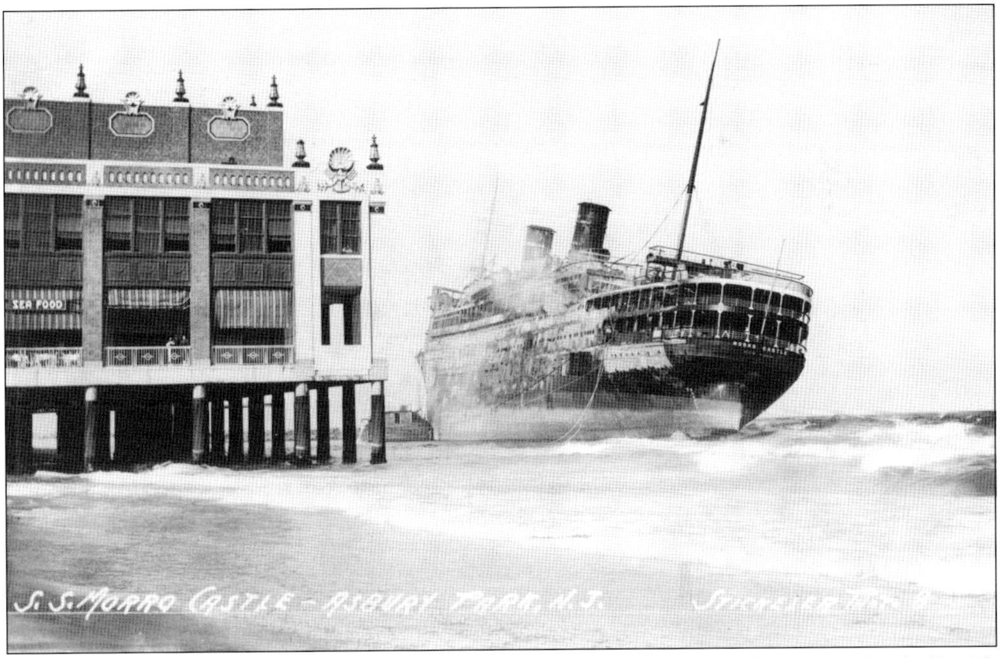


There were concerns that the *Morro Castle* would move and crash into the convention hall with the change of tides, but she remained in place, smoldering for days after coming to rest. The barge next to the *Morro Castle* in this image eventually extinguished the fire, using high-powered pumps to send tons of water into the ship.

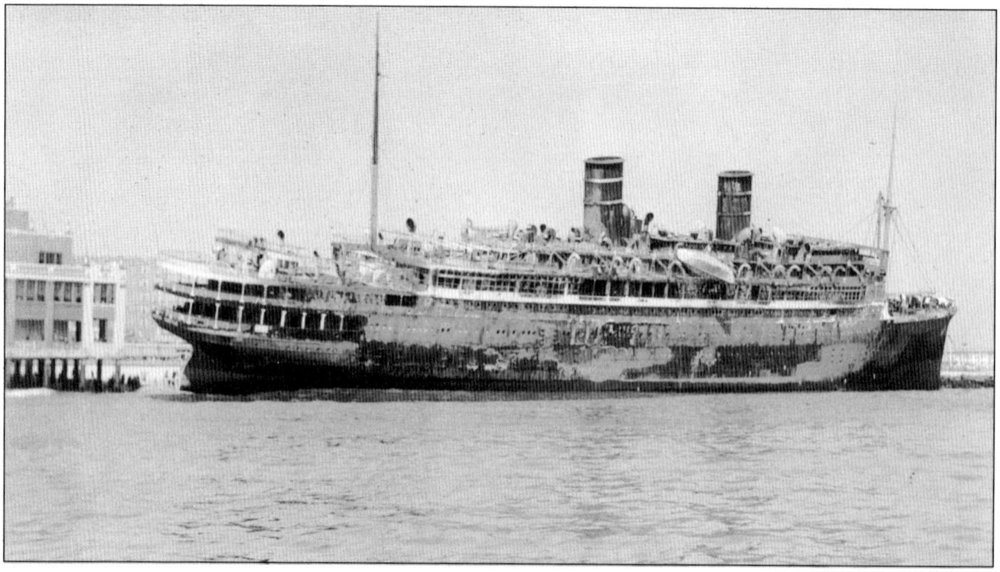

The cause of the fire aboard the *Morro Castle* has never been satisfactorily determined, but suspicion largely rests on radio operator George Rogers. Though originally hailed as a hero for staying with the ship to man its radio transmitter, two years after the disaster, Rogers was investigated for arson unrelated to the wreck. In 1938, Rogers was convicted of attempted murder after sending a bomb to a coworker who suspected him of setting the *Morro Castle* fire. George Rogers was released in 1942 but convicted of double murder in 1954, and died in jail in 1958.

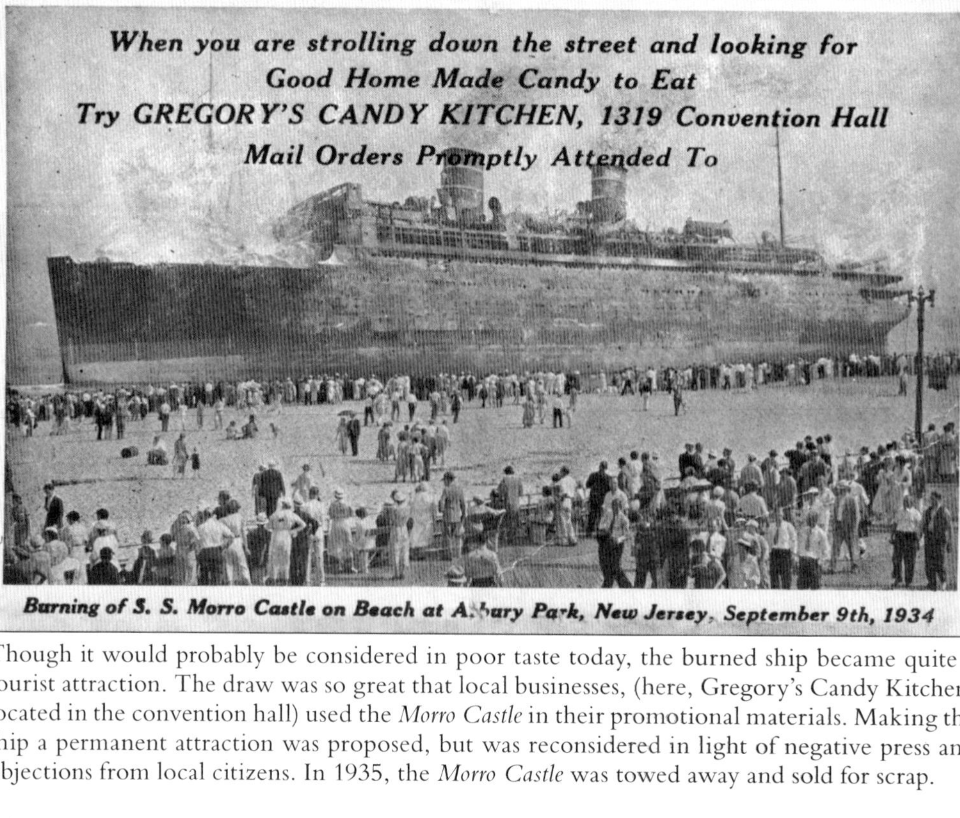


**Burning of S. S. Morro Castle on Beach at Asbury Park, New Jersey, September 9th, 1934**

Though it would probably be considered in poor taste today, the burned ship became quite a tourist attraction. The draw was so great that local businesses, (here, Gregory's Candy Kitchen, located in the convention hall) used the *Morro Castle* in their promotional materials. Making the ship a permanent attraction was proposed, but was reconsidered in light of negative press and objections from local citizens. In 1935, the *Morro Castle* was towed away and sold for scrap.

## *Eight*

# The Great Atlantic Hurricane of 1944

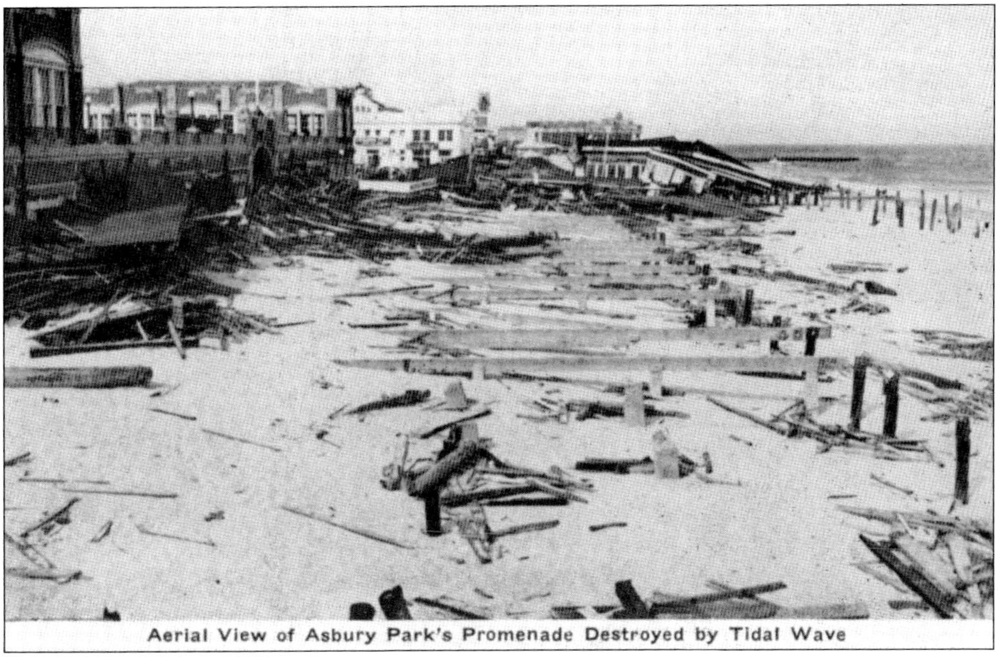

Aerial View of Asbury Park's Promenade Destroyed by Tidal Wave

In September 1944, a late summer hurricane struck the Eastern Seaboard, causing $50 million in damage from the Carolinas to Massachusetts. New Jersey was particularly hard hit by the storm, with $30 million of damage reported in the Garden State alone. Depicted here is the damage to Asbury Park's boardwalk as seen facing north from the Casino.

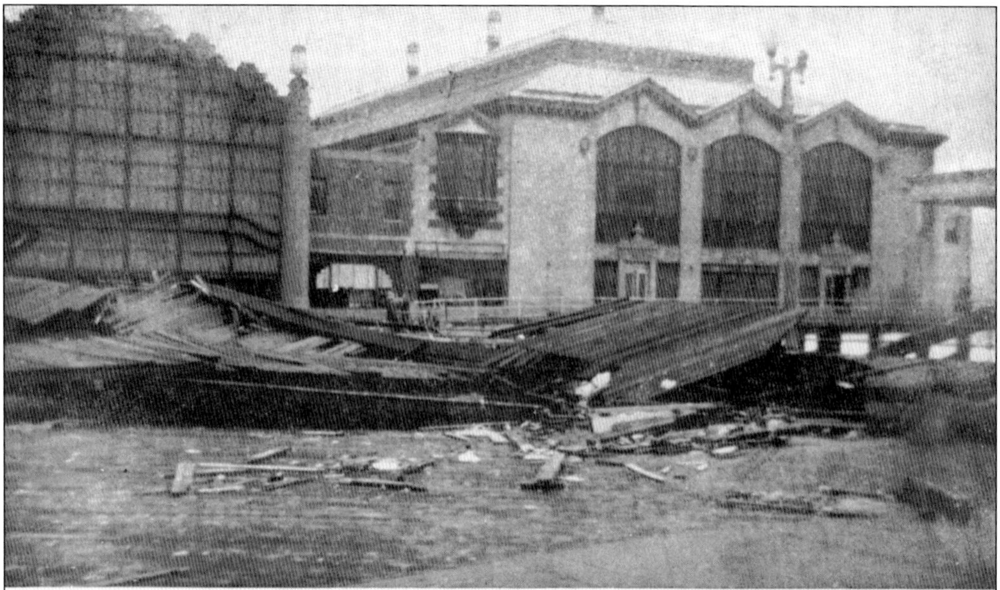

Wreckage in front of Asbury Park, N. J., Casino after the Hurricane of Sept. 14, 1944

Though the hurricane of 1944 brought sustained winds in excess of 75 miles per hour, it was the storm surge that caused the worst of the damage in Asbury Park. Here, boardwalk debris is seen in front of the Casino, looking north from Ocean Grove.

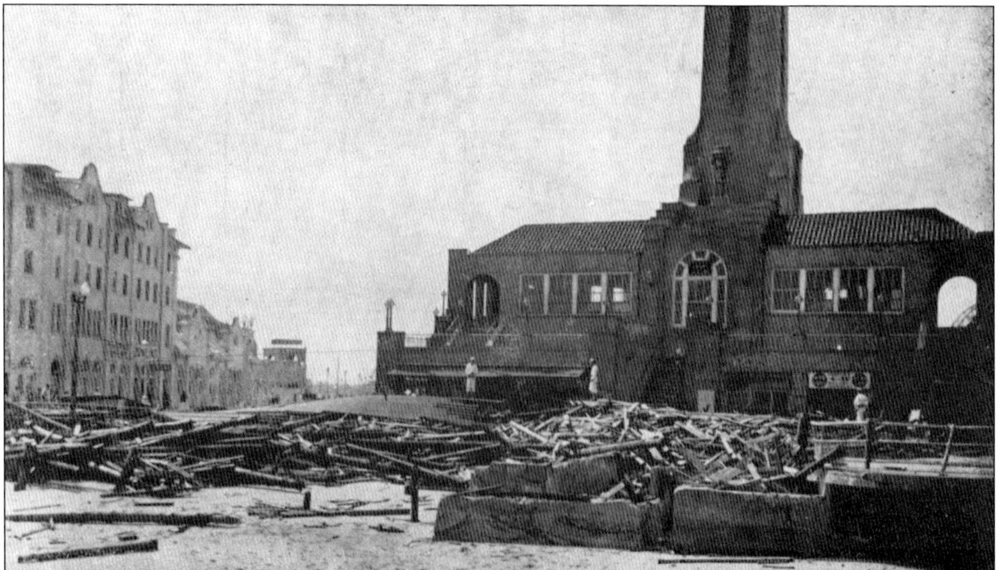

The Boardwalk 'aint' where it used to be in Asbury Park and Ocean Grove, N. J., Sept. 14, 1944 Hurricane

The boardwalk has washed up against Asbury Park's heating plant in this image. The Casino would be to the right of the photographer.

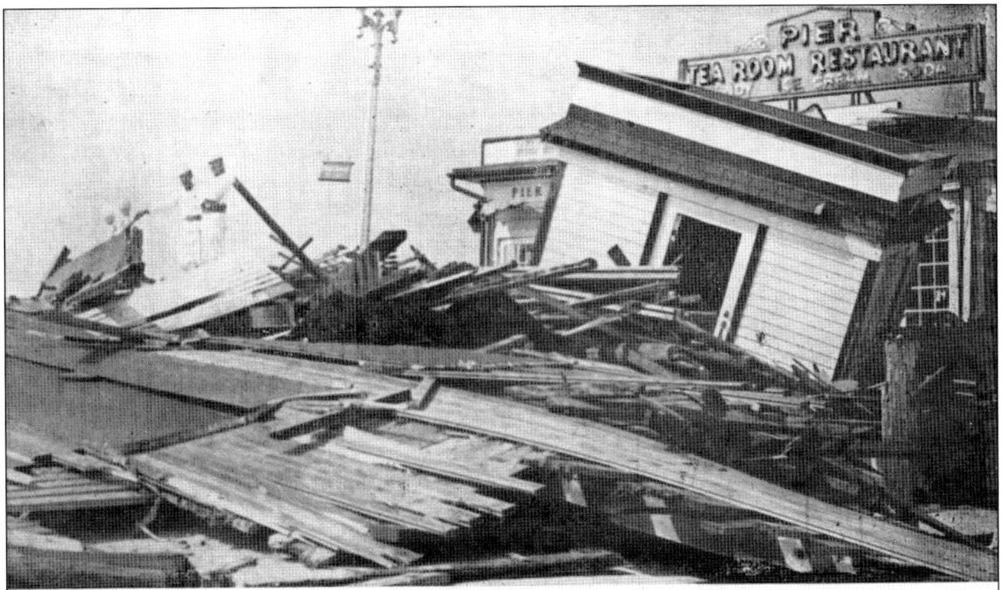


**Damage to Fishing Pier and Concessions near Casino at Asbury Park, N. J. in Storm of Sept. 14, 1944**

Asbury Park's fishing pier and concessions at First Avenue are pictured here. The Navy set up patrols in the aftermath of the storm to prevent looting; two sailors can be seen at left.

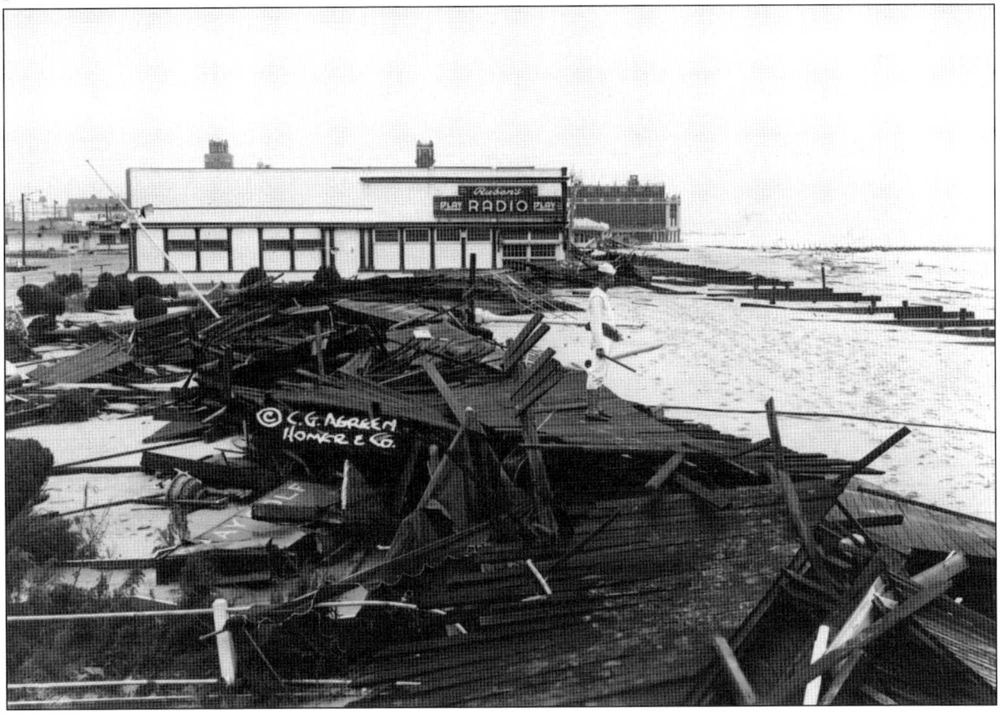


This image shows the damage to what had been a mini-golf course at Third Avenue. Locals reported a 50-foot tidal wave that washed nearly the entire boardwalk between Third and Fifth Avenues inland to Kingsley Street with its railing and light posts still attached. The convention hall is visible in the distance.

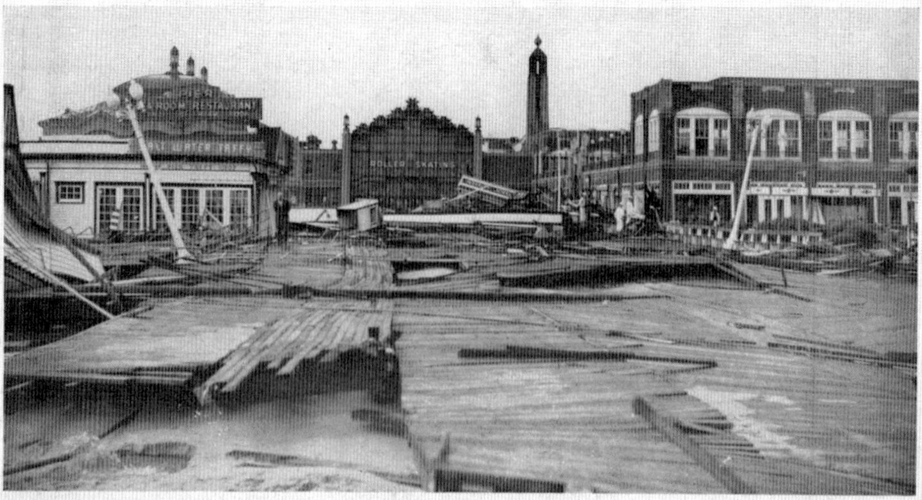

The brick and steel buildings weathered the storm, but the massive waves cut through the wooden structures like a giant knife through paper-mache.

Although the boardwalk and pavilions were destroyed, the Casino and convention hall survived the storm, though not without damage. The doors to the convention hall's arcade were torn from their hinges, and the Casino would remain closed until 1950.

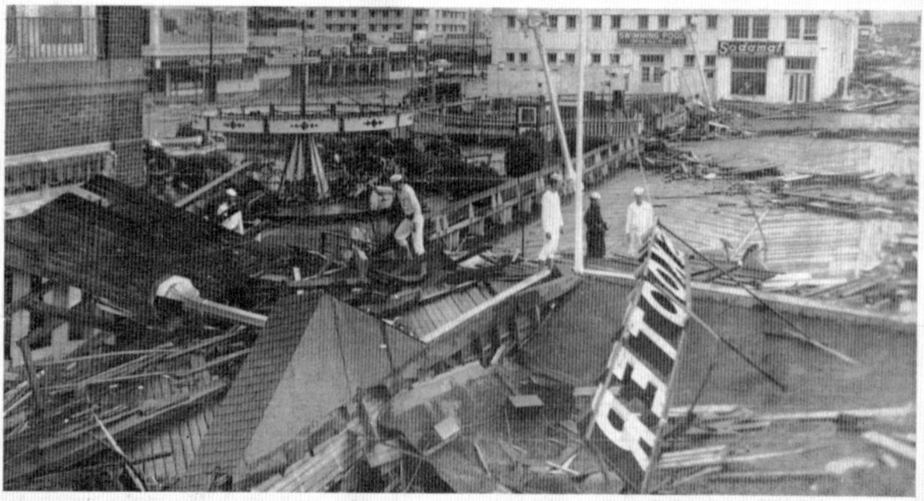


Aerial view looking north from First Avenue and Boardwalk, showing wooden building east of Boardwalk telescoped against buildings that stood sixty feet to the west.

Looking north, parts of the buildings on what had been the foot of the First Avenue fishing pier have washed up against the First Avenue pavilion. The hurricane destroyed 200 feet of the pier proper as well as all of the pavilions that once lined the eastern side of the boardwalk; these would not be rebuilt.

# *Nine*

# The Boardwalk and the Beach

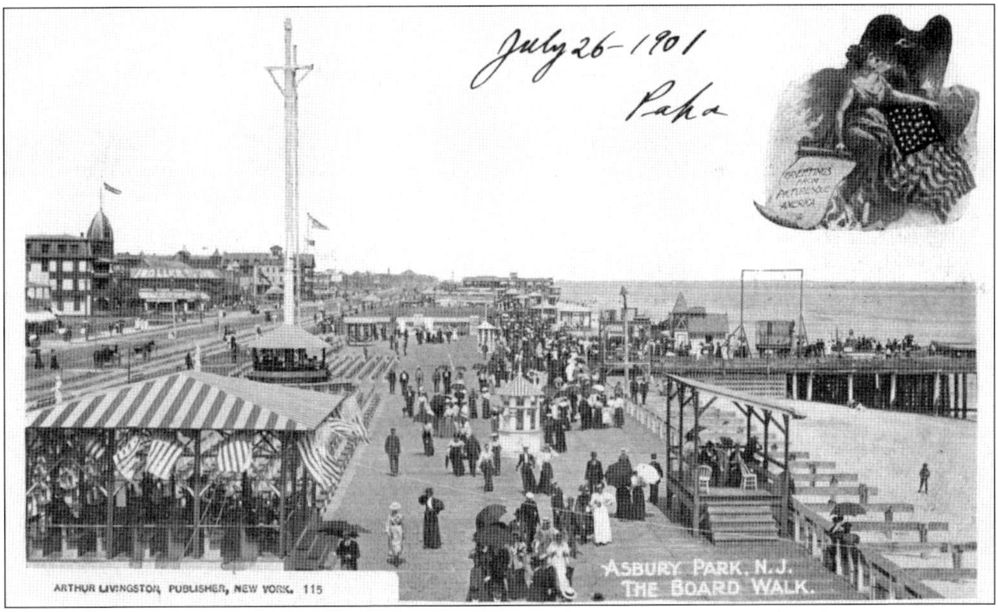


Asbury Park's earliest boardwalk was a narrow walkway that was removed and put into storage at the end of the summer. Just wide enough for two people walking side by side, a second strip was added before it was eventually expanded to the permanent wide promenade seen here around 1901. Founder Bradley was fond of placing random items like marble bathtubs, old boats, and animal cages along the boardwalk, ostensibly for the enjoyment of children. These were removed once the city gained control of the beachfront.

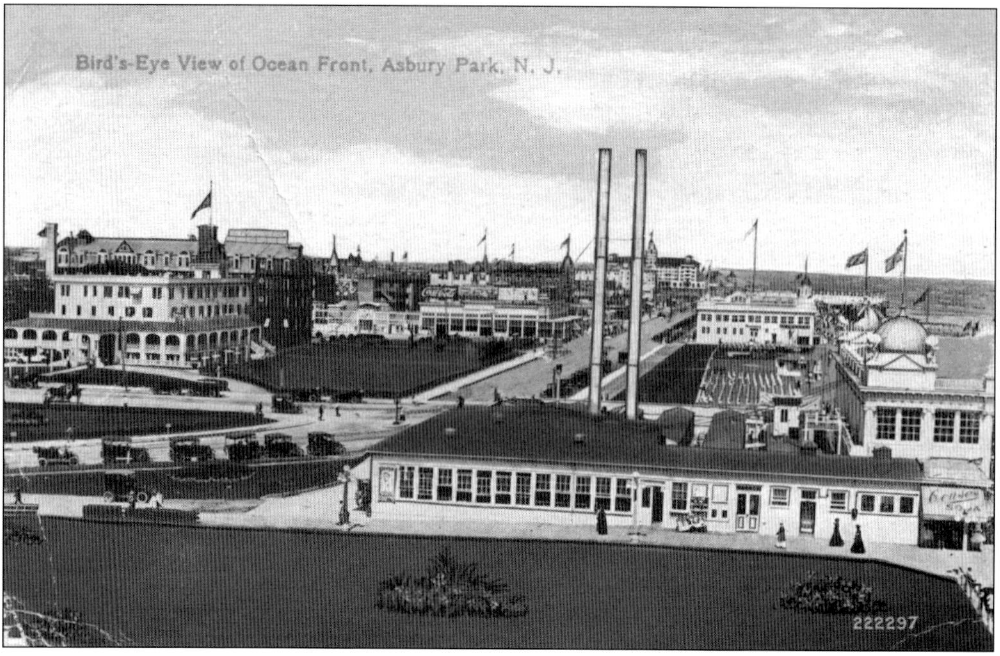

In this north-facing bird's-eye view of the oceanfront from about 1918, the Casino's restaurant can be seen in the foreground. North of the Casino along the boardwalk are rows of benches, the Natatorium, and the Fifth Ocean Avenue. The building at left is the Coleman House hotel, and in the far distance is the Monterey hotel.

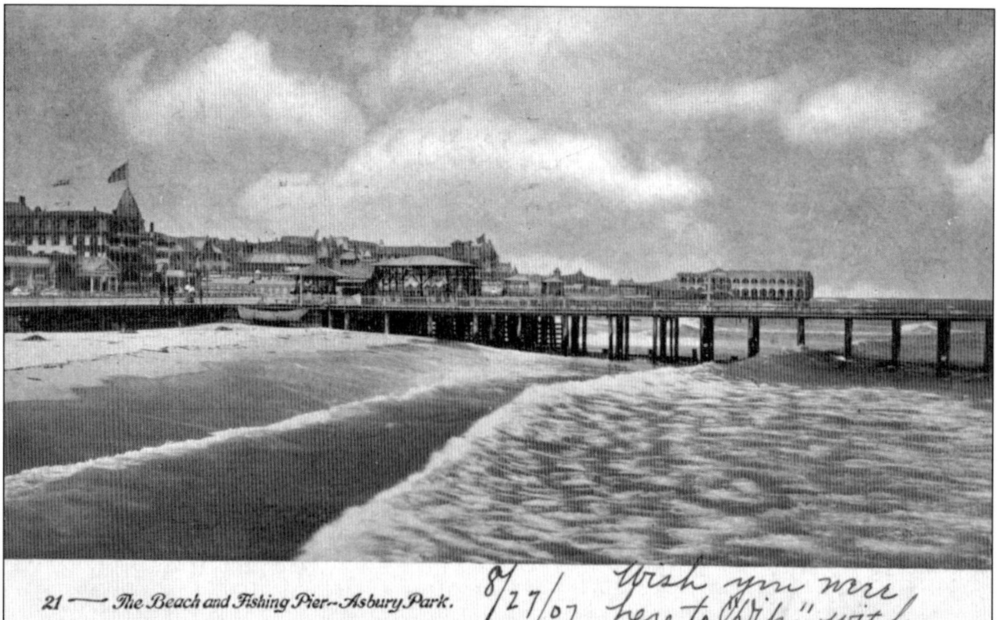

This is the view of the waterfront from the portion of the Casino that extended out over the ocean. The fishing pier at First Avenue is seen here in 1907, and in the distance is the Fifth Avenue Arcade, where famous bandleader Arthur Pryor led multiple daily concerts in the summer.

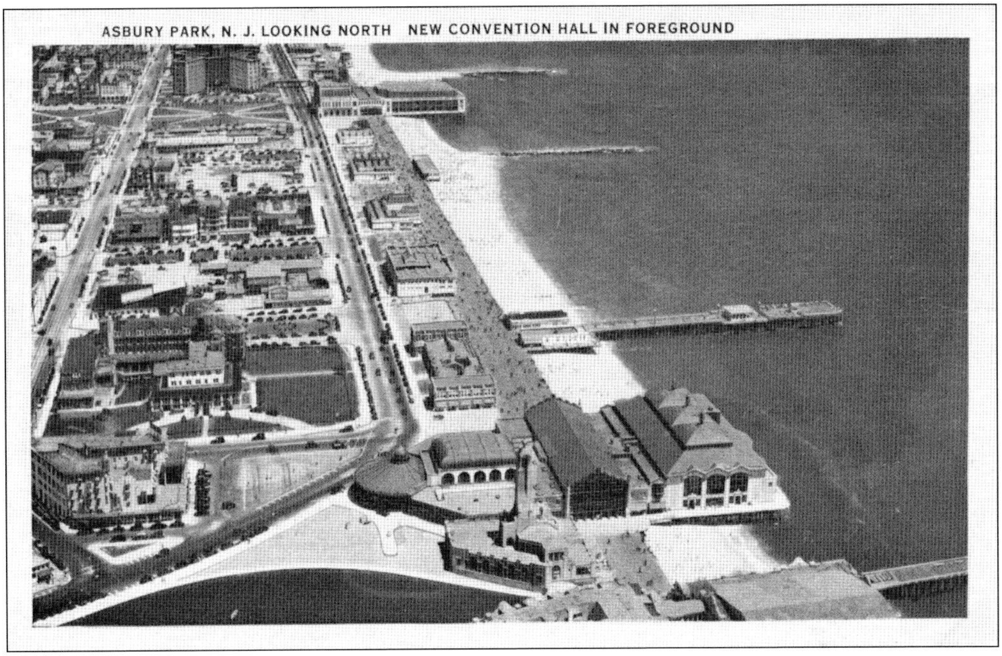


Looking north along the boardwalk, this aerial view shows the heating plant, the Casino, the fishing pier, pavilions, and the convention hall. The large lot to the west of the Asbury Avenue pavilion contains the Coleman House hotel; the hotel directly south of the Coleman House is the Plaza Hotel.

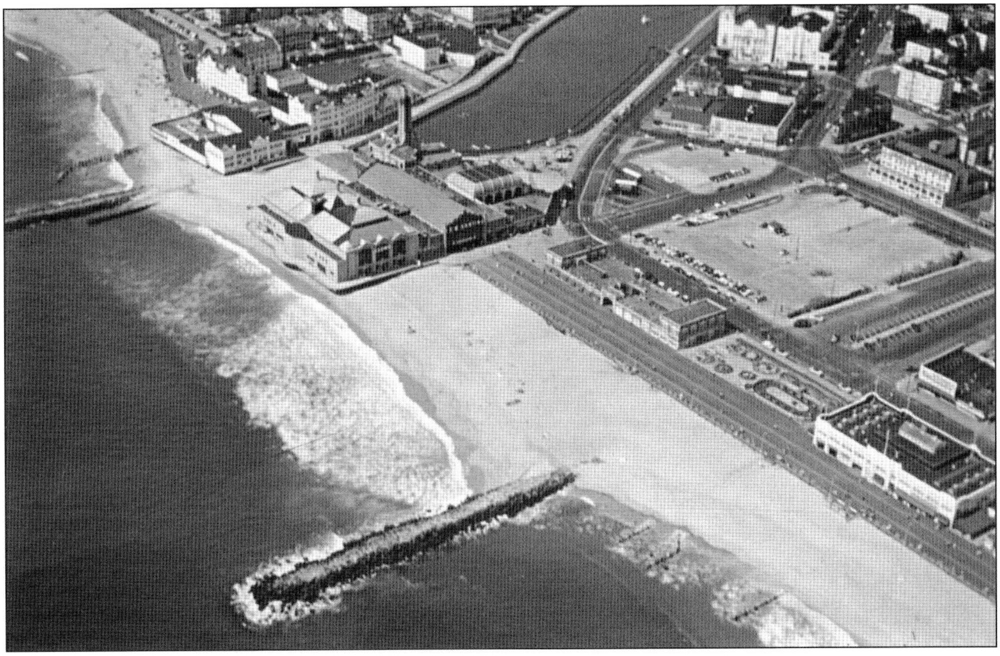

Looking in the opposite direction of the previous image, the southern end of Asbury Park's boardwalk is visible, including the Casino and the Asbury Avenue pavilion. The Coleman House hotel and Plaza Hotel have been demolished, and the First Avenue fishing pier has been replaced by a jetty. In the upper right are Palace Amusements and the Mayfair Theater.

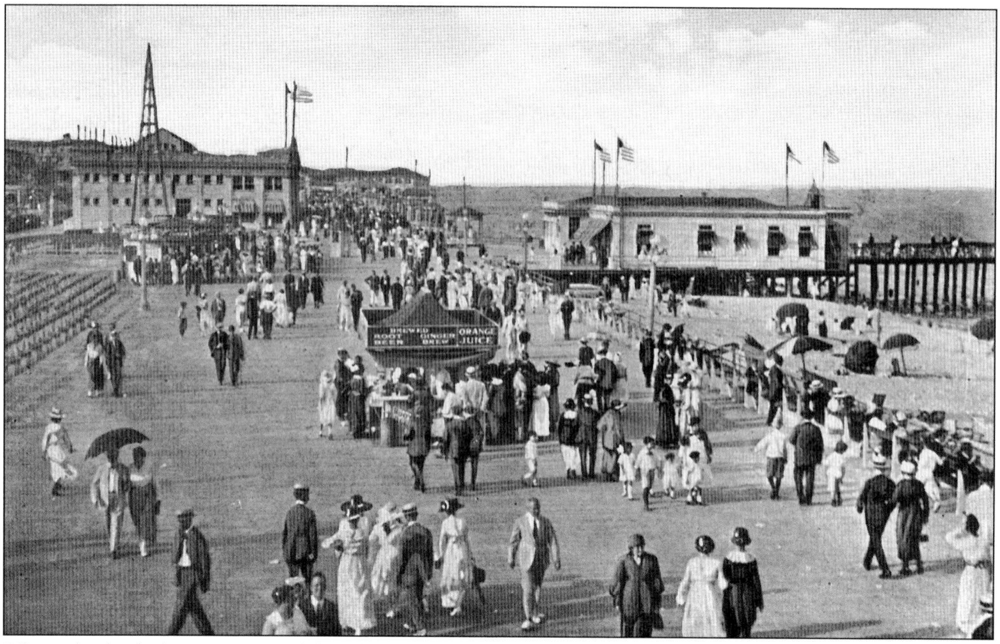


Though alcohol was not available for sale on the boardwalk, root beer, ginger brew, and orange juice were available. On the right, the buildings at the foot of the fishing pier can be seen.

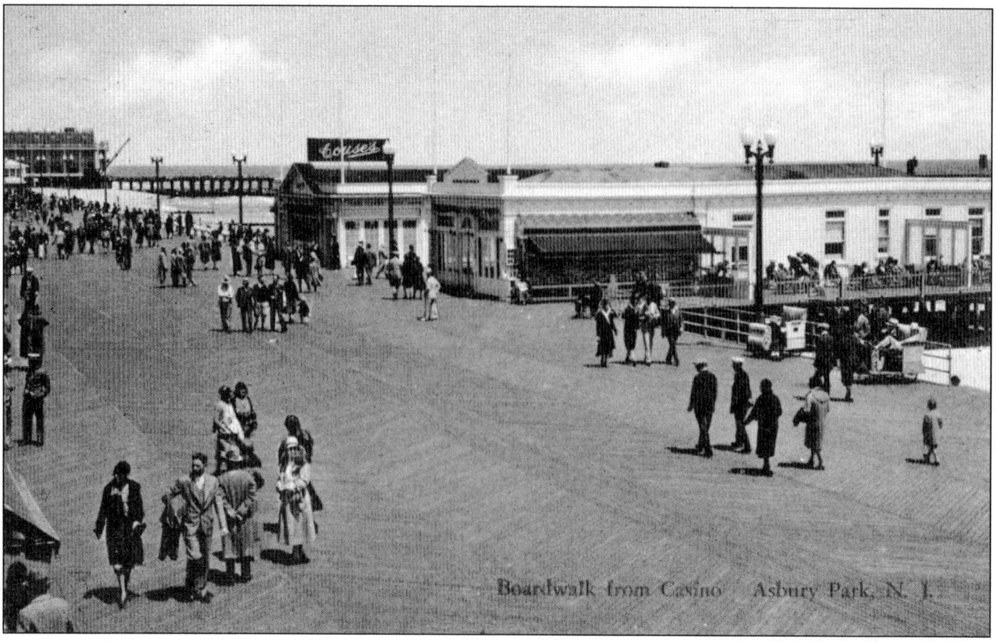


In this early 1940s postcard, one of Couse's four Asbury Park locations can be seen at the foot of the fishing pier. Couse's advertised that they made their own crushed fruits and ice cream.

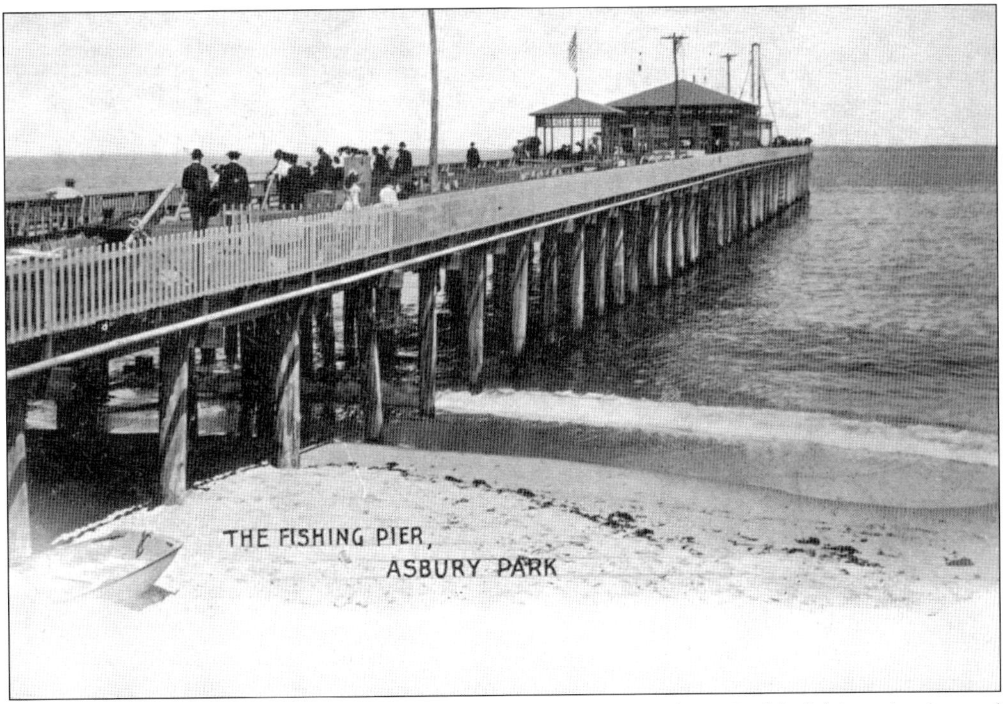


Founder Bradley paid $10,000 of his own money to construct Asbury Park's fishing pier, located at First Avenue. The pier was home to the largest fishing club in the United States in 1915. Fishing enthusiasts reportedly came from all over the country to catch tuna, striped bass, blue fish, mackerel, snapper, and flounder.

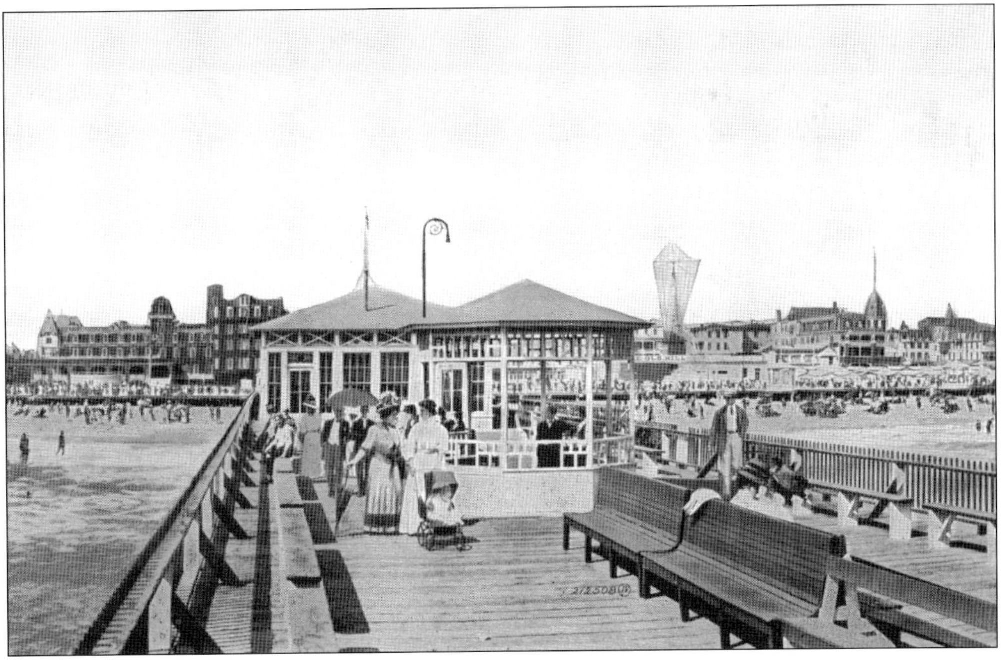

Looking west toward the boardwalk from the end of the fishing pier at First Avenue, the Coleman House hotel is seen at left in this card, mailed on August 18, 1910.

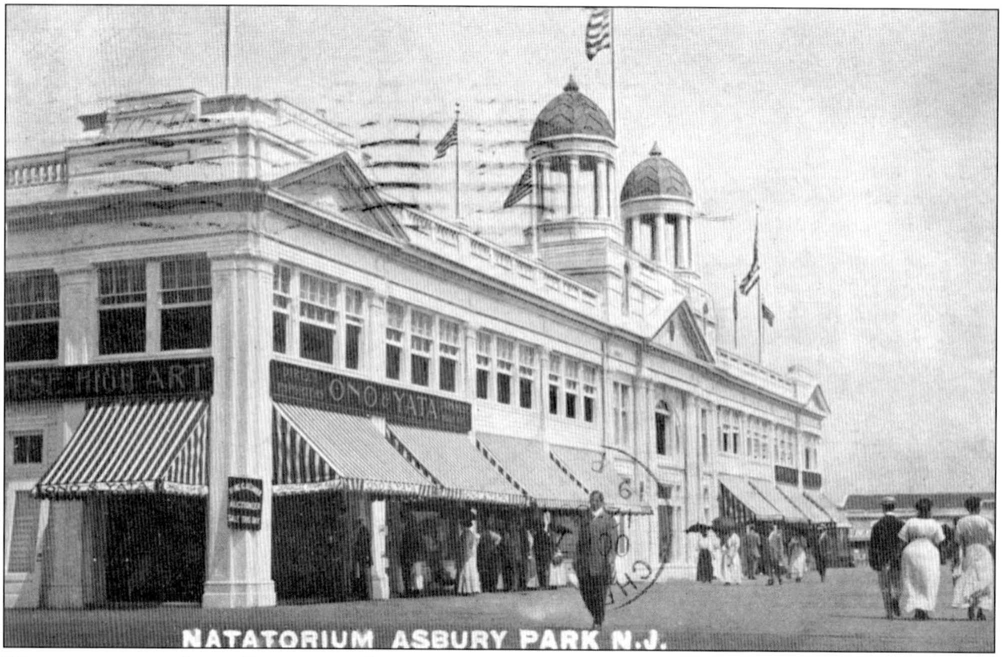


The two-story Greco Roman–style Natatorium, located at First Avenue on the boardwalk, housed a large indoor swimming pool and hot and cold saltwater baths. Shown here in 1911, the building was open year-round. The Natatorium also had restrooms, reading parlors, a barber shop, and stores like the art shop seen to the left.

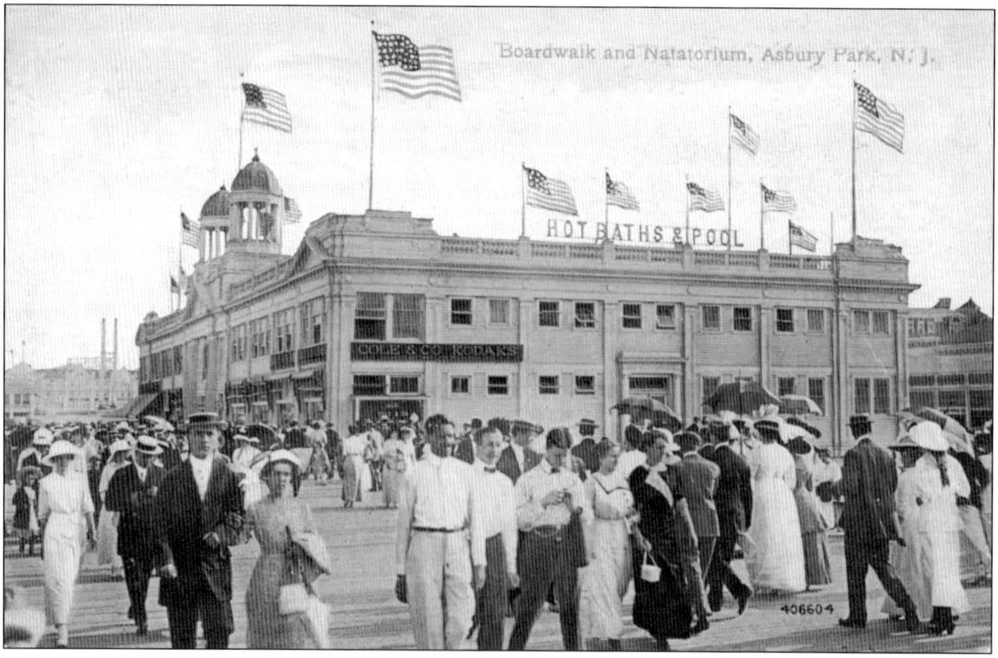


On April 5 1917, faulty wiring in the Natatorium started a fire that destroyed four blocks of Asbury Park's waterfront between First and Second Avenues, from the boardwalk to Grand Avenue. Winds coming off of the water from a nor'easter made fighting the fire particularly difficult. All told, nearly 50 buildings were destroyed, and the damage was estimated at $1 million at the time.

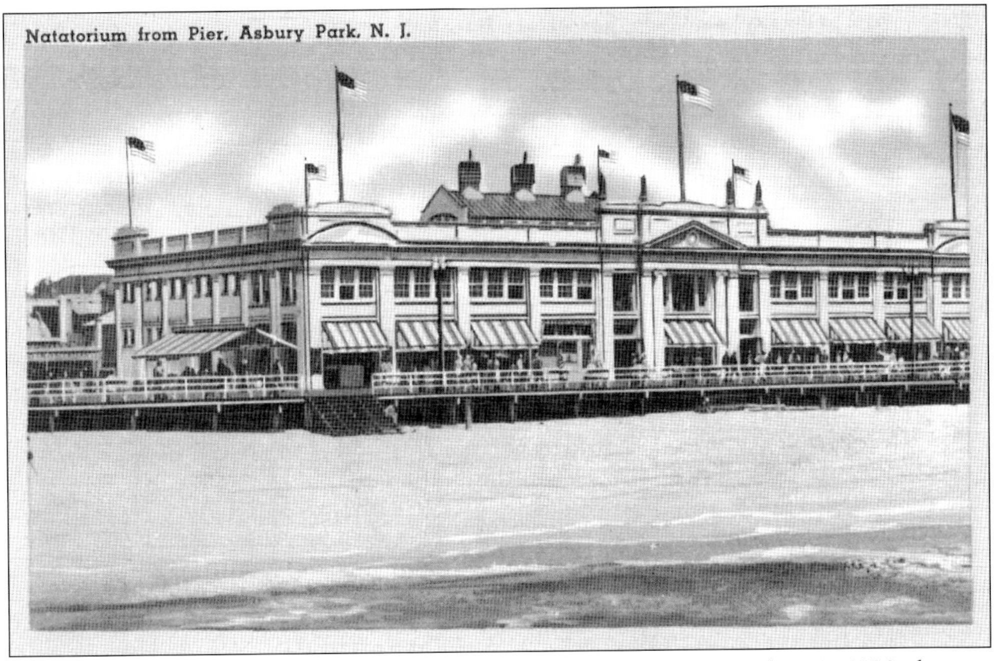


The Natatorium was rebuilt in the same location after the great fire. Seen here in 1920, the new building housed many of the same amenities as the one it replaced. MacDonald & Ely Real Estate Agents had offices in the building in the 1920s, and Michals Seafood Restaurant was located in the Natatorium before moving to its location at Ocean and Second Avenues.

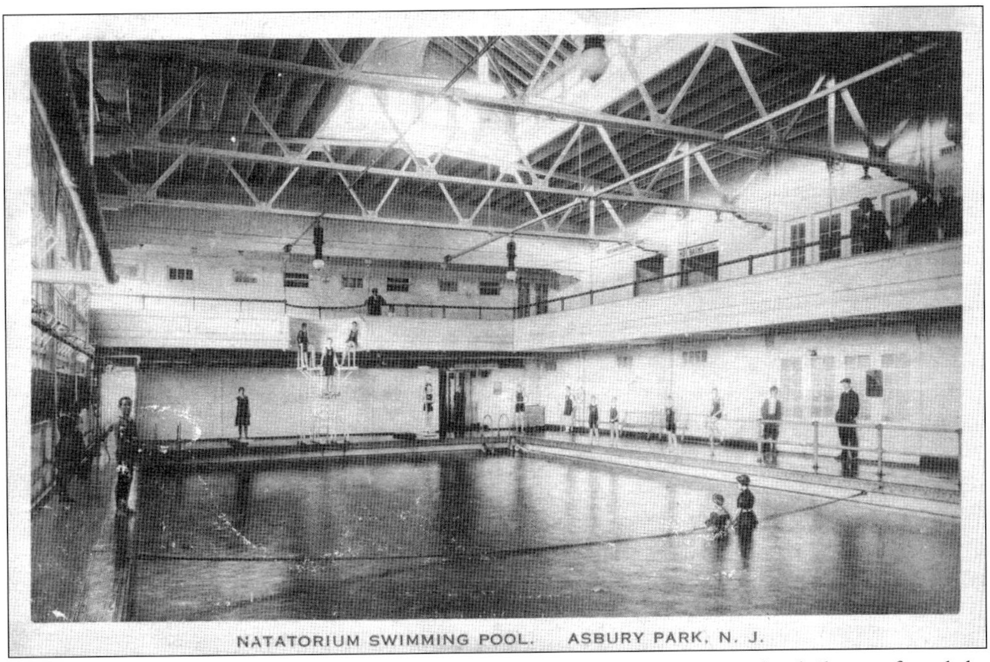


The Natatorium's large indoor tile-lined pool is seen here. In the 1940s, the daily rate for adults was 60¢. The city demolished the Natatorium in 1962.

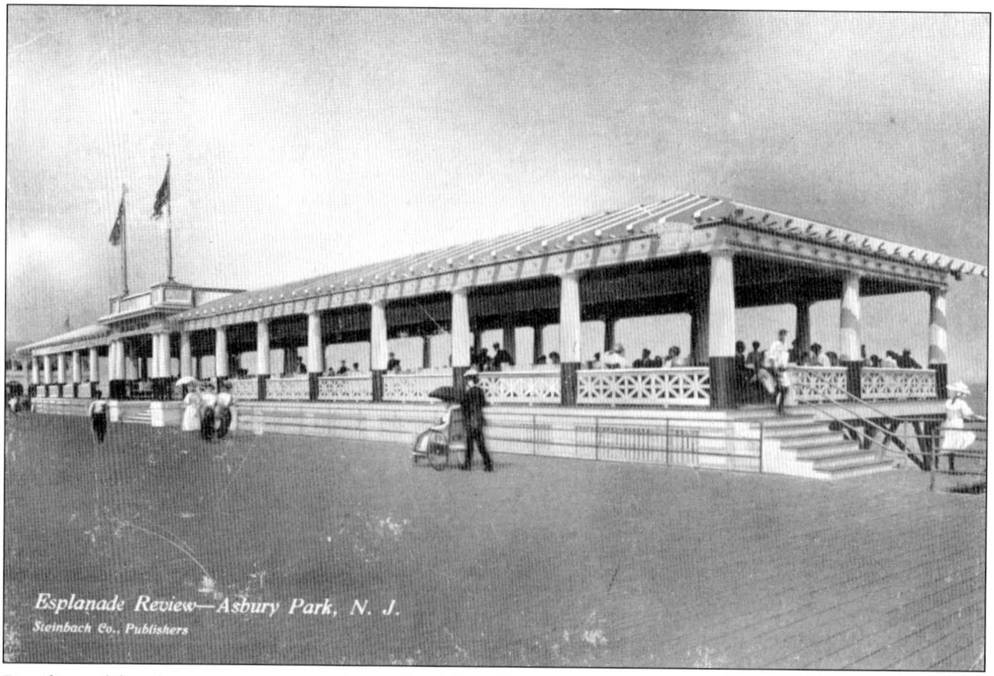


Pavilions like the one seen here, located at Fourth Avenue, were available for patrons to rest and enjoy a view of the beach.

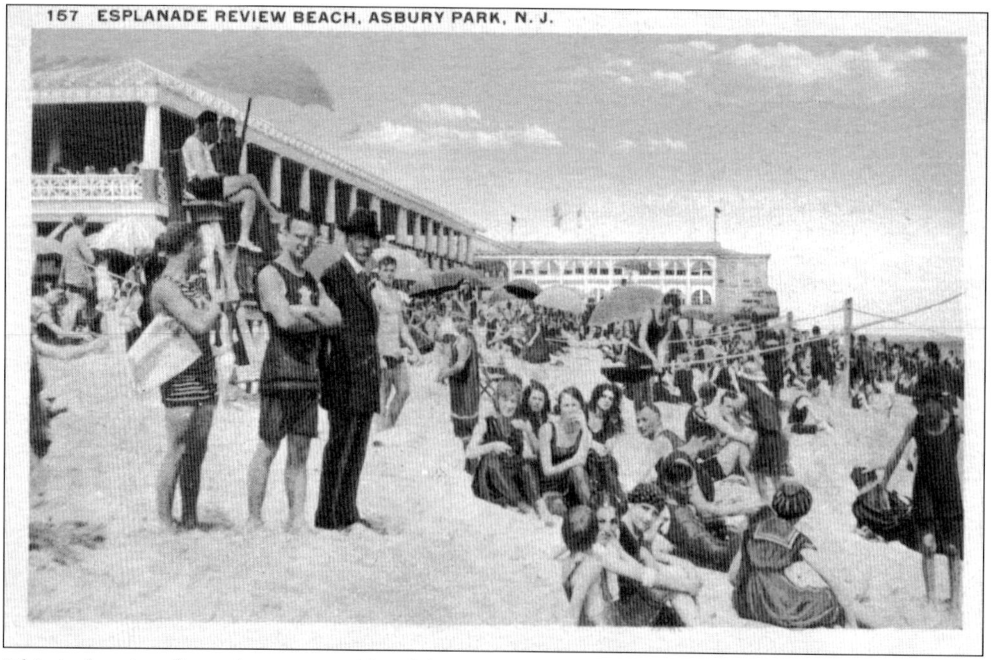


This is the view from the eastern side of the Esplanade Review at Fourth Avenue. The building in the distance at center is the Fifth Avenue Arcade.

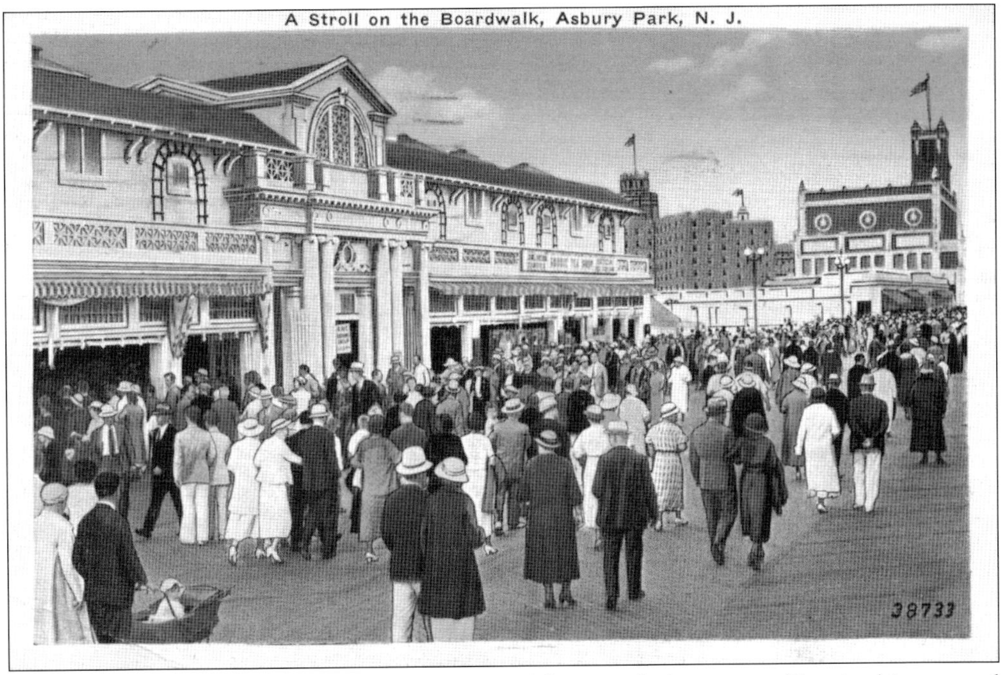


Men and women enjoy the boardwalk in front of the Fourth Avenue pavilion in this postcard postmarked June 26, 1939. The Paramount Theater and Berkeley-Carteret hotel can be seen on the right.

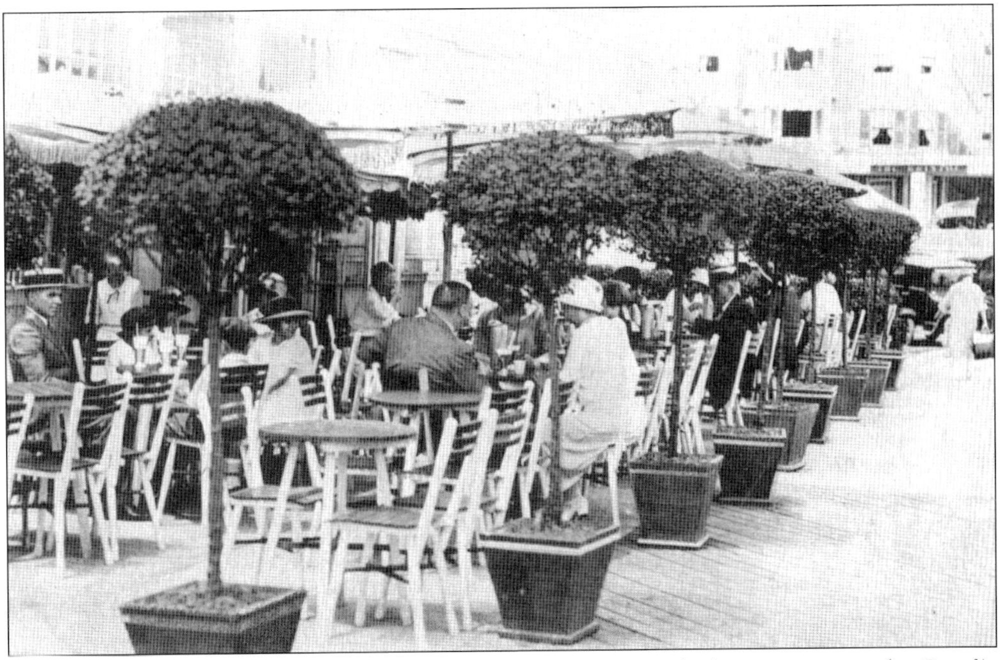

In this postcard, mailed in July 1931, patrons enjoy open air refreshments next to the Goodie Tea Shoppe in the Fourth Avenue pavilion.

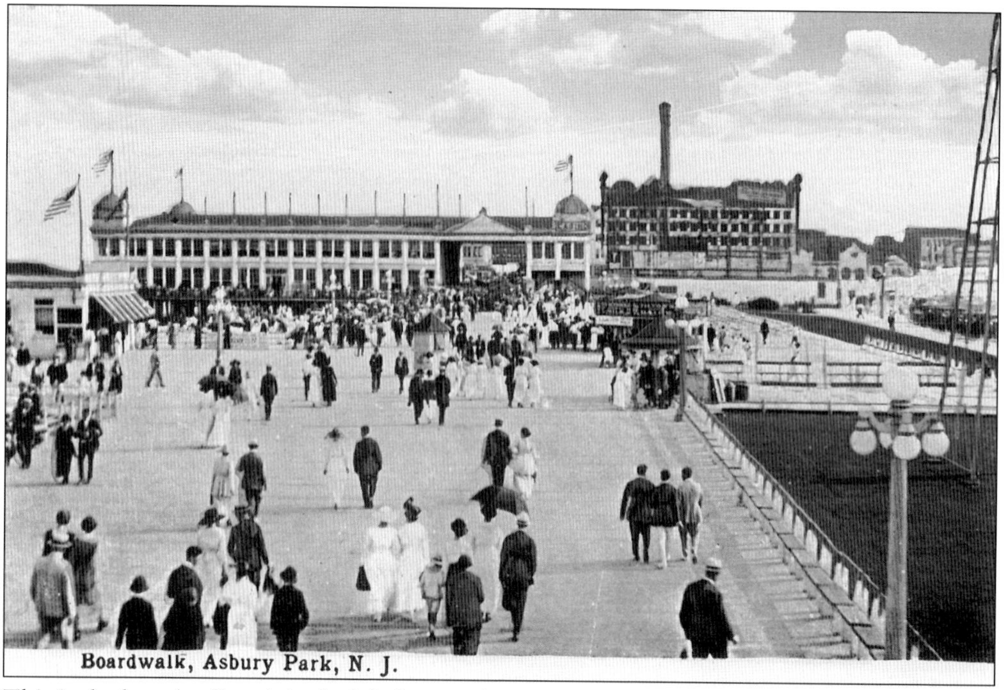


This is the boardwalk as it looked facing south toward the old Casino in the early 1900s. The concessions at the foot of the fishing pier can be seen at left.

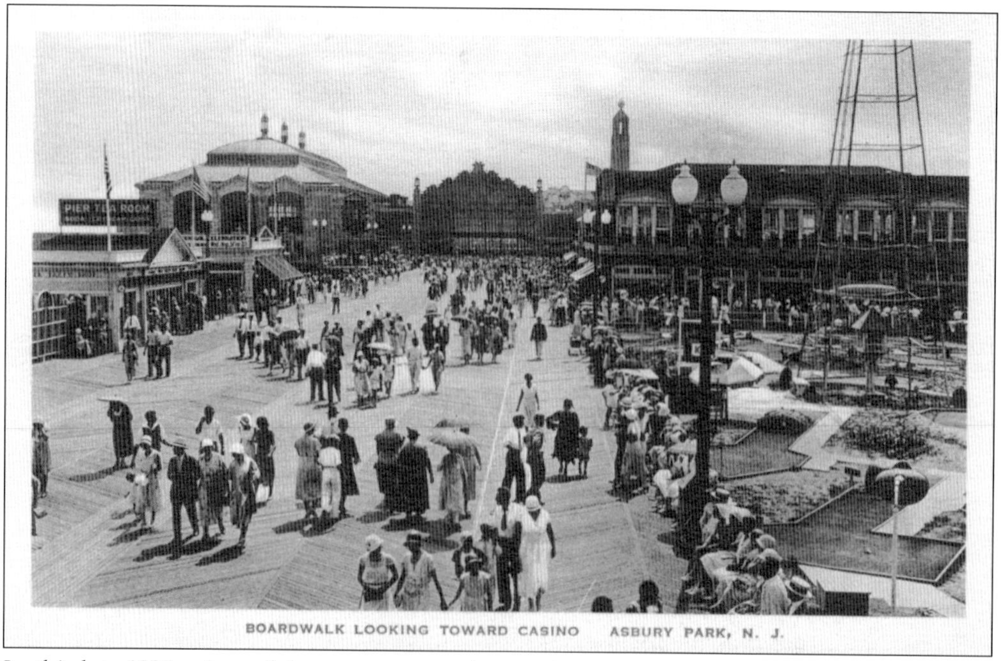


In this late 1930s view of the same area as the previous image, the original Casino has been replaced by Warren and Wetmore's Casino. The Asbury Avenue pavilion has been built where rows of benches once were, and one of the boardwalk's many mini-golf courses has replaced what was open space.

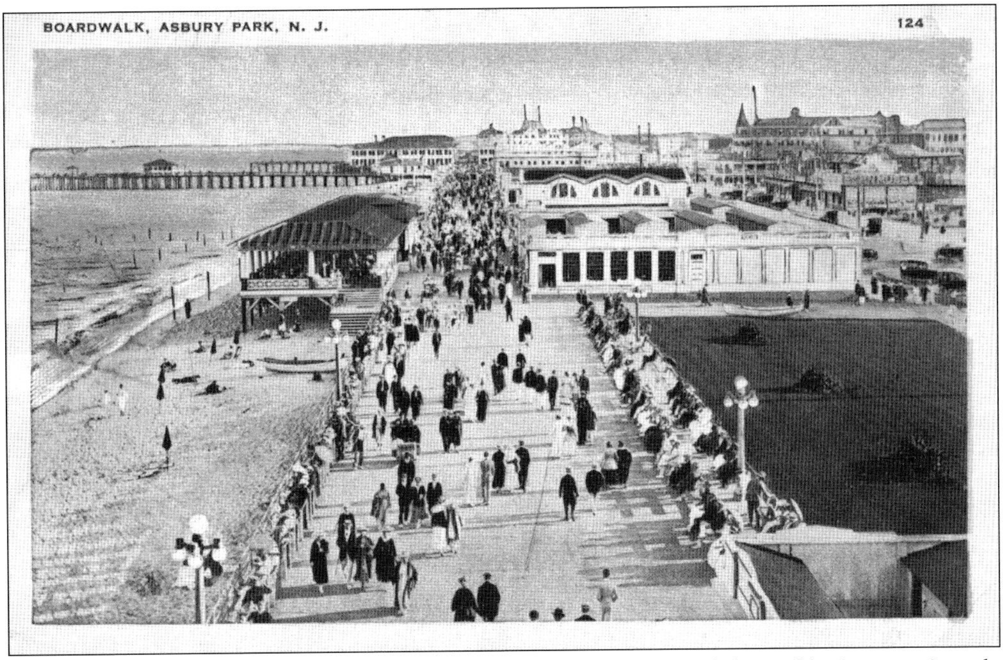


This is the beachfront as it appeared from the second story of the Fifth Avenue Arcade in 1926.

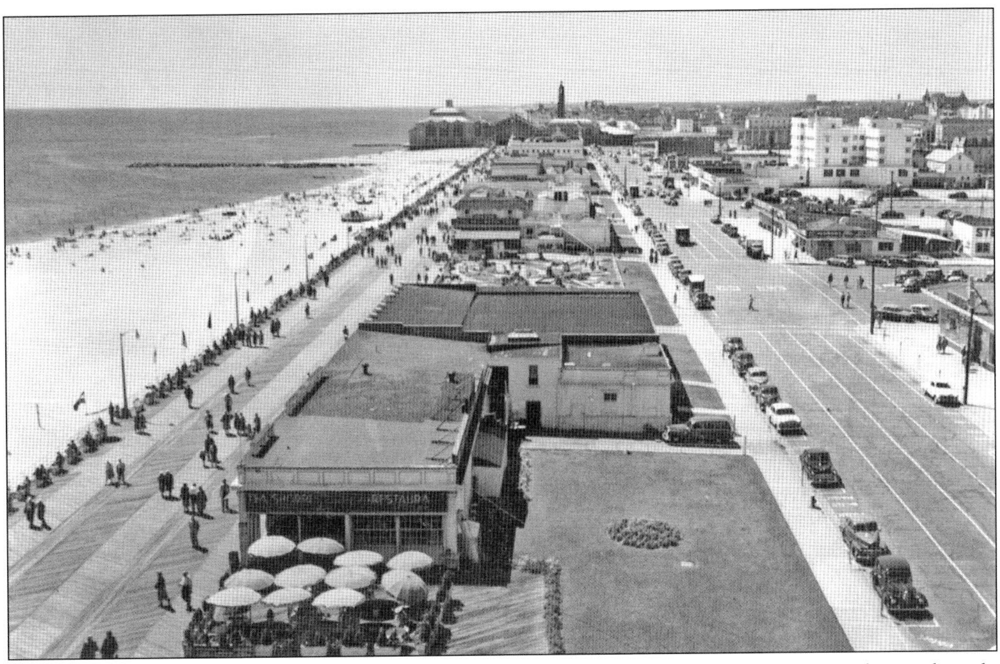

In this later view, the new Casino has replaced the older wood-frame structure. The Esplanade Review at Fourth Avenue is gone, and the First Avenue fishing pier has been replaced by a jetty.

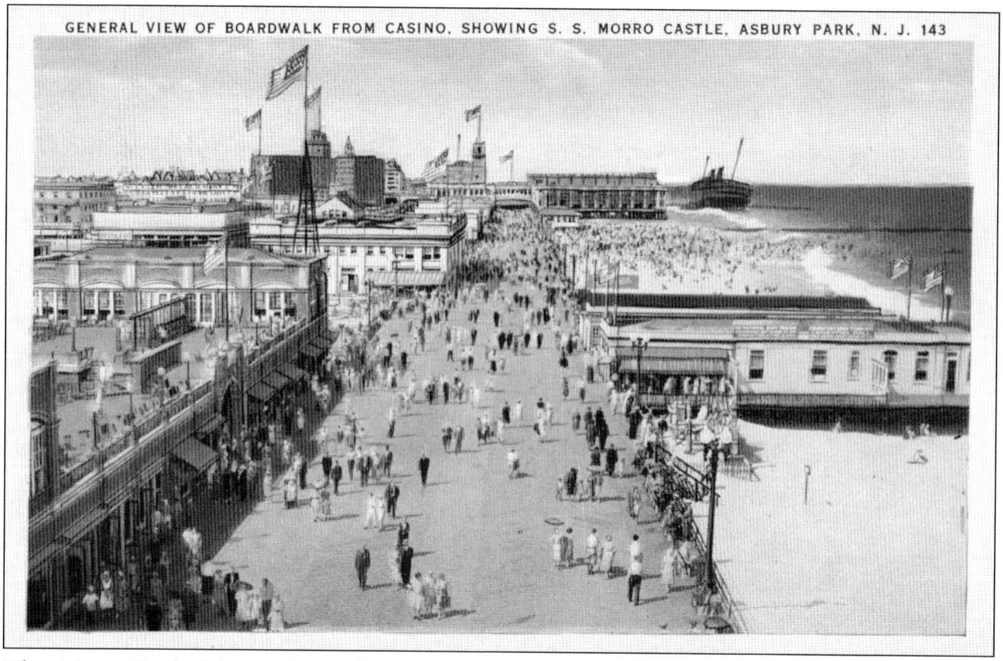


The *Morro Castle* shipwreck can be seen in this view of the boardwalk looking toward the convention hall from the second story of the Casino.

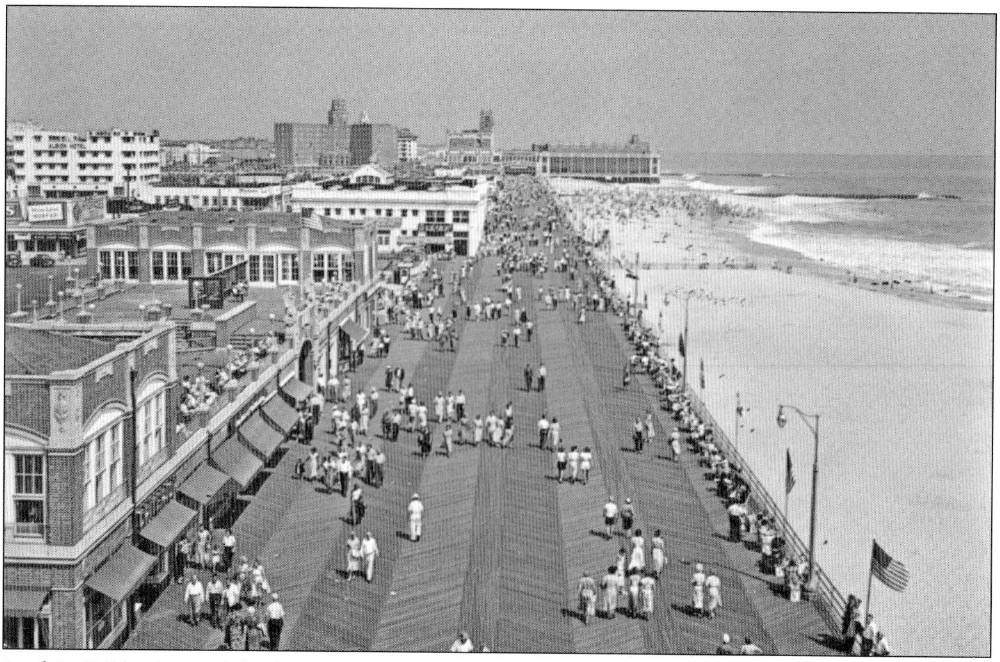

In this 1950s view of the boardwalk from the Casino, the boardwalk looks much as it did 20 years earlier, though the structures to the right of the boardwalk are no longer there.

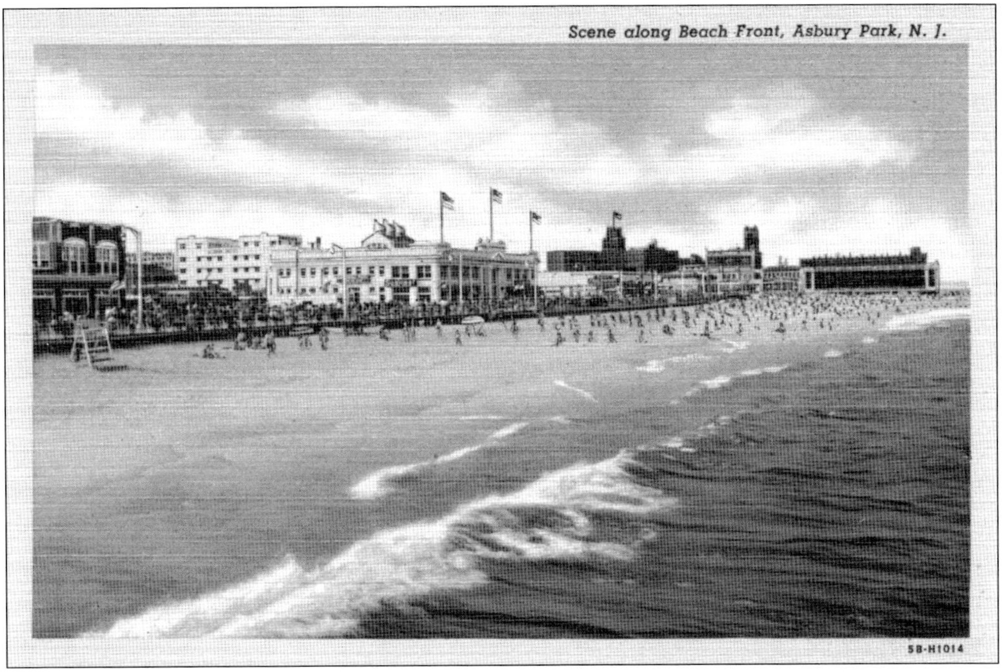


This is the scene along the beachfront as it looked in the 1930s. From left to right are the Asbury Avenue pavilion, Albion hotel, Natatorium, Berkeley-Carteret hotel, and convention hall.

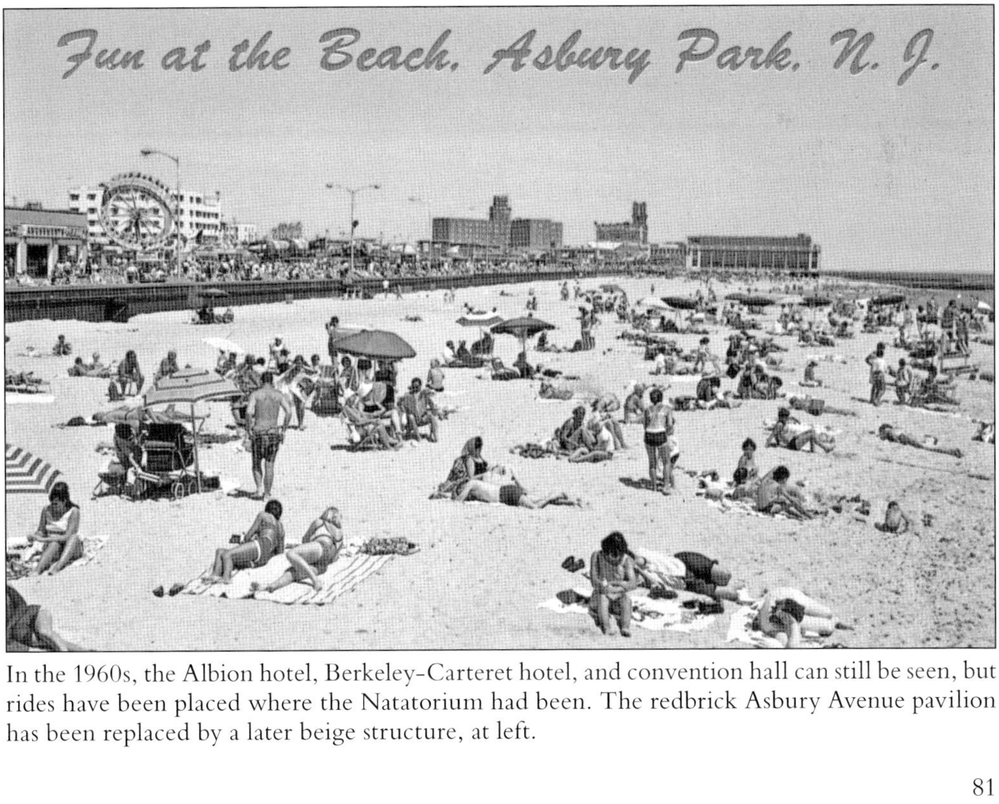


In the 1960s, the Albion hotel, Berkeley-Carteret hotel, and convention hall can still be seen, but rides have been placed where the Natatorium had been. The redbrick Asbury Avenue pavilion has been replaced by a later beige structure, at left.

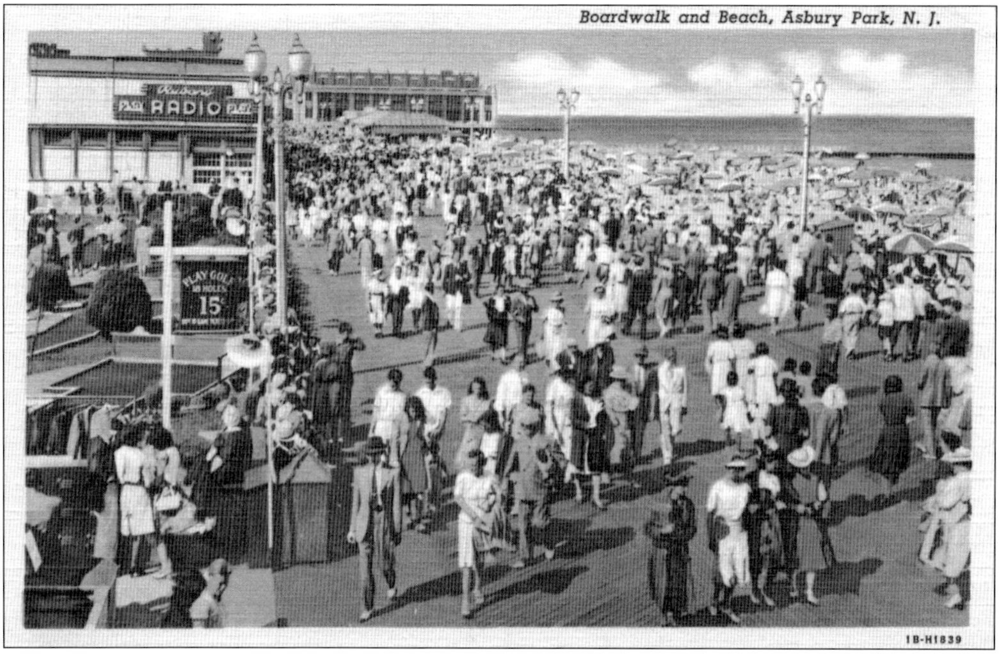


Ruben's arcade and a mini-golf course can be seen in this postcard, postmarked August 20, 1943. Around this time, during World War II, Asbury Park installed dim-out curtains along the boardwalk so patrons could enjoy the boardwalk at night without fear of ships being silhouetted against the lights of the boardwalk.

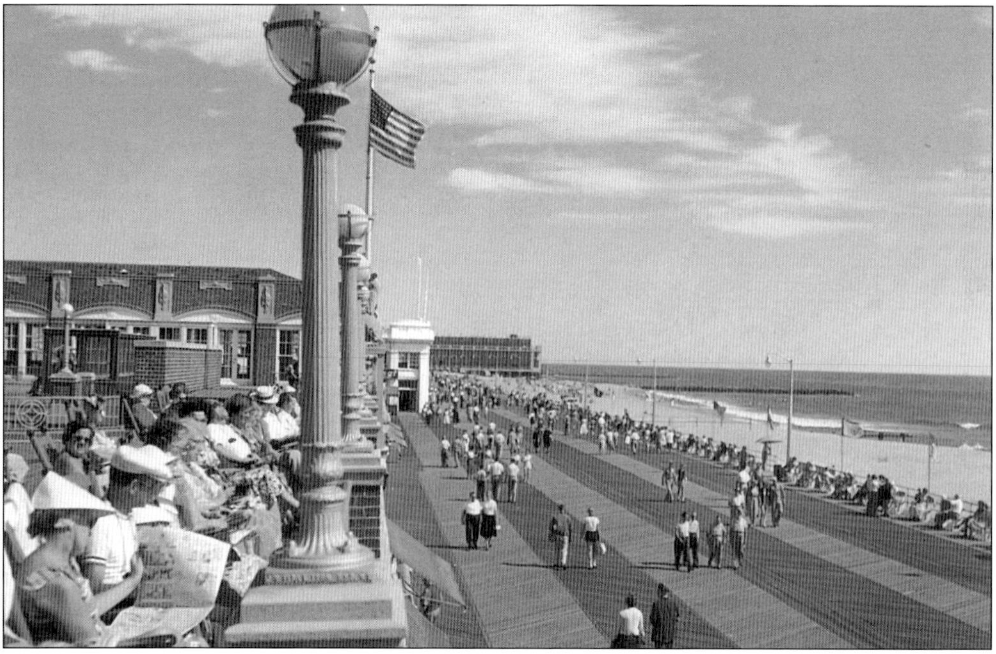

Reading the newspaper atop the Asbury Avenue pavilion was a relaxing way to pass the time along the boardwalk.

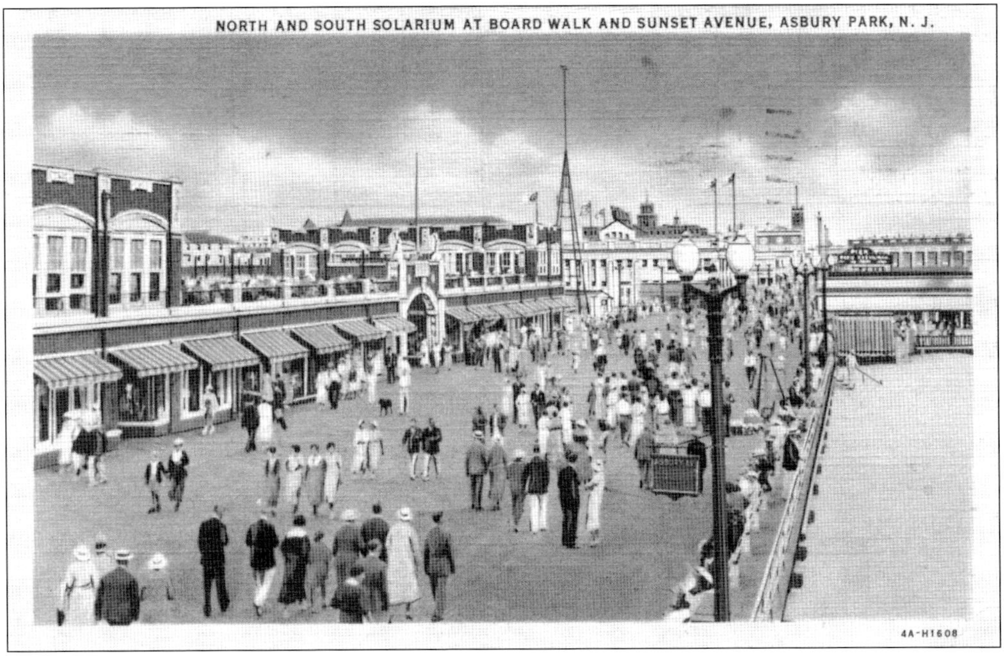


Though this card is captioned "North and South Solarium at Boardwalk and Sunset Avenue," this image actually depicts the Asbury Avenue pavilion as it appeared in the 1930s.

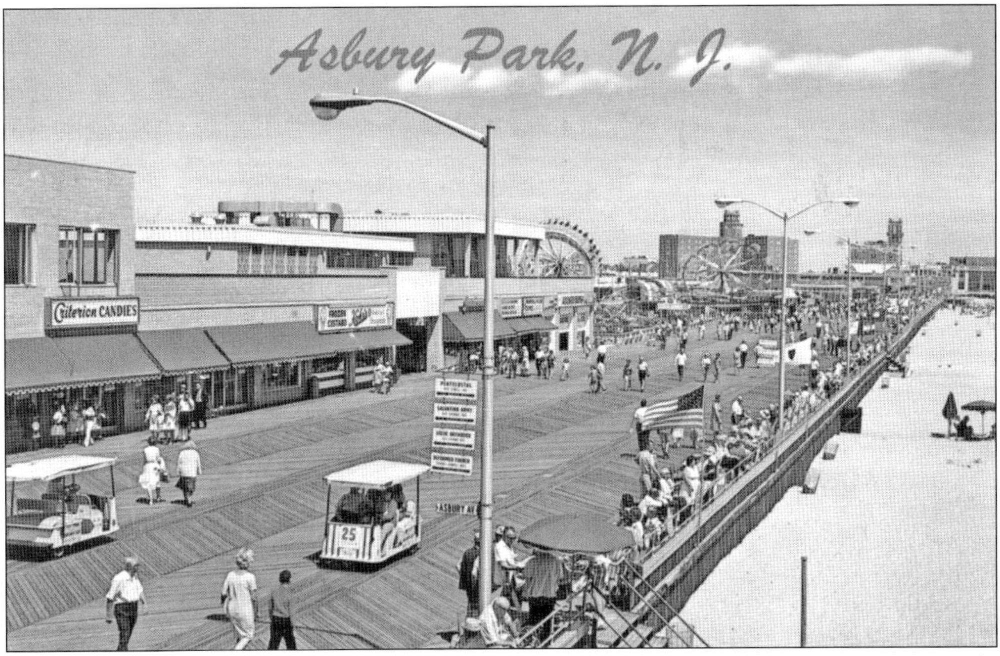


The redbrick Asbury Avenue pavilion was destroyed by fire in September 1963, just five weeks after a fire gutted the Sunset Avenue pavilion to the north. The beige building pictured here was built to replace the original pavilion. Criterion Candies and Kohr's Frozen Custard were two of the ground floor tenants in 1967.

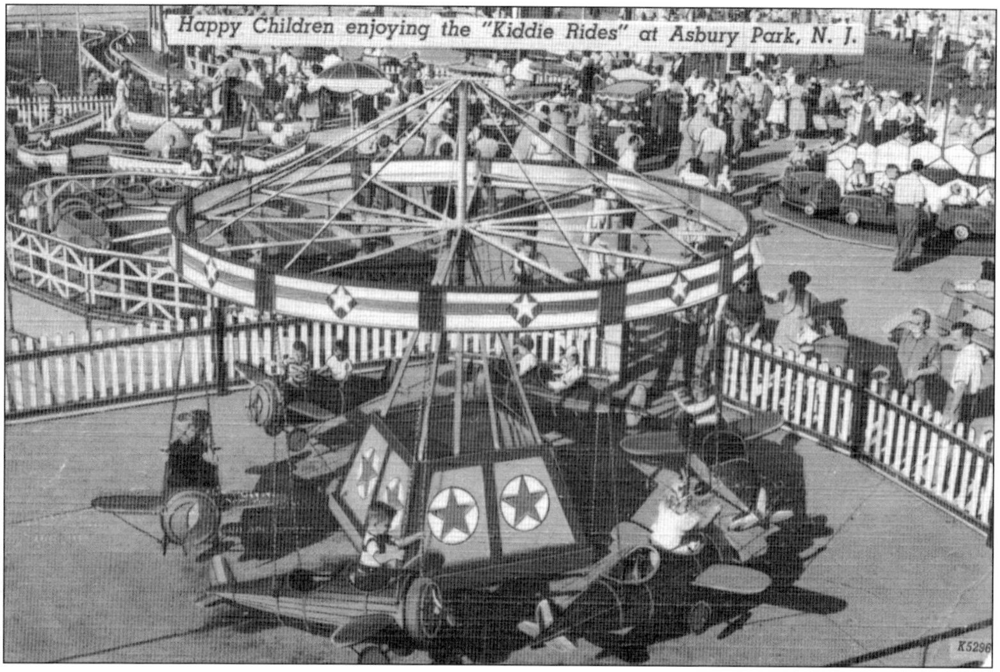


Kiddie rides like the airplane ride seen here were a popular draw for Asbury Park's boardwalk in the mid-20th century.

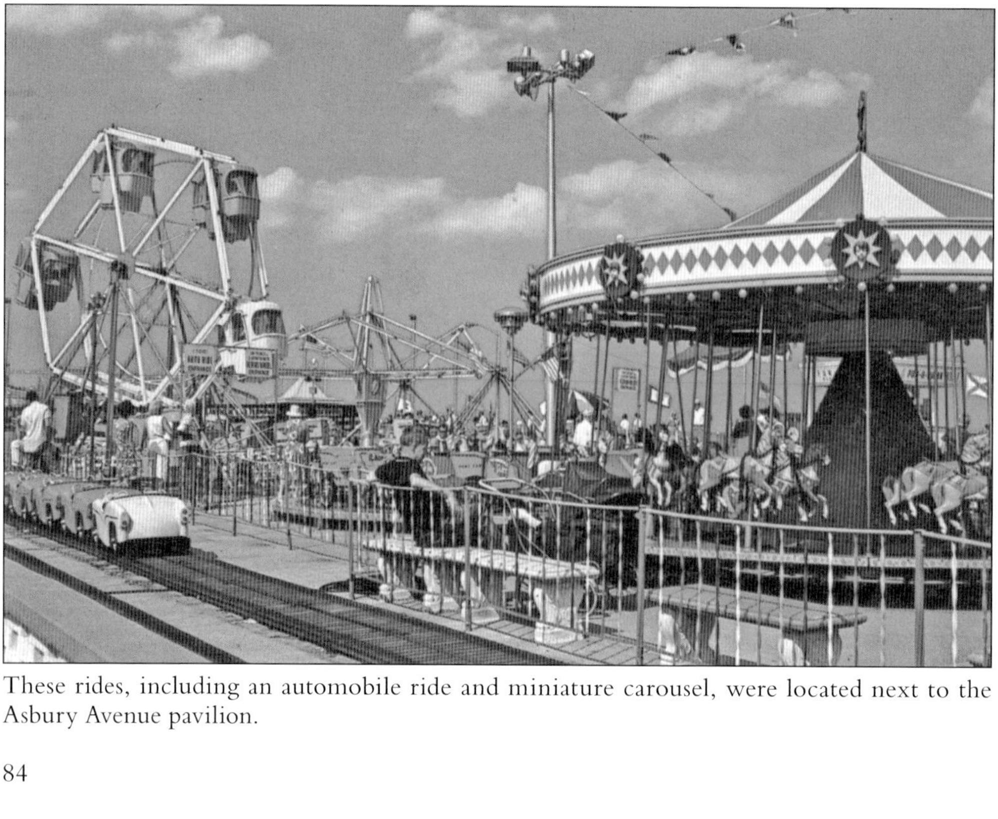

These rides, including an automobile ride and miniature carousel, were located next to the Asbury Avenue pavilion.

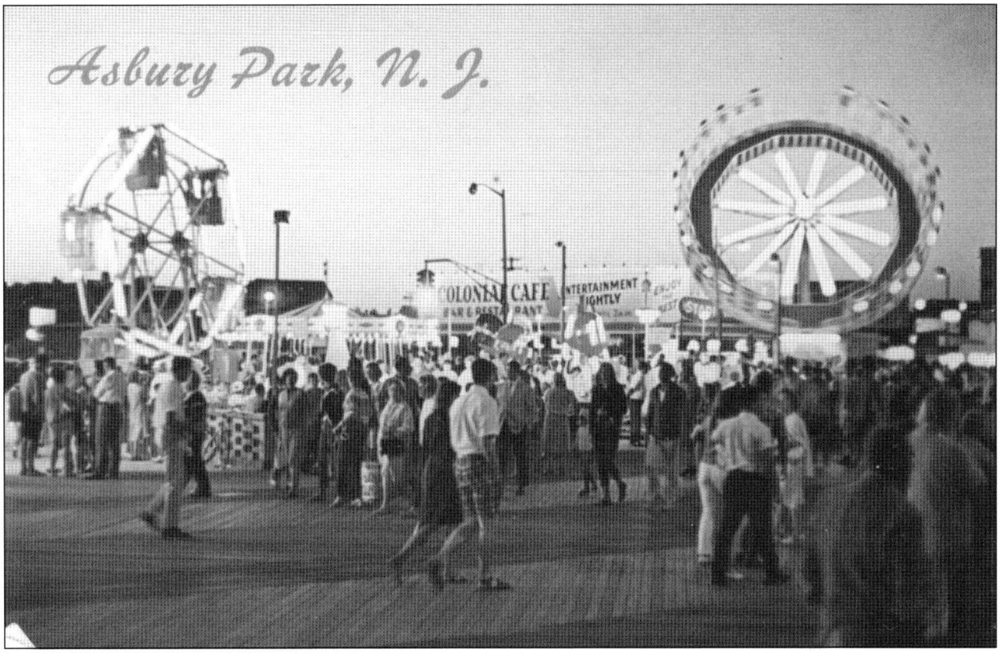


In this view of the boardwalk at dusk, the Colonial Café Bar and Restaurant can be seen behind the brightly lit rides at First Avenue.

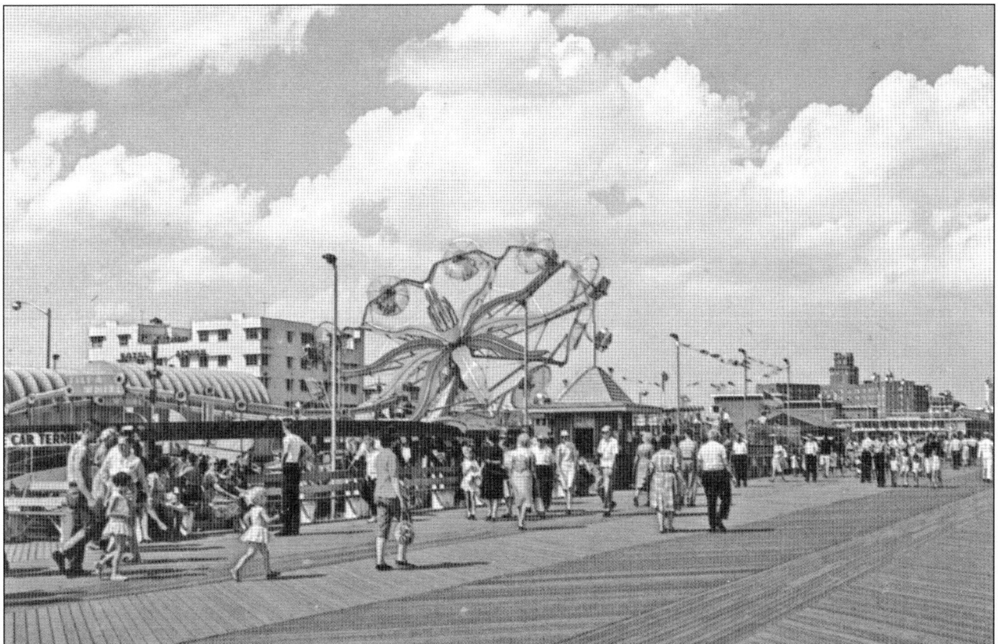

In addition to kiddie rides, attractions like the parachute ride and Tilt-a-Whirl seen here were available for visitors looking for thrills.

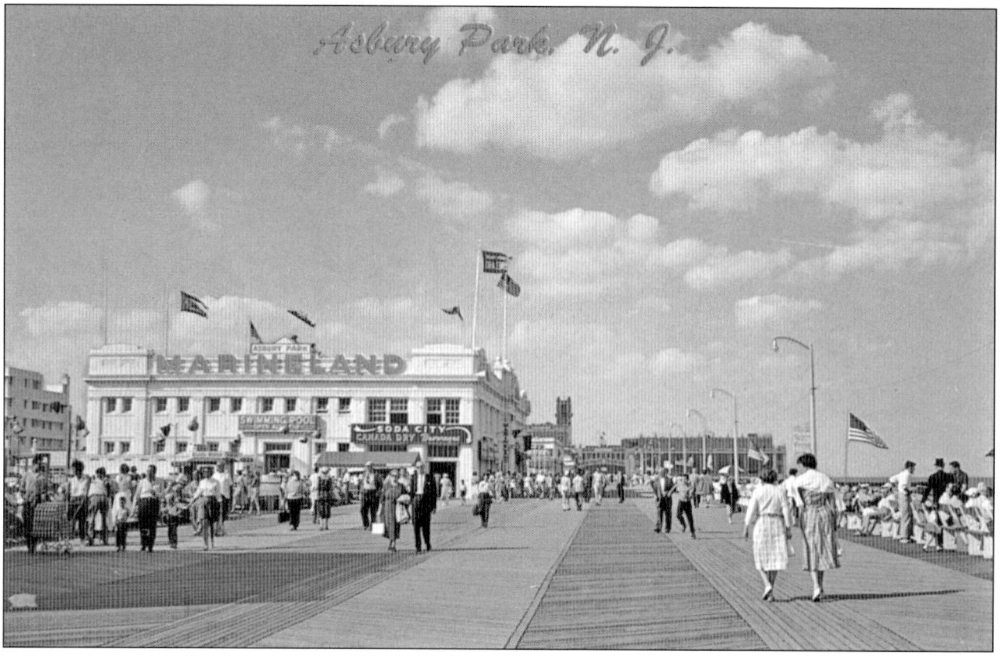


The Natatorium, which was called "Marineland" at the time this photograph was taken, can be seen at left. On the right in the distance is the convention hall.

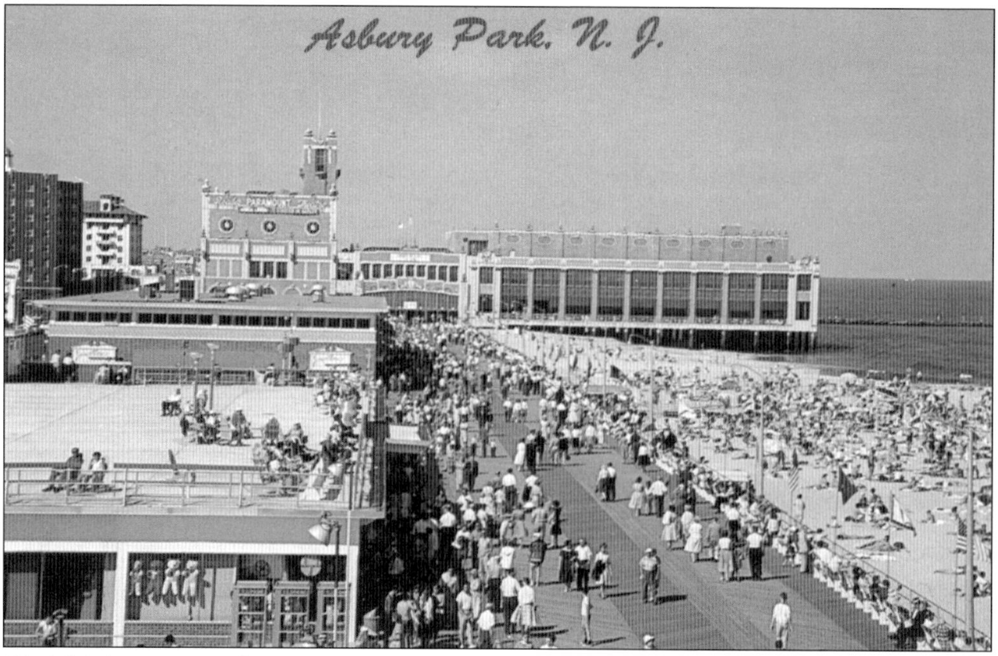


The Third Avenue pavilion's sun deck can be seen on the left in this postcard depicting a crowded day on Asbury Park's beach. On the left, the Berkeley-Carteret and Monterey hotels are visible in the distance.

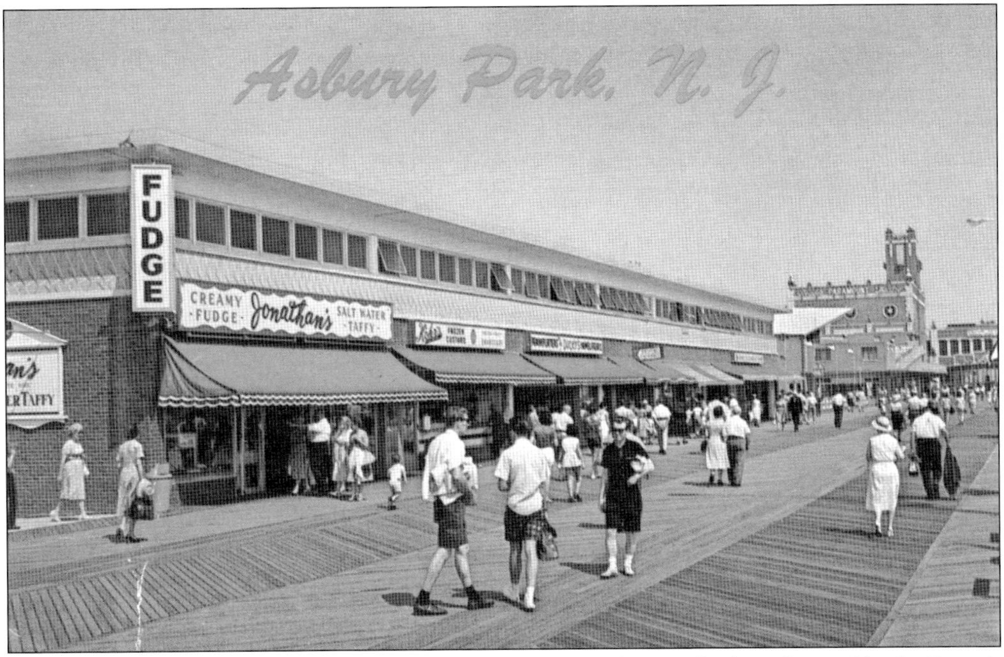


The Arbes family operated Jonathan's, seen here in 1969. This candy shop, located in the Fourth Avenue pavilion, sold the fudge and saltwater taffy typical to the Jersey Shore. Kohr's Frozen Custard shop next to Jonathan's served orangeade made with freshly squeezed oranges in addition to their famous orange and vanilla swirl custard.

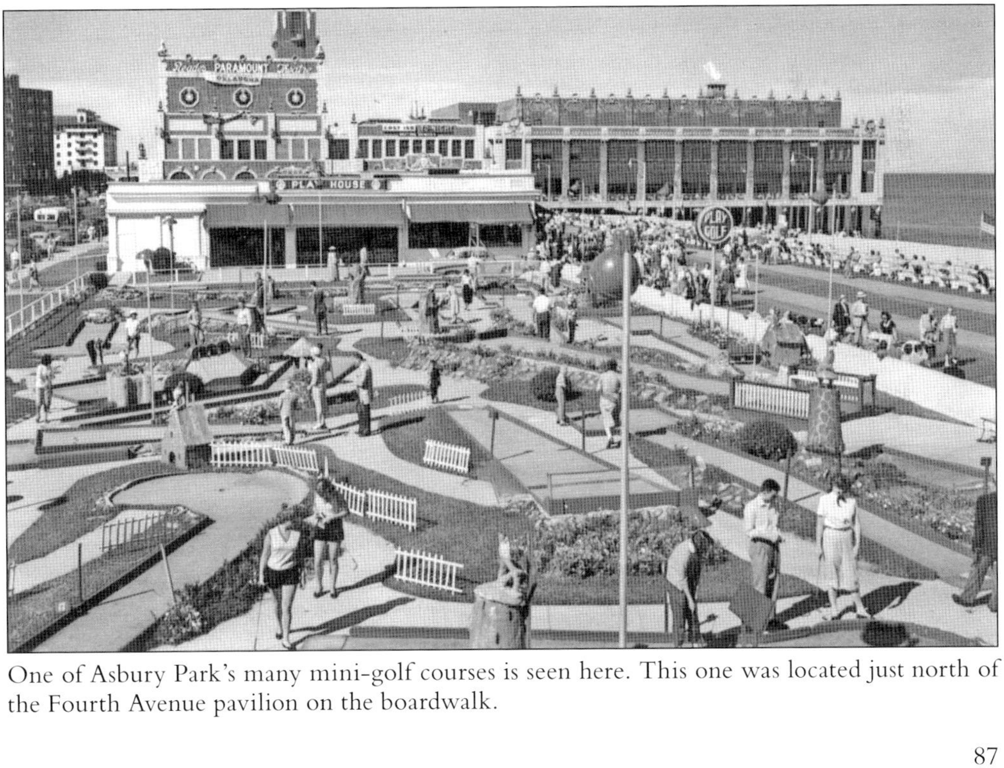


One of Asbury Park's many mini-golf courses is seen here. This one was located just north of the Fourth Avenue pavilion on the boardwalk.

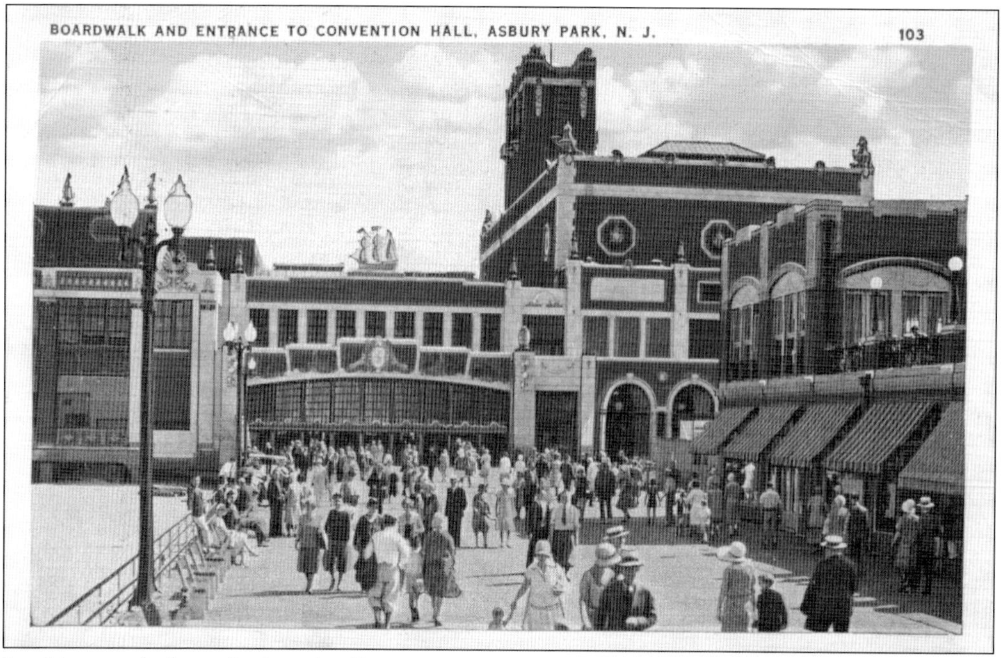


Looking south from the boardwalk at Sunset Avenue, the entrance to the convention hall and Paramount Theater is at center. To the right is the Sunset Avenue pavilion.

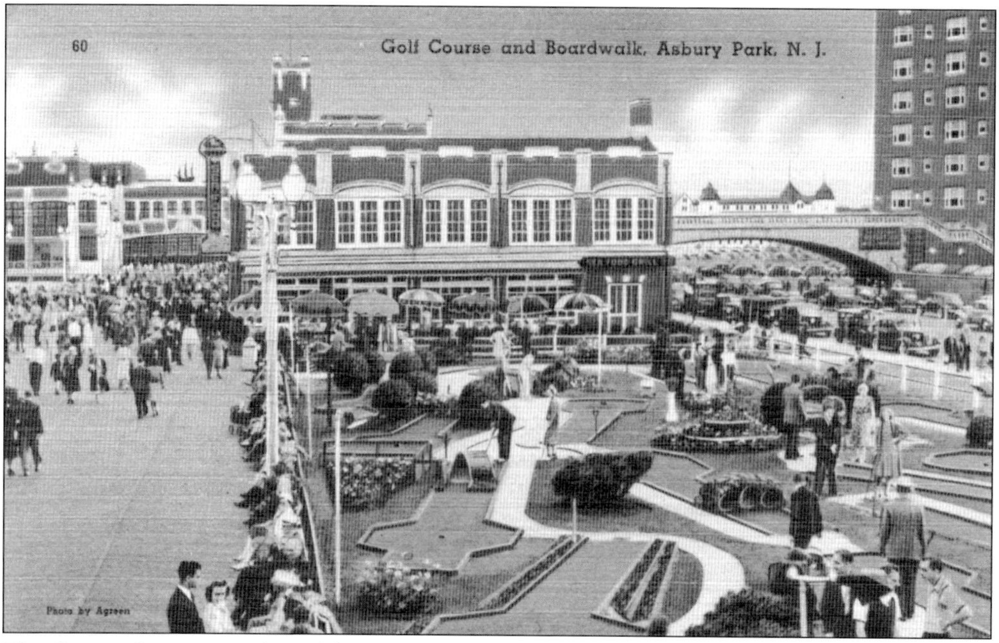


The Sunset Avenue pavilion, like the Casino, convention hall, and Asbury Avenue pavilion farther south on the boardwalk next to the Casino, was designed by Whitney Warren.

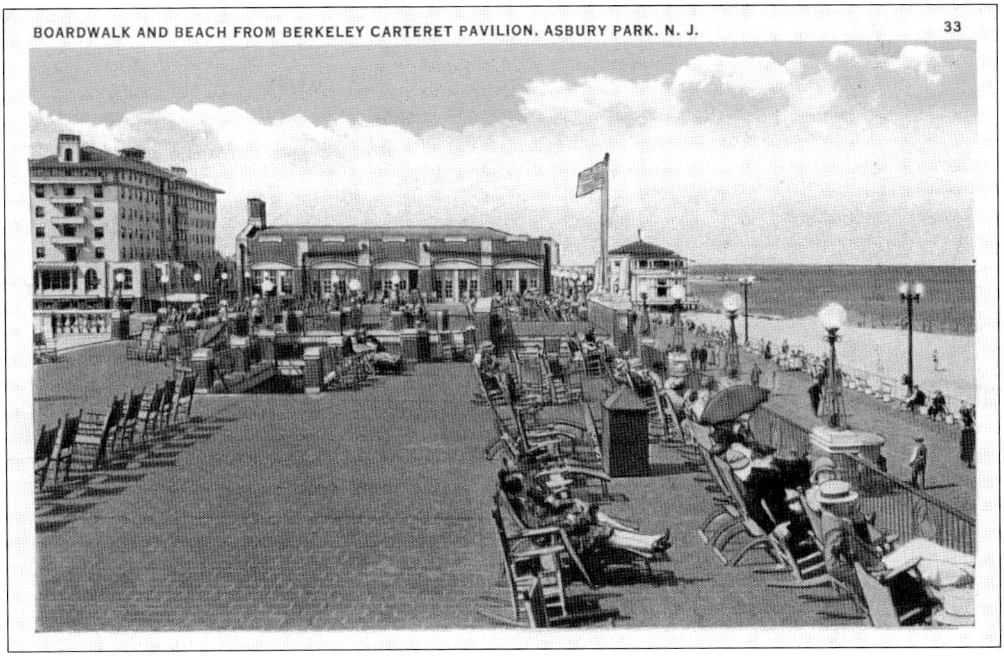


The Sunset Avenue pavilion featured a sun deck where visitors could relax and enjoy a view of the Atlantic Ocean. The Monterey hotel (left) and the Seventh Avenue pavilion (right) are visible in the distance.

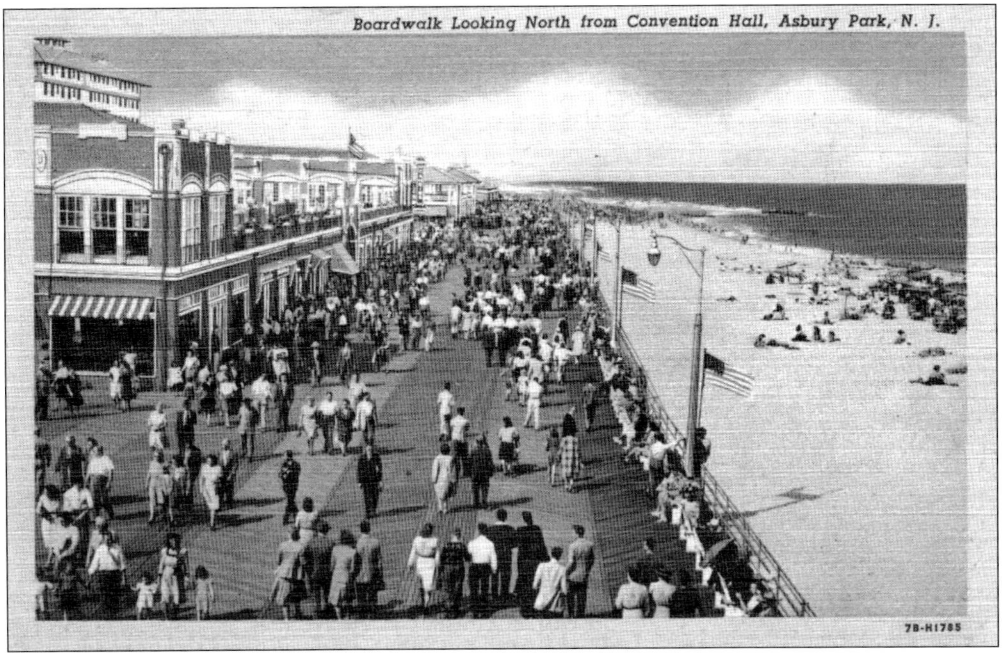


This 1952 view shows the boardwalk looking north from the convention hall. The Sunset Avenue pavilion at left was destroyed by a fire in August 1963 that caused an estimated $1 million in damage to the boardwalk.

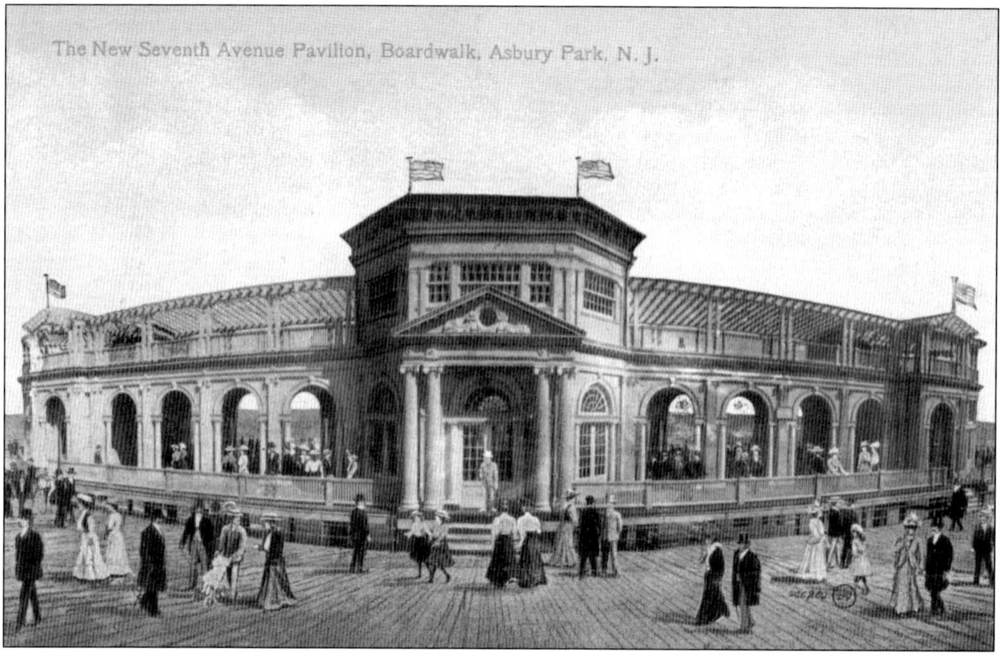


The Victorian Seventh Avenue pavilion was designed by architect Clarence W. Brazer, who graduated from high school in Asbury Park. Brazer was also responsible for the design of Asbury Park's Trinity Episcopal Church, located on Asbury Avenue.

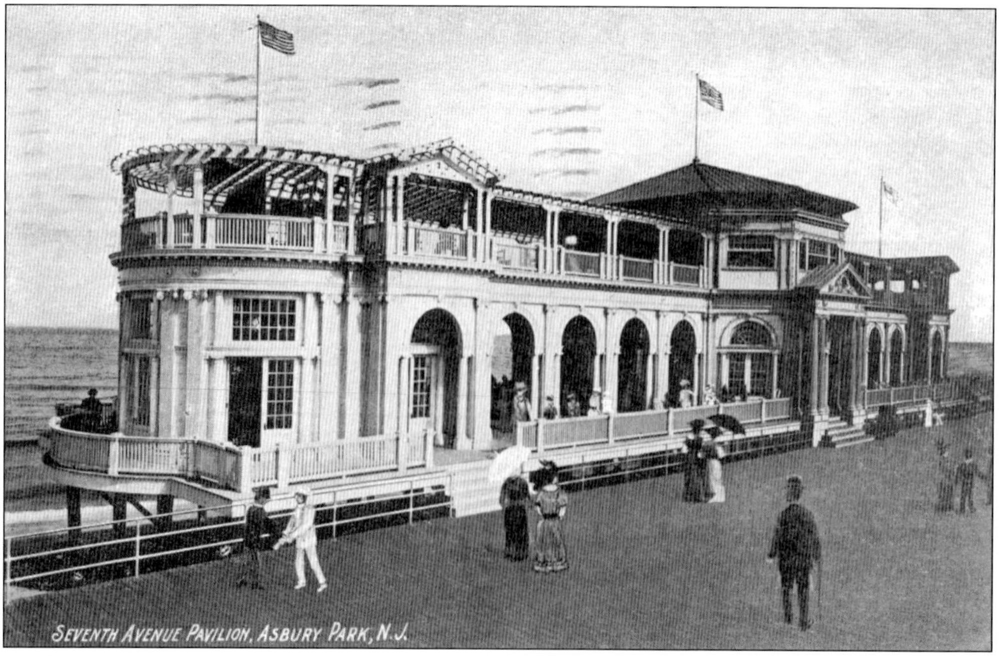


With rounded edges and decorative latticework, the Seventh Avenue pavilion was nicknamed the "Birdcage." Rocking chairs were provided for those who wished to rest a while on the porch that wrapped around the pavilion.

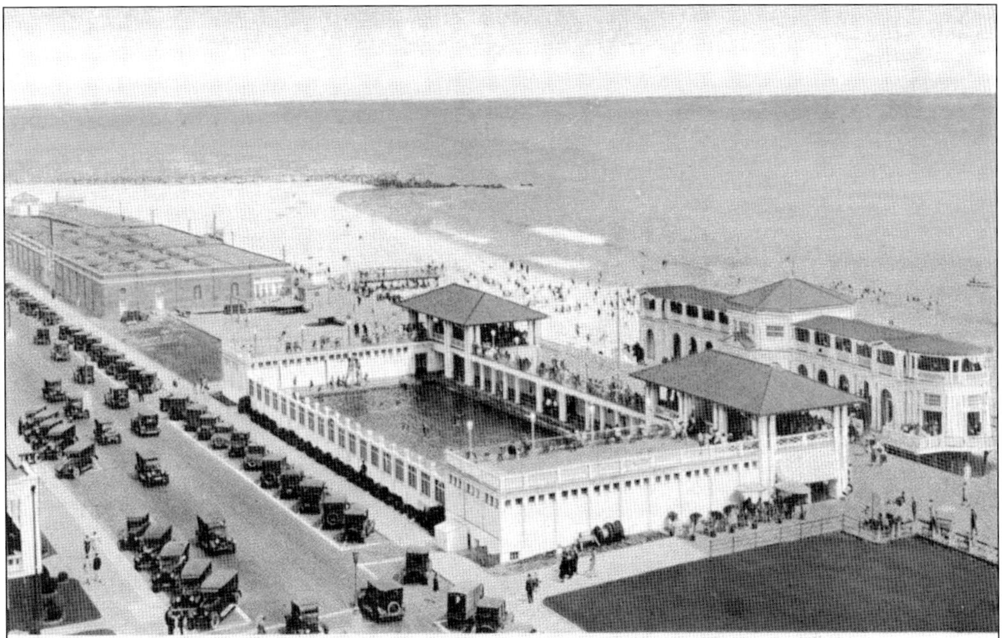

BIRD'S EYE VIEW OF SEVENTH AVENUE SWIMMING POOL AND BOARDWALK, ASBURY PARK, N. J. 106697

Across from the Seventh Avenue pavilion was another of the boardwalk's saltwater swimming pools. Like many buildings of the time in Asbury Park, the pool was built in the Spanish Revival style, with terra-cotta tile roofing on its pavilions.

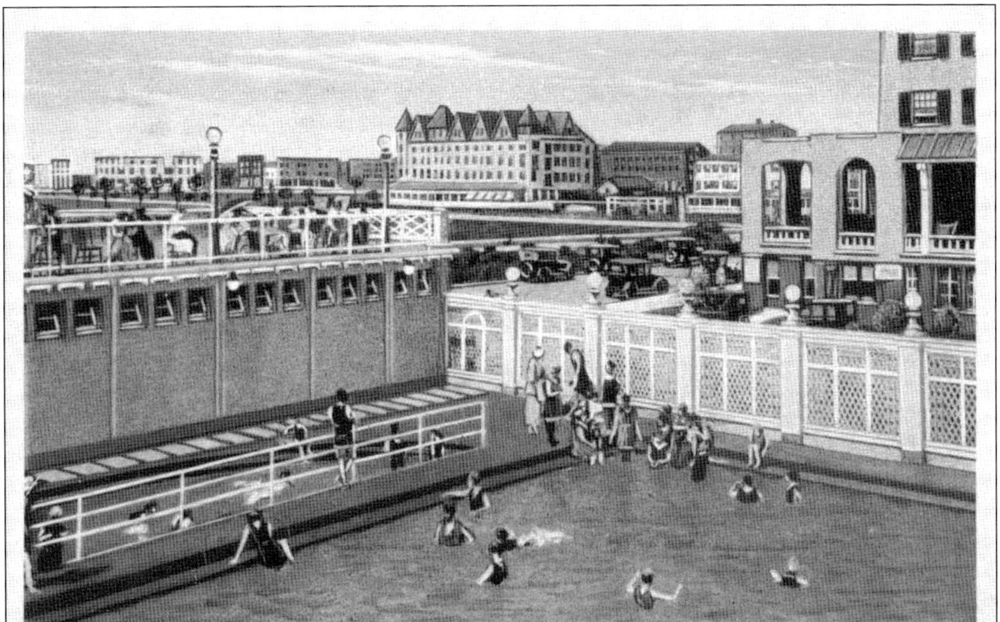

THE NEW POOL, ASBURY PARK, N. J.

The Seventh Avenue pool faced the Monterey hotel, which was located on the opposite side of Ocean Avenue. A portion of the hotel can be seen at right.

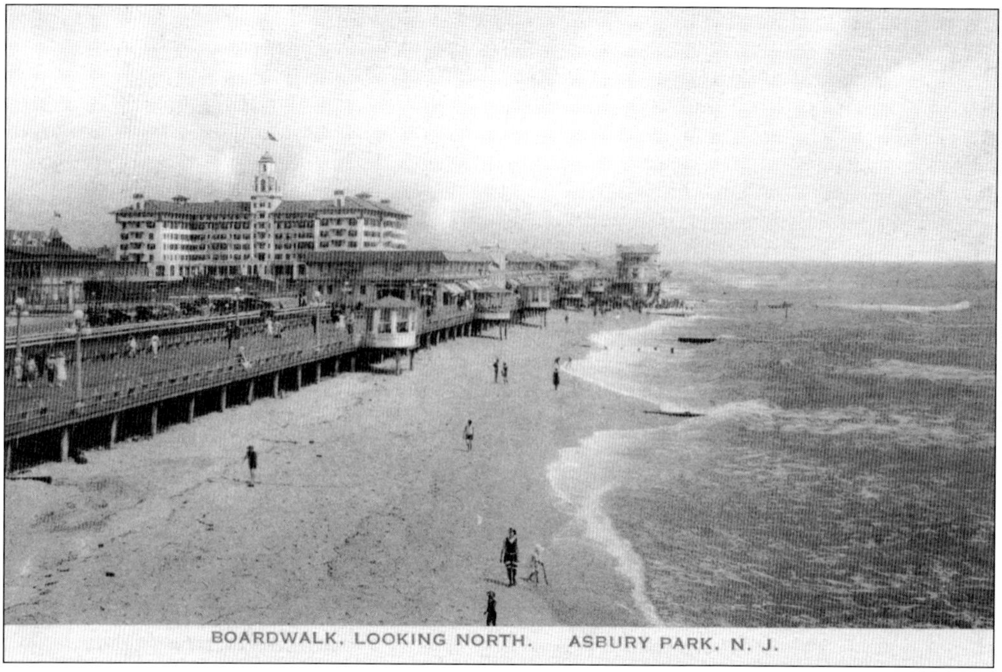


In this early view, numerous small octagonal pavilions that once dotted the beach side of the boardwalk are visible. On the left, to the south of the Monterey hotel, is one of Asbury Park's two auditoriums. This building was replaced by the Berkeley-Carteret hotel after Founder Bradley passed away and his estate sold the land where the auditorium stood.

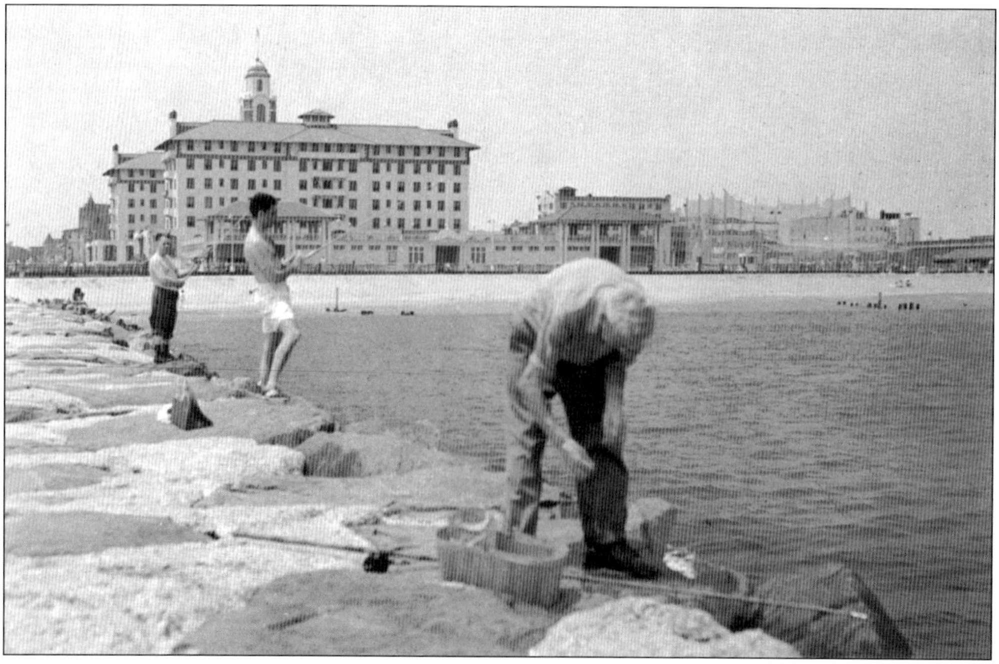

Looking west from the fishing jetty, the Seventh Avenue pool and Monterey hotel are pictured here.

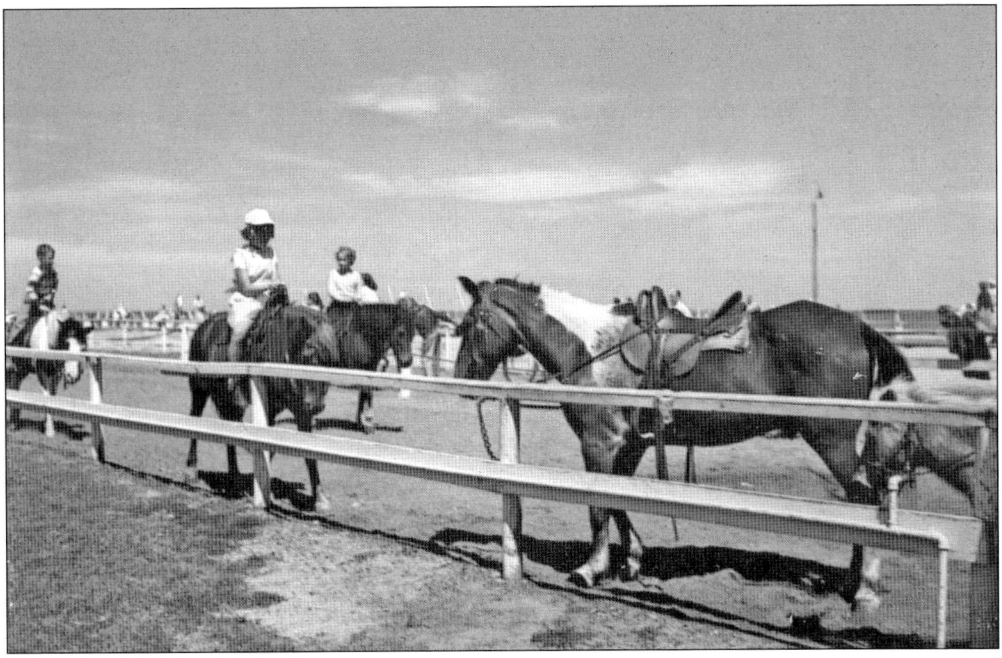

In the 1950s, pony rides like those seen here at Eighth Avenue were just one of the many activities available for visitors to enjoy.

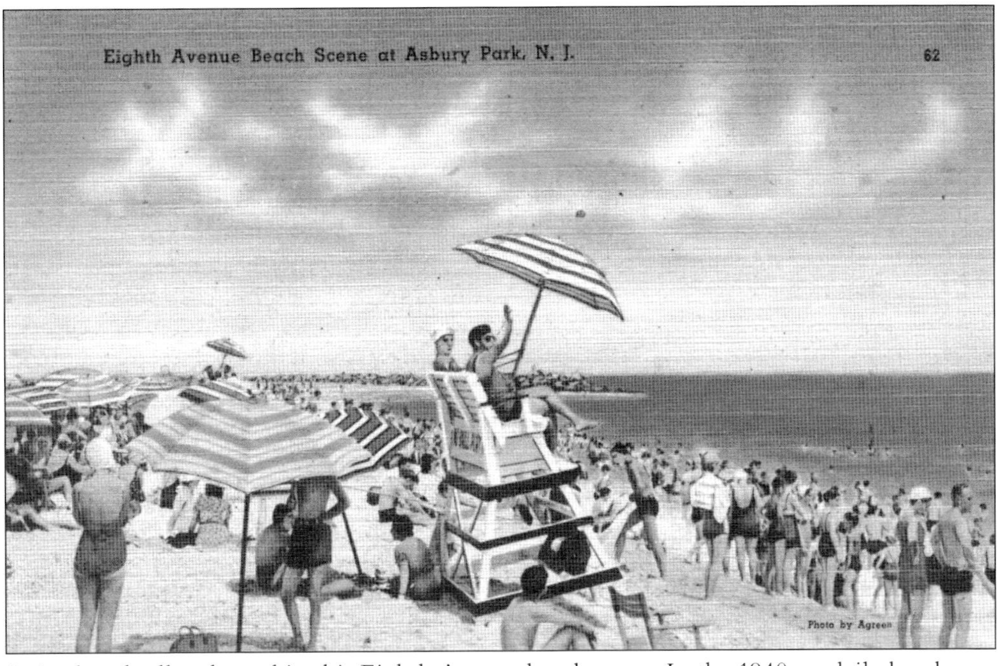


Striped umbrellas abound in this Eighth Avenue beach scene. In the 1940s, a daily beach pass was 50¢, and a season pass was $20 for residents, $30 for nonresidents.

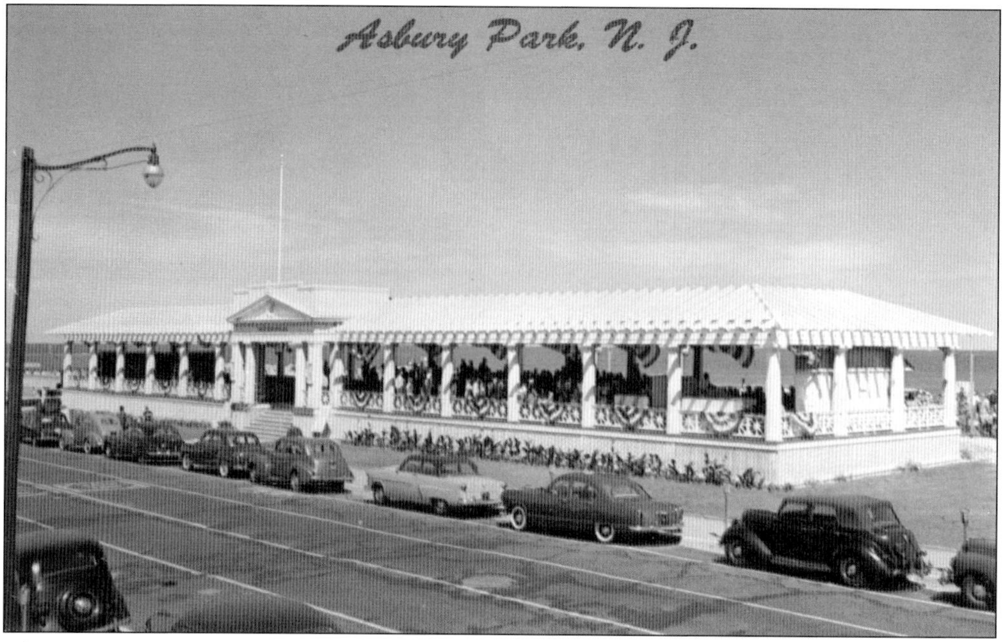


The Eighth Avenue pavilion had a seating capacity of 400. It was home to the Asbury Park Municipal Band, which performed concerts here four times a week in the summer. The Asbury Park Municipal Band moved to the Fifth Avenue band shell when it opened in 1962, and this pavilion was demolished shortly after.

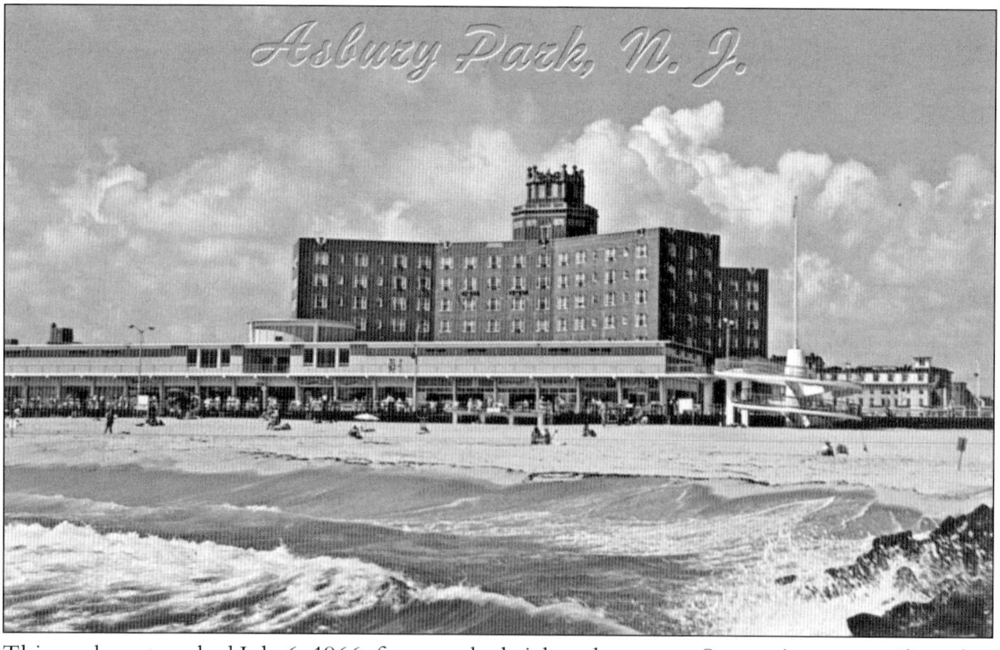


This card, postmarked July 6, 1966, features the brick and concrete Sunset Avenue pavilion that replaced the previous pavilion, which was destroyed by fire in 1963. This structure was designed by John Fridy of Philadelphia, who also designed the Howard Johnson's at Fifth Avenue. The ground floor of the pavilion had 12 shops, and the second story housed bathing facilities that were reached by the circular poured-concrete ramp visible at right.

# *Ten*

# Places to Stay and Dine

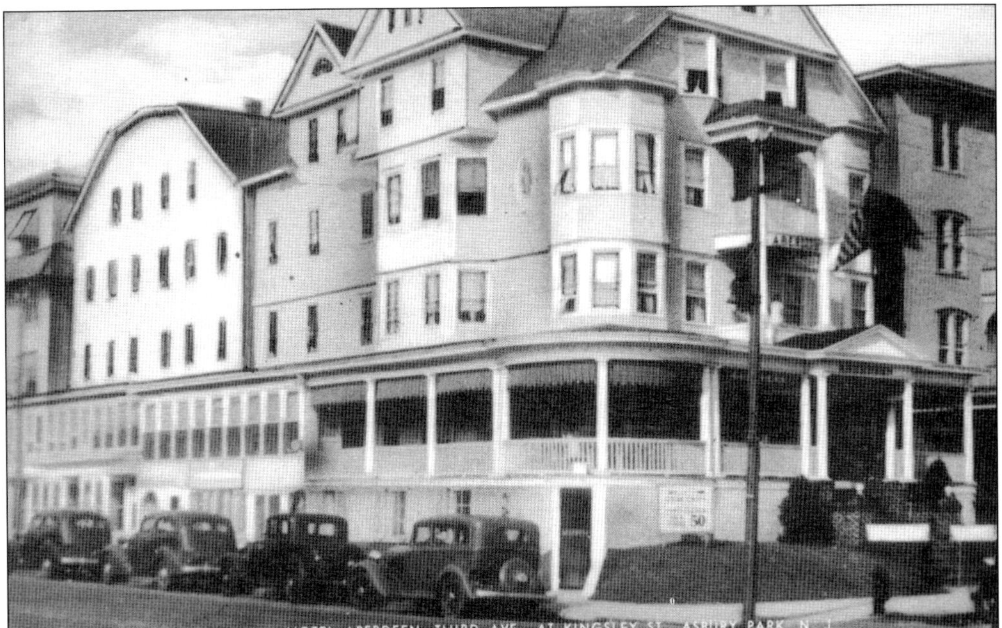


Hotel Aberdeen, operated by Mrs. C.H. Wettlin, was one of the more than 200 hotels and rooming houses operating in Asbury Park in the first half of the 20th century. Located at Third and Kingsley Streets, the hotel had accommodations for 100 patrons and was open year-round in the 1940s.

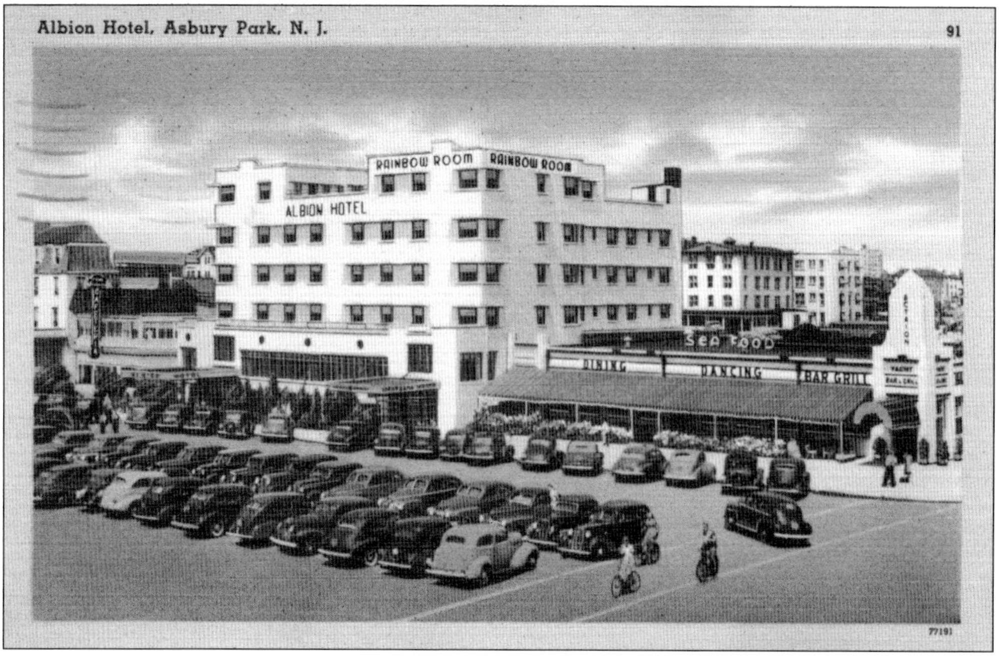


The Albion hotel, seen here around 1951, replaced an earlier wood-frame structure that was destroyed in a 1940 fire that also destroyed the adjacent Steeplechase Park. The public's fear of fire prompted advertising materials and postcards to call out the "completely fireproof" nature of the new building. The Actaion Yacht Bar and Grill can be seen next to the hotel on the right.

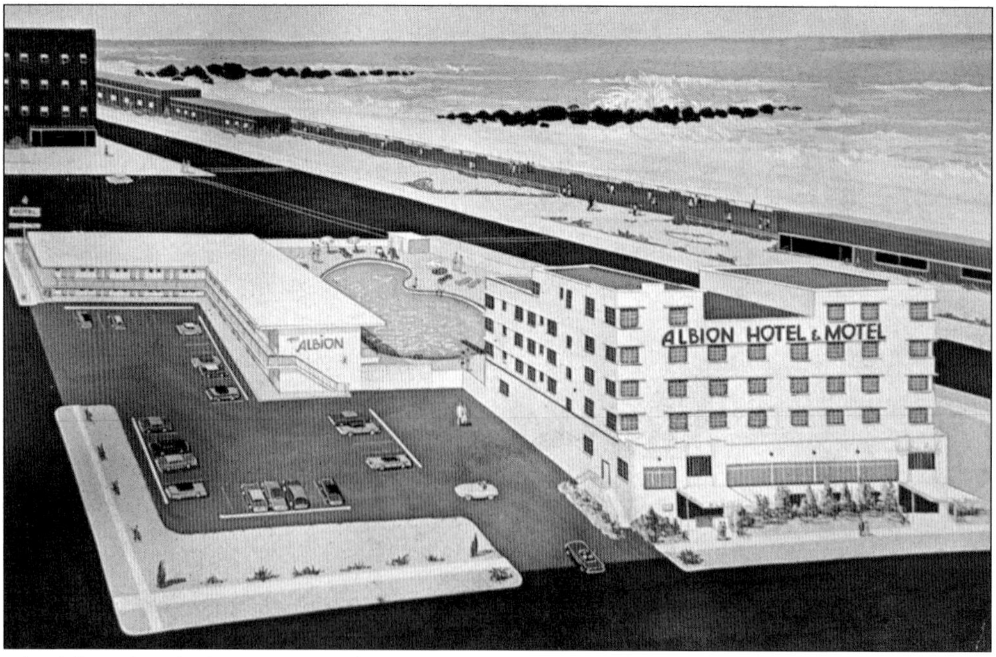


The Albion hotel advertised soundproof rooms and "modernistic furnishings," which included murals and fixtures from the 1939 New York World's Fair. The hotel's popular Rainbow Room nightclub could accommodate banquets of up to 500 people and claimed to be the finest place to dine and dance along the Jersey Shore.

The Albion hotel closed for business in the late 1980s. There was interest in restoring and reopening the hotel, but the hallways were too narrow to meet modern building codes, and it was demolished in 2001. The Rainbow Room sign was salvaged from the demolition, and in 2011 it was restored and now hangs in the transportation center, next to city hall.

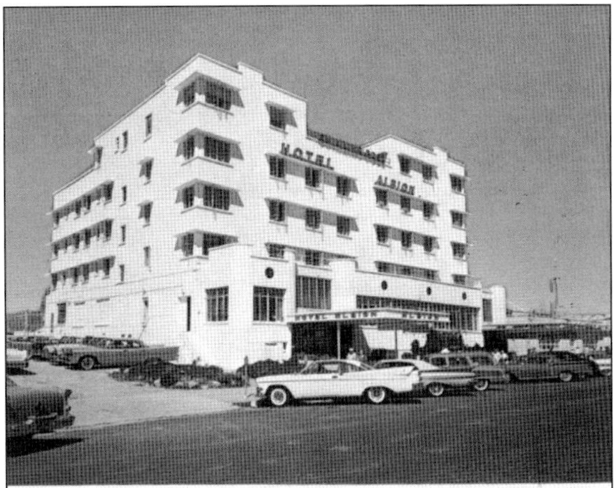

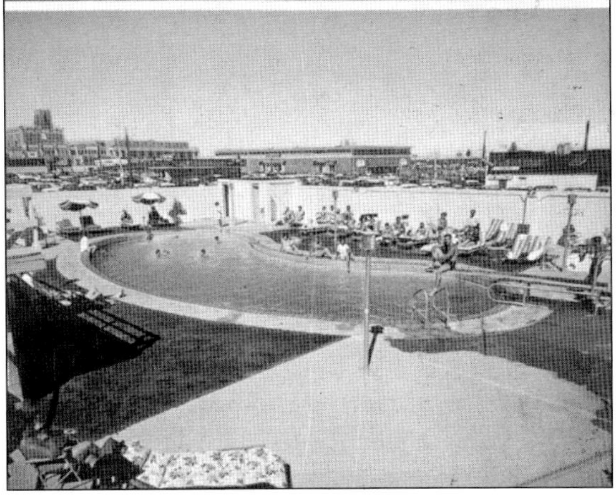

Actaion Yacht Bar and Grill, next to the Albion hotel, offered dining and dancing. Its advertised specialty was daily fresh-broiled live Maine lobster, which could be had at a price of $1.25. A yacht-shaped bar and porthole-shaped sconces completed the restaurant's nautical theme. In later years, this building would house Michals Seafood Restaurant.

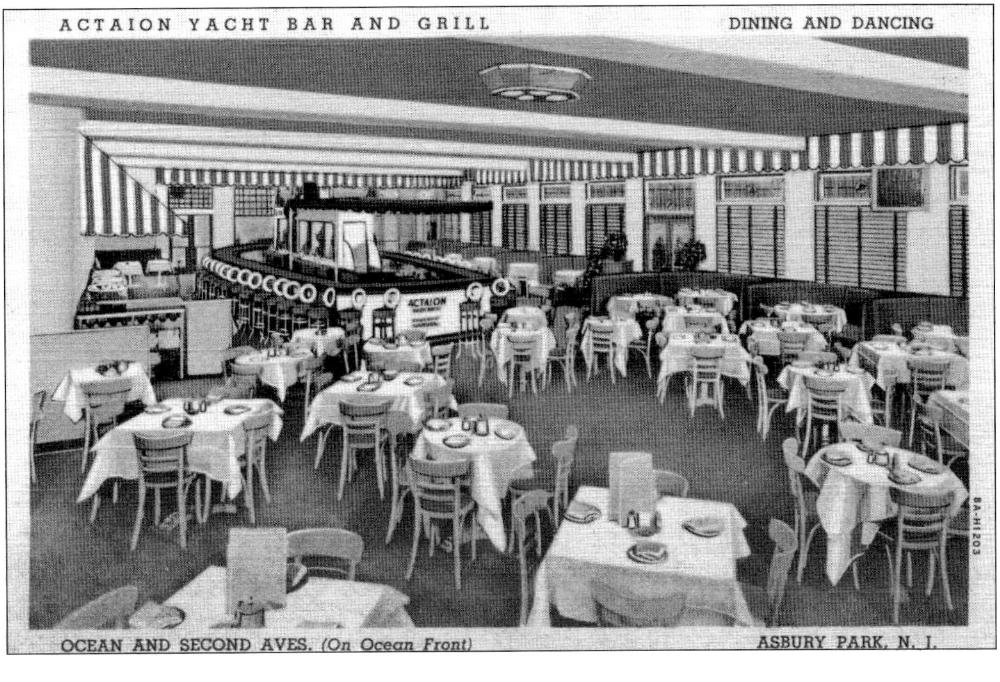

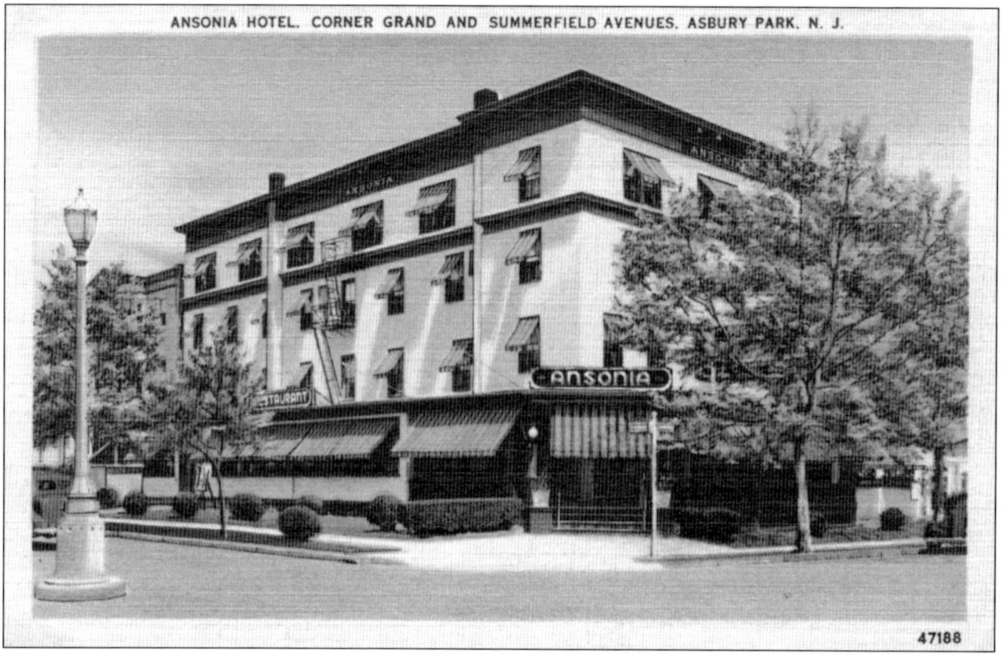


The 50-room Ansonia Hotel was located at the corner of Grand and Summerfield Avenues. At $6 for a weeklong visit, the hotel was one of the more moderately priced places to stay in Asbury Park in 1939, when it was operated by J.E. Thornton. Today there are condominiums at the corner of Grand and Summerfield Avenues.

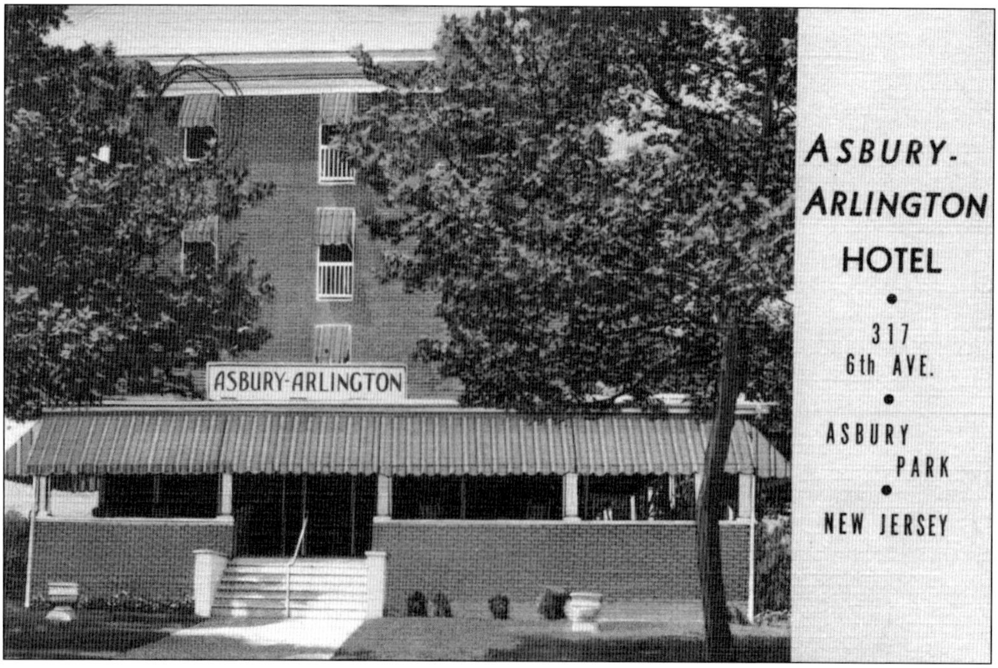


The Asbury Arlington Hotel on Sixth Avenue, seen here around 1947, was originally built in 1905. Hot and cold water was available in all rooms in the late 1940s, but not all had a private bath. Today, the building has been restored and converted into condominiums.

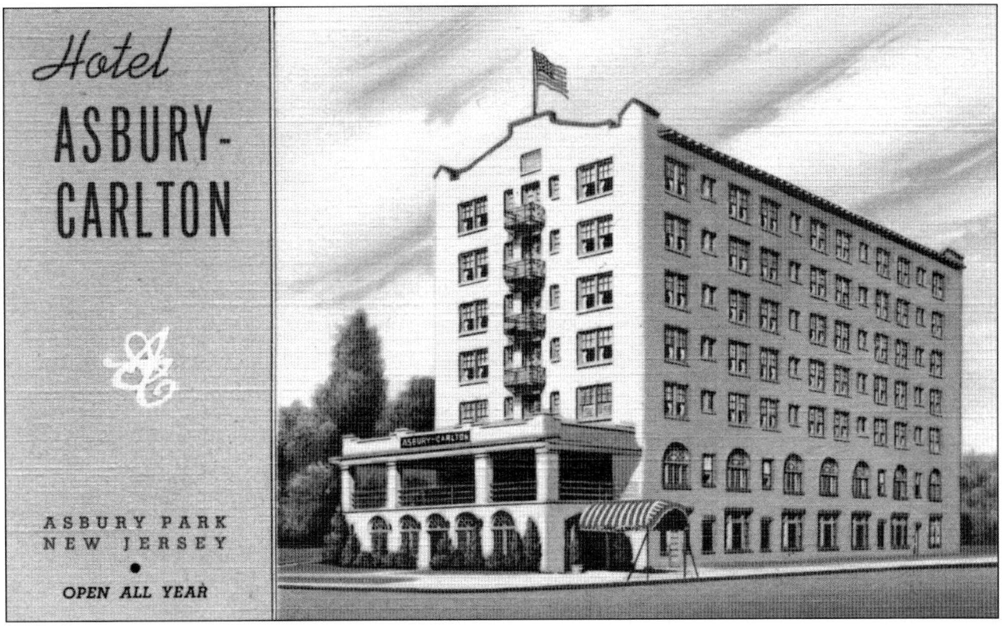


The seven-story Hotel Asbury-Carlton was one block from the boardwalk at Seventh Avenue and Kingsley Street. In the summer, patrons could enjoy a view of the ocean from the hotel's front porch. For winter visitors, the hotel had a steam-heated lobby that took up nearly an entire floor. The Asbury-Carlton's 100 rooms were outfitted with Simmons furniture, and each room had a private toilet and running water. This view dates to the early 1940s, when Harry S. Jackson was the hotel's manager.

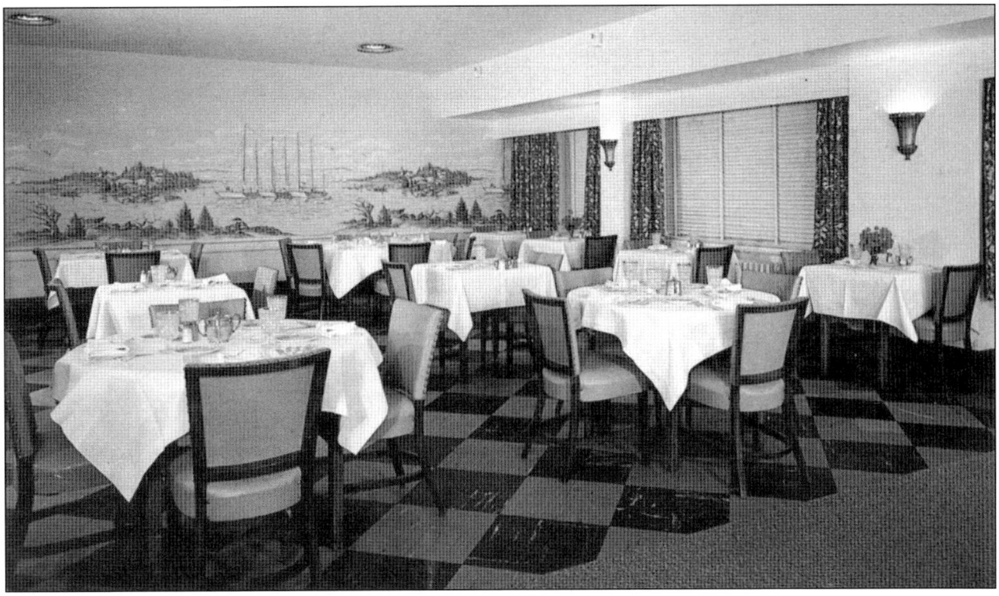

The Asbury-Carlton's dining room is seen here around 1965. The restaurant received daily supplies of local meats, seafood, and dairy for its dishes. Not long after this postcard was mailed, the Asbury-Carlton became the Asbury-Carlton Sheltered Care Home, housing some of the many mentally ill and disabled people who were deinstitutionalized in New Jersey in the 1970s. Today, the lot where the Hotel Asbury-Carlton stood is empty.

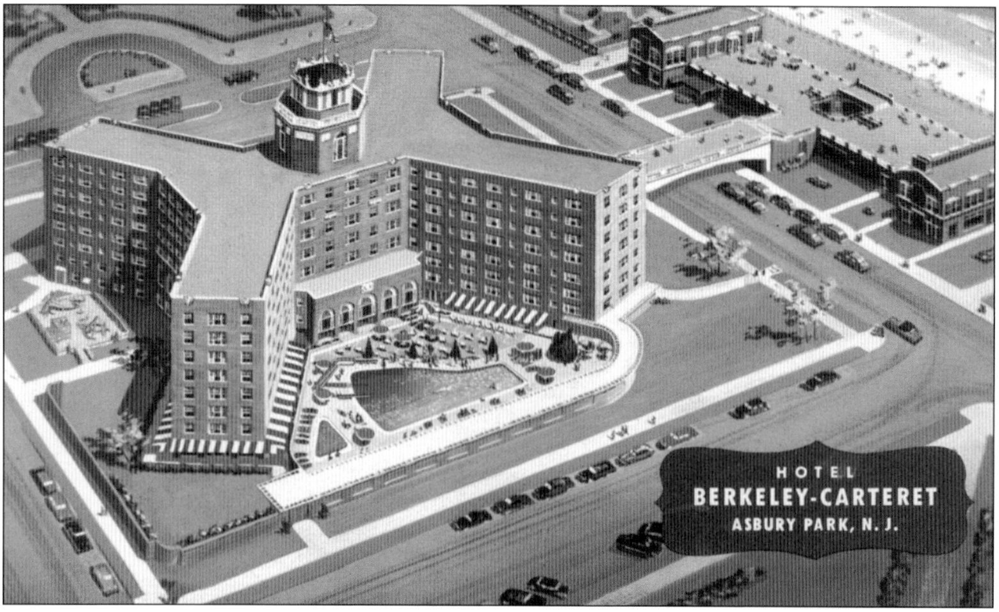


After Founder Bradley died, Arthur Steinbach, of the family that owned the Steinbach's department store downtown, negotiated with the Bradley estate to purchase the block at Ocean and Sunset Avenues, which had been the location of Bradley's auditorium. Steinbach hired Whitney Warren to design a new hotel, which he called the Berkeley-Carteret after Colonial New Jersey landowners. With 420 rooms, the Berkeley-Carteret was the largest and most luxurious hotel in the city.

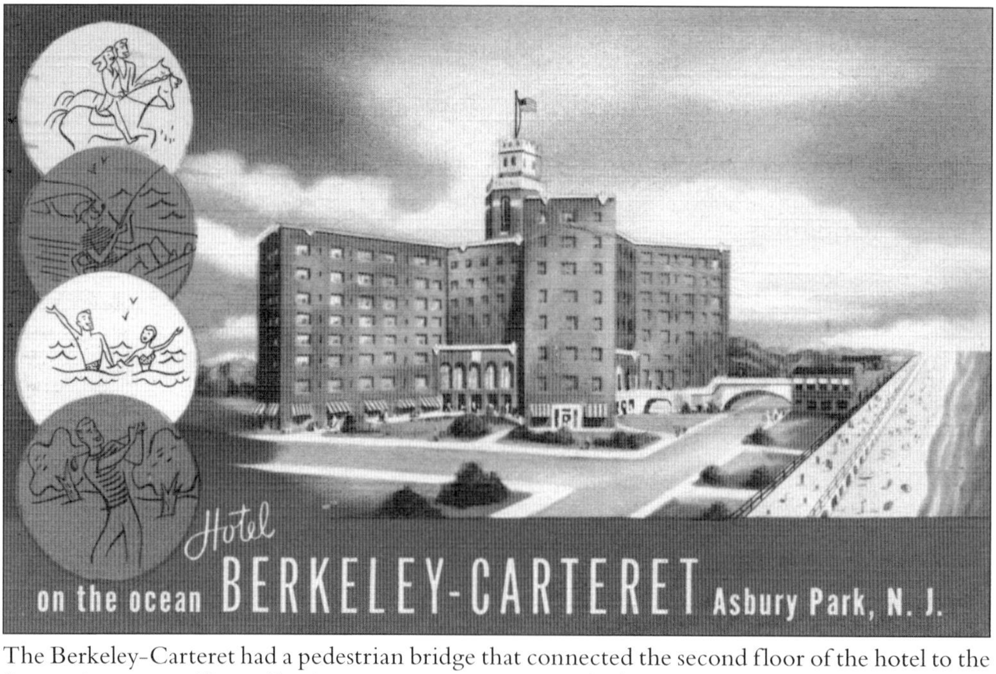


The Berkeley-Carteret had a pedestrian bridge that connected the second floor of the hotel to the Sunset Avenue pavilion, allowing patrons easy access to the boardwalk. In addition to amenities like telephone service and hot and cold running saltwater in each room, in 1949, a stay at the Hotel Berkeley-Carteret included "a round of your favorite sport," including horseback riding, fishing, swimming, golf, or tennis.

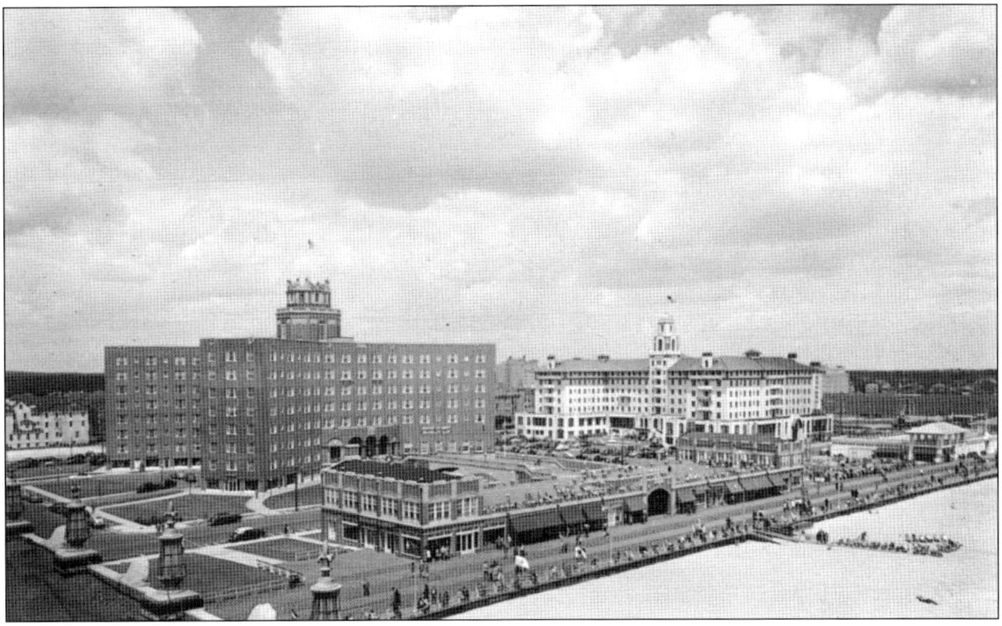

This view from the roof of the convention hall shows both the Berkeley-Carteret and Monterey hotels. Both of these buildings were used as receiving stations by the British Royal Navy during World War II. The Monterey was torn down in 1963, but the Berkeley-Carteret has been restored and reopened as the Berkeley Oceanfront Hotel.

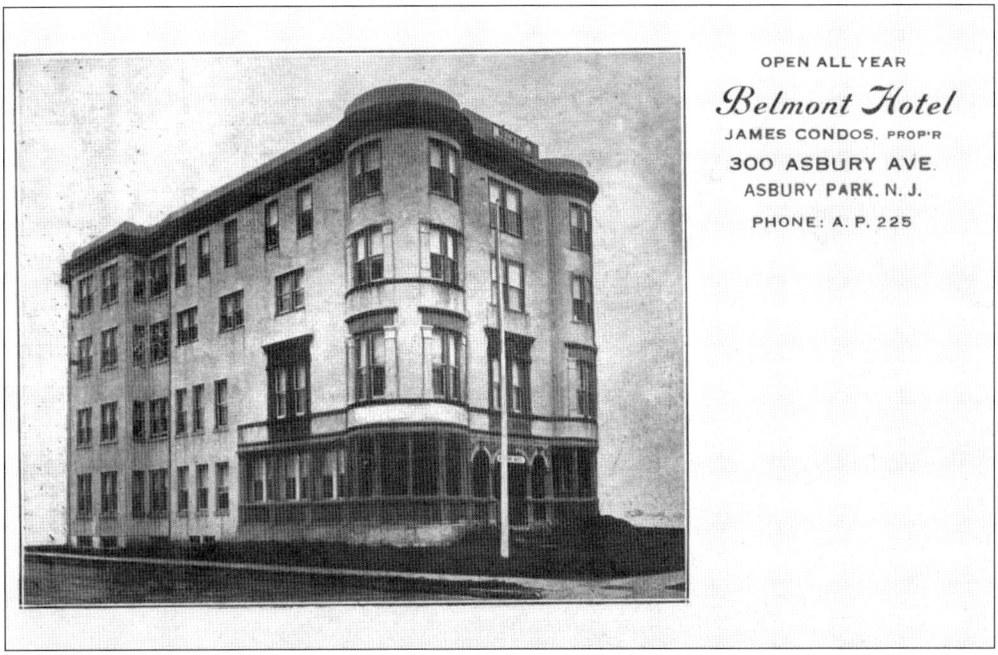


The 50-room Belmont Hotel was located on Asbury Avenue. James Condos was the hotel's proprietor in the late 1940s, when it was open year-round and a room cost $2.50 per night. The Belmont and adjacent Atlantic Hotel were due to be demolished and developed into condominiums, but before that could happen, both buildings were destroyed in a five-alarm fire in February 2006.

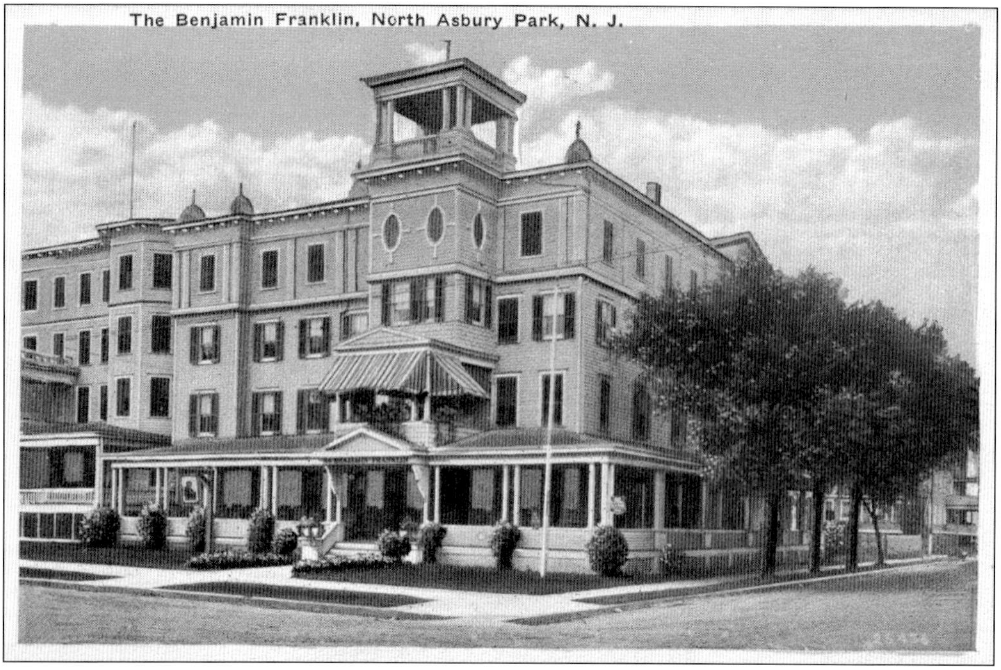


The Benjamin Franklin Inn opened in 1887, making it one of the oldest hotels in Asbury Park. Located on Sixth Avenue and Webb Street, the hotel had 105 rooms and was open from May until October in the 1940s.

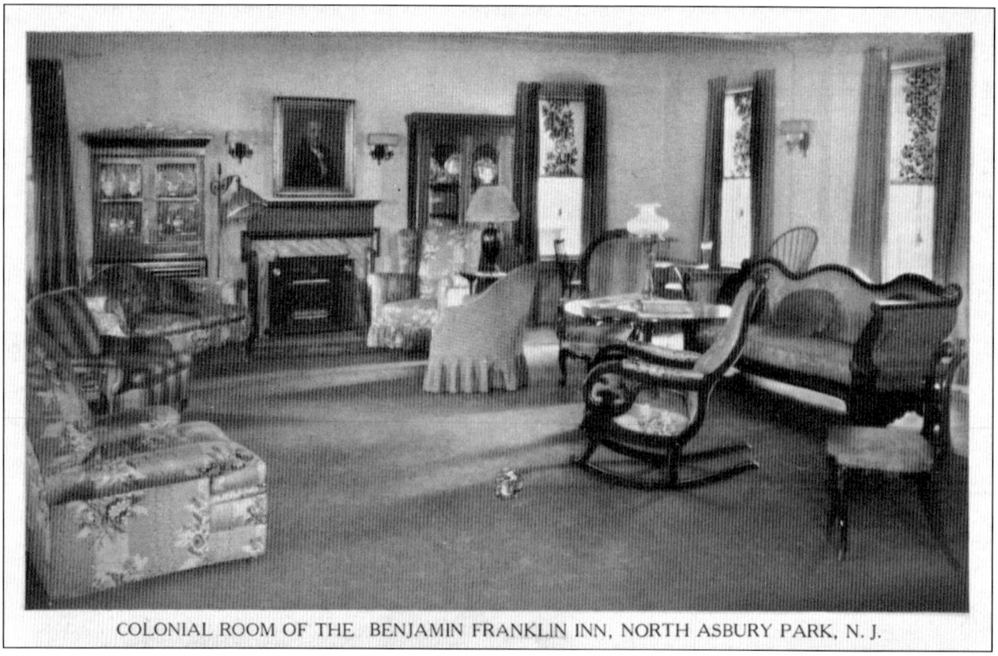


The Benjamin Franklin Inn was advertised as "an inn with the charm of New England on the Jersey coast." Its décor was designed to evoke an earlier time, as is evident in this image of the hotel's Colonial Room. The proprietor in the 1930s and 1940s was Carrie E. Stroud, who had assumed ownership from her parents in 1925.

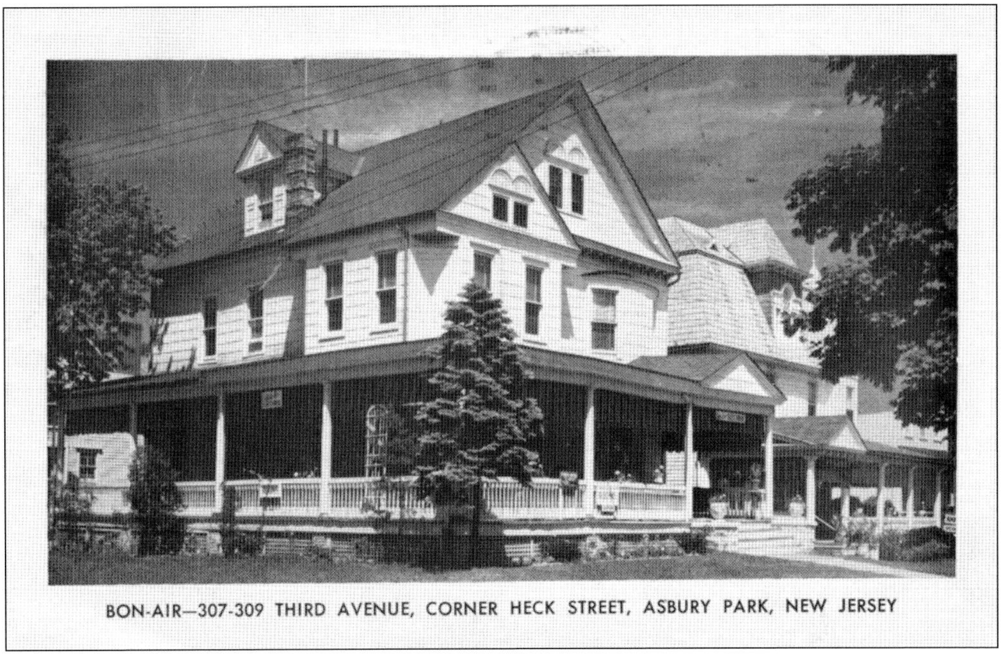


The Bon-Air was located at the corner of Third Avenue and Heck Street. This "exclusive guest house" was owned and operated by Mr. and Mrs. M. Gurbach in the 1950s. Today, the house at the corner of Third Avenue and Heck Street is a private residence.

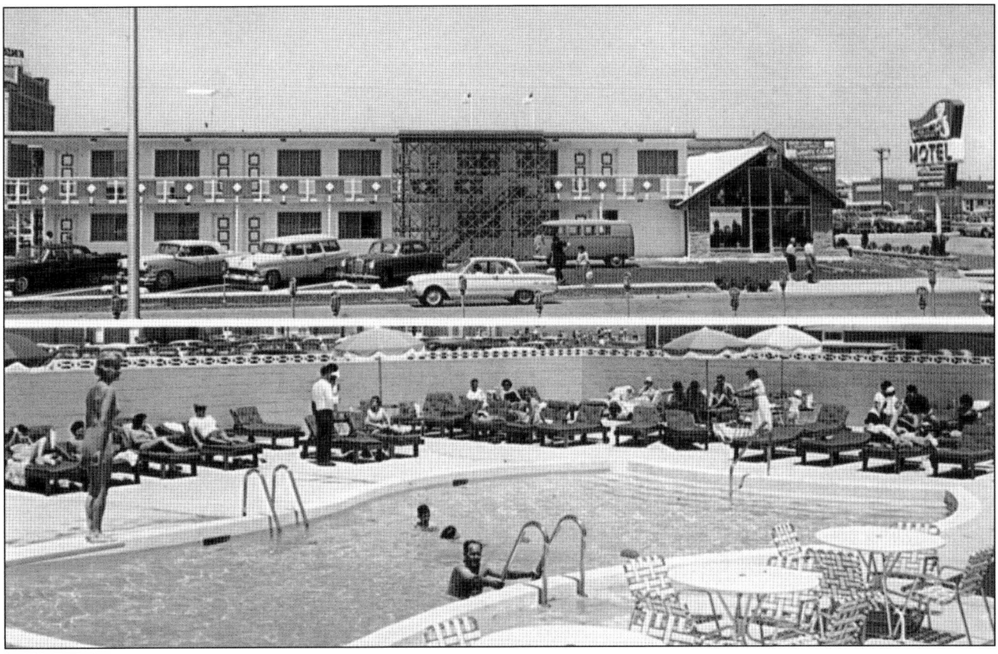


The Cavalier Motel on Seventh Avenue had a spacious pool area with chaise lounges and sun umbrellas. Patrons could enjoy night swimming, with the pool area being "beautifully lighted" in the evening. Additionally, the motel offered free use of the nearby Monte Carlo Beach Club with a stay.

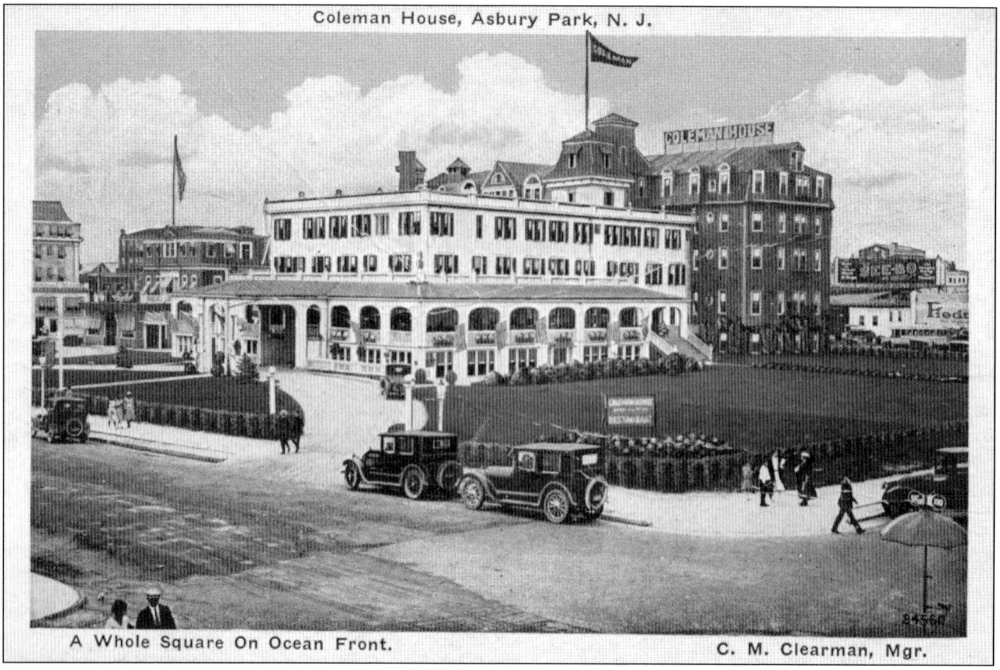


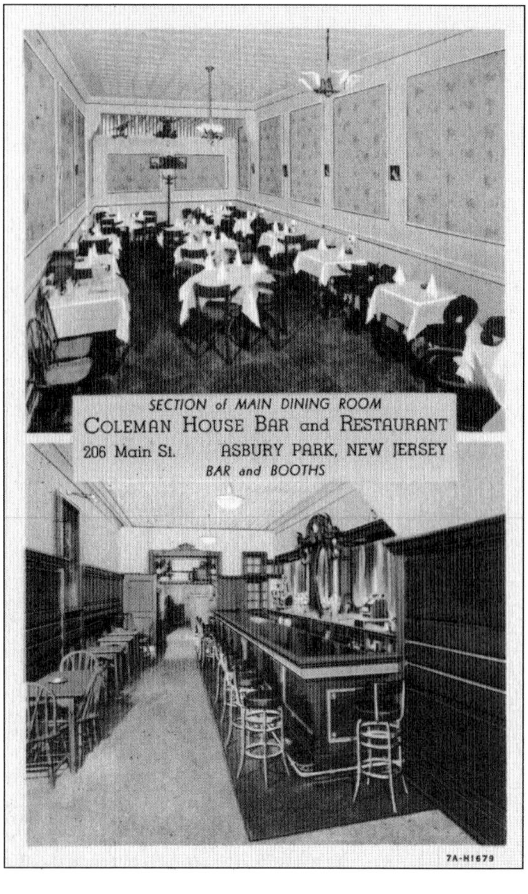


The Coleman House was one of the earliest hotels established in Asbury Park. Built in 1876, it was expanded twice during the 1800s, and ultimately occupied the entire block at Asbury and Ocean Avenues. With room for 350, the Coleman House was one of the largest hotels in the city. The land where the Coleman House was located became the site of a municipal parking lot after the hotel was demolished in 1934.

The Coleman House Bar and Restaurant was located at 206 Main Street, opposite the Asbury Park train station. The restaurant, seen here around 1937, offered "quality food at popular prices." Today, this building houses Johnny Mac House of Spirits, where the mirrored bar at the bottom can still be seen.

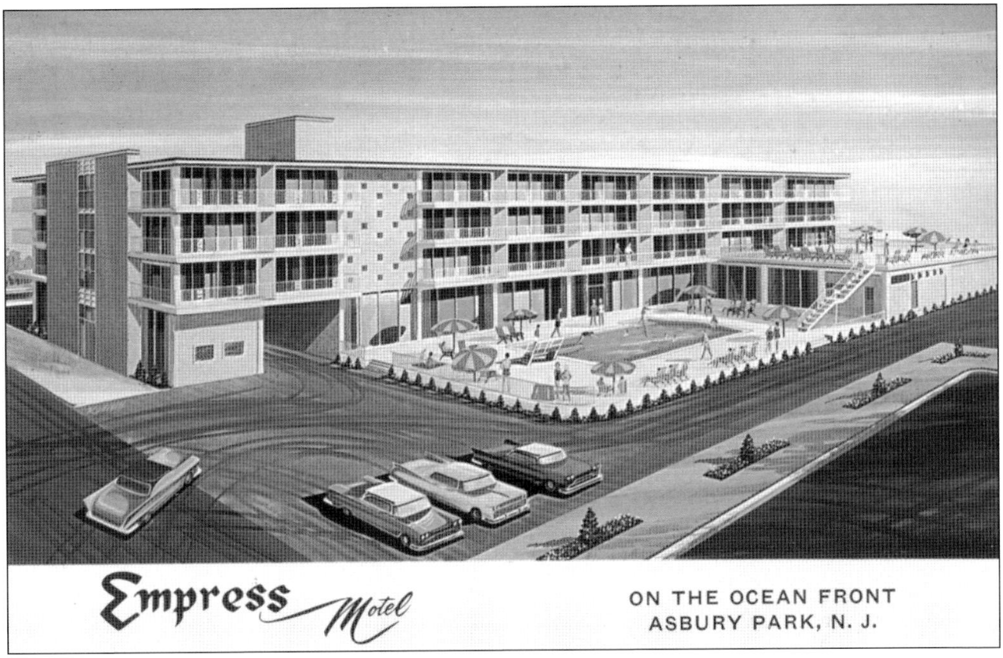


The 101-room Empress Motel was built in the 1950s at the corner of Asbury and Ocean Avenues on a portion of the block where the Coleman House previously stood. Open all year, the mid-century motel boasted amenities like 21-inch televisions and winter swimming. After years of declining business, the Empress closed in the late 1980s.

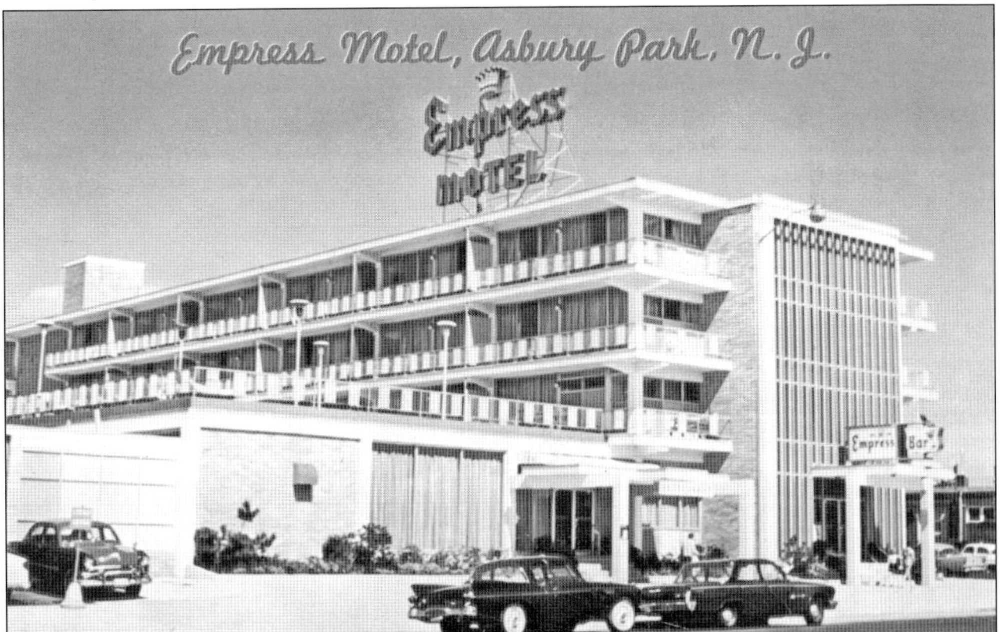


In 1998, New York record producer Shep Pettibone purchased the Empress Motel building. He renovated the motel's nightclub, which was reopened as Club Paradise in 1999. Pettibone completely restored the derelict motel portion of the building as well, and in 2004, the Empress was reopened as an LGBT friendly hotel.

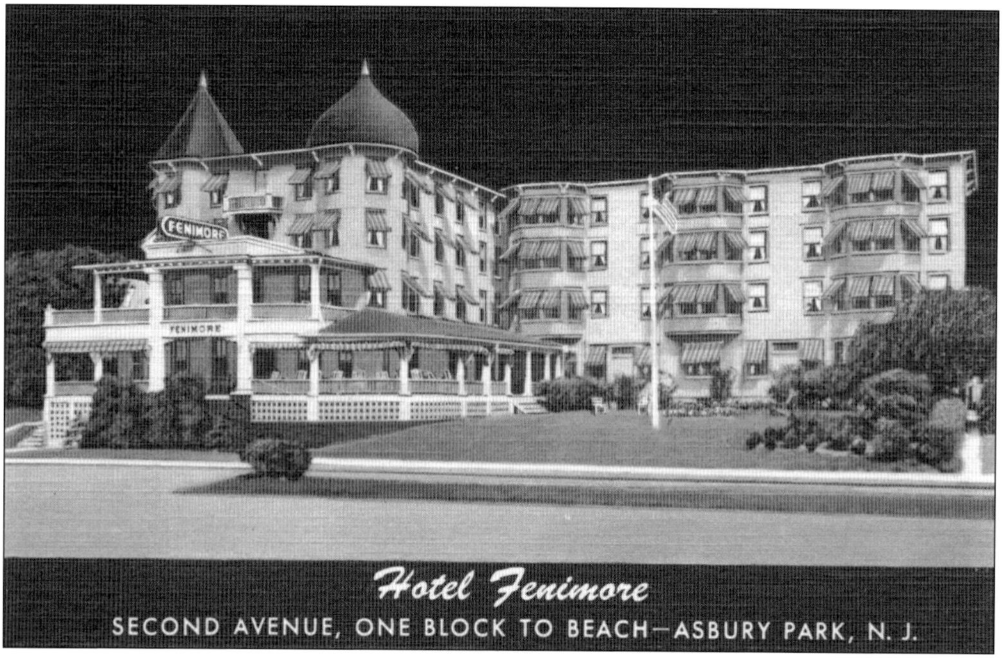


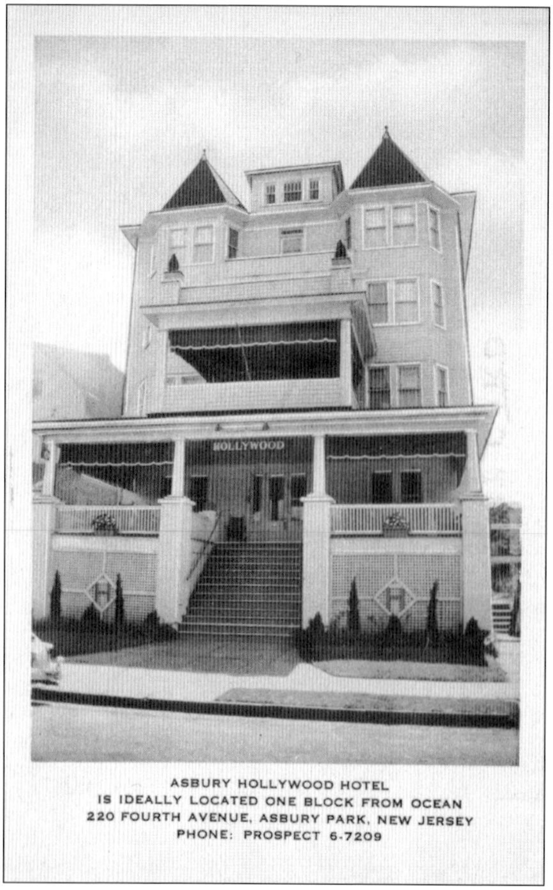


The Hotel Fenimore, located on Second Avenue, offered a complementary continental breakfast to those who chose to stay here. In this 1949 postcard, the four-story hotel, which had 130 rooms, advertises that it caters to a "select clientele." Today, an apartment building occupies the lot where the Fenimore once stood.

The four-story Asbury Hollywood Hotel was located one block from the beach at 220 Fourth Avenue. In addition to ocean bathing, visitors could enjoy the hotel's club room, which was outfitted with ping-pong and pool tables. H. Moloughney owned the hotel in the 1940s; later, Mr. and Mrs. Fred J. Erichsen took over as owners. Today, there is an apartment building where the Asbury Hollywood Hotel once was.

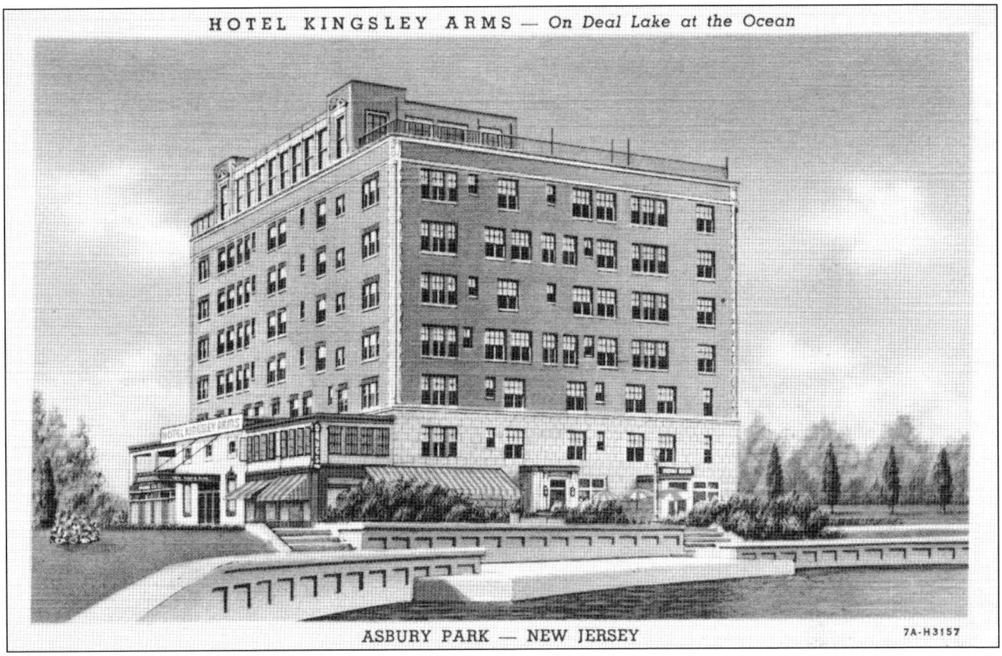


The Kingsley Arms Apartment Hotel was built in 1931; this is how the hotel appeared in 1948. The Kingsley Arms overlooked Deal Lake and the Monte Carlo Beach Club, and had a sun deck that offered a view of the Atlantic Ocean. There were multiple dining options for those staying at the Kingsley Arms, including a coffee house, cocktail lounge, and the Flaming Dining Room, which was advertised as having "an atmosphere of good taste and refinement."

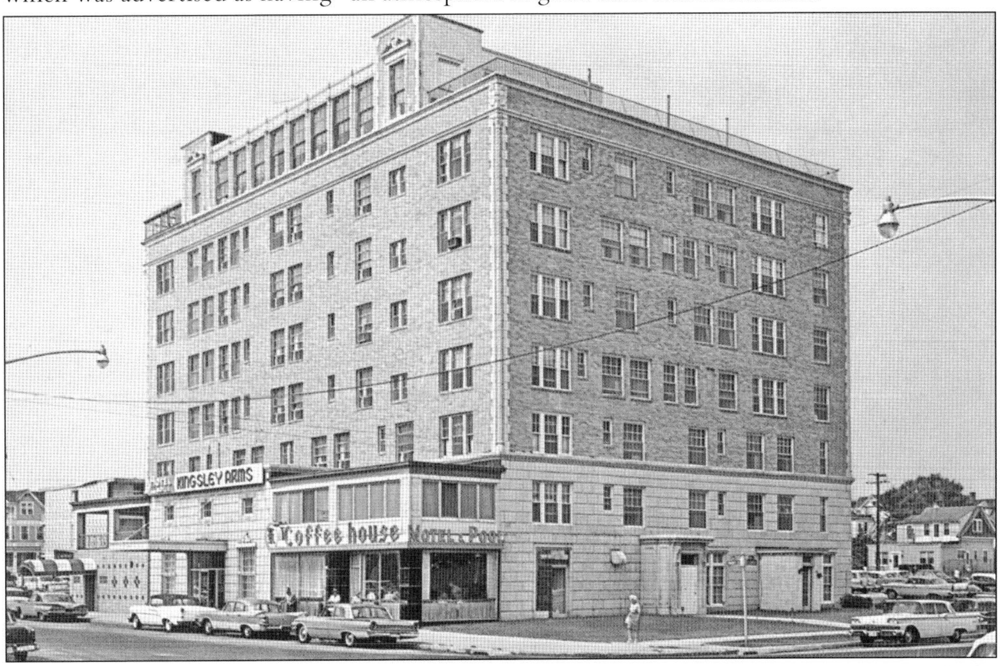


This postcard shows the Kingsley Arms as it looked in 1965. When it operated as a hotel, the eight-story Kingsley Arms had 200 rooms and apartments. Today, it has been converted into a 98-unit apartment building.

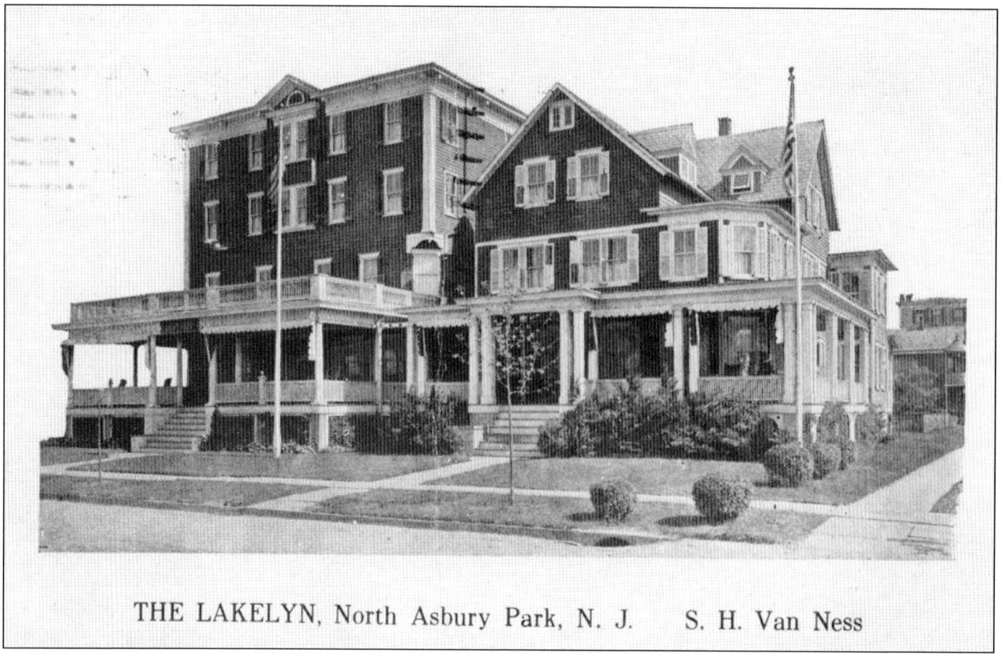


The 40-room Hotel Lakelyn overlooked Sunset Lake. This postcard depicts the hotel as it looked around 1930, when it was open from May to October. Advertisements promised a restful atmosphere and excellent cuisine. Located on Sunset Avenue, the hotel was a short walk to Asbury Park's convention center and offered special rates for convention-goers.

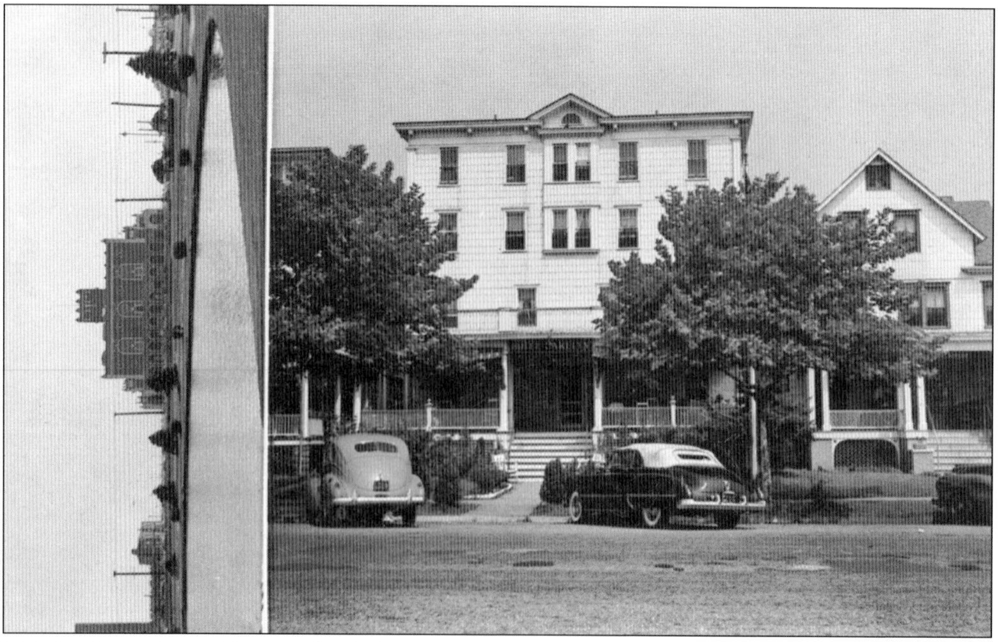

This is a later view of the Hotel Lakelyn. By this time, K.T. Basmajian had taken over ownership from S.H. Van Ness. Today, the building on the right side of the image is still standing; the left-hand portion of the hotel has been replaced by a parking lot.

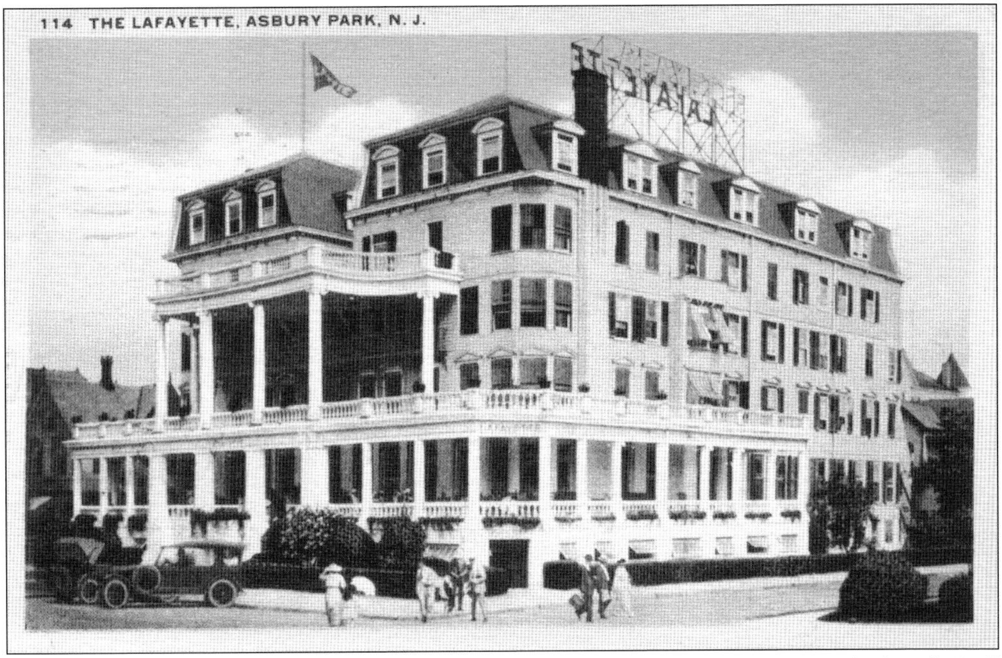


The Lafayette Hotel, at 301 Fourth Avenue, was constructed in the late 1880s. The hotel's "H" shape allowed every room to have a window, making it one of the best-ventilated hotels in the city, which was important in a time before air-conditioning. Margaret Frost owned the Lafayette with her husband; when he died, she took over as sole owner, which was unusual at the time. Later, the Frosts' son Charles joined her in operating the Lafayette.

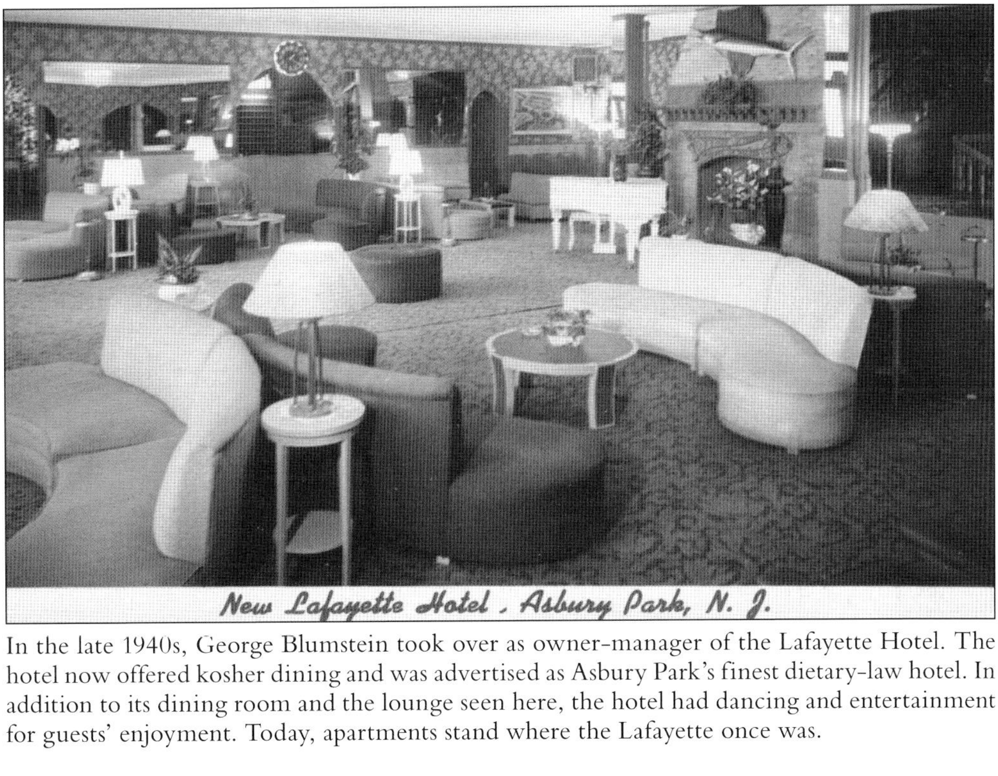


In the late 1940s, George Blumstein took over as owner-manager of the Lafayette Hotel. The hotel now offered kosher dining and was advertised as Asbury Park's finest dietary-law hotel. In addition to its dining room and the lounge seen here, the hotel had dancing and entertainment for guests' enjoyment. Today, apartments stand where the Lafayette once was.

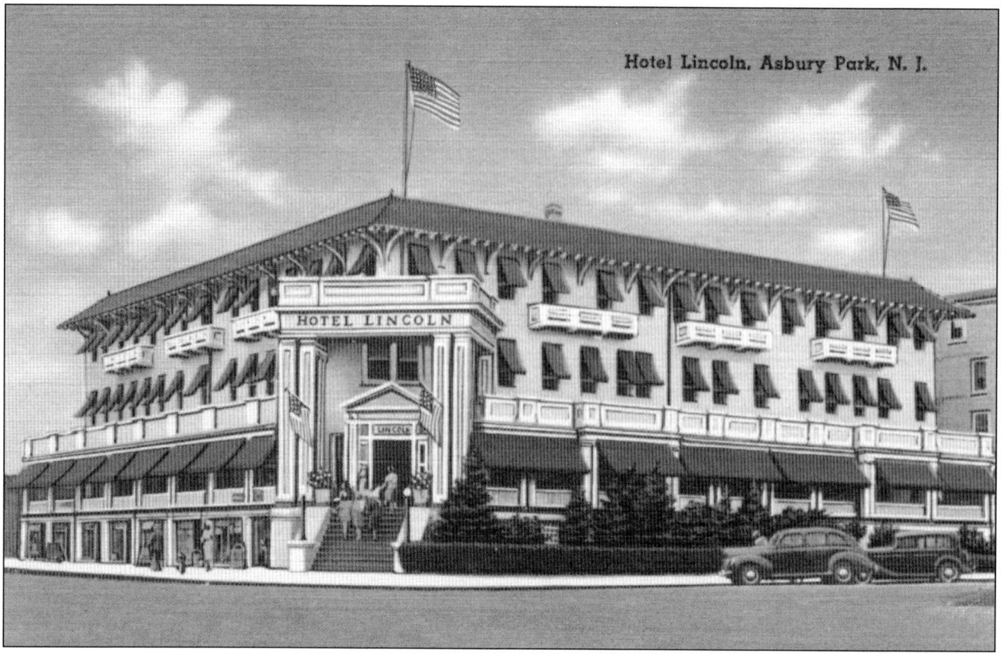


The Hotel Lincoln was located at Fourth Avenue and Kingsley Street, across from the Baronet Theater. Boasting a steam-heated lobby, the hotel's 100 rooms could sleep 250 guests. In 1949, L. Welkowitz was the owner. Advertising dating to that time called the hotel "a select hotel for select people" and touted the delicious food served by the hotel's kosher kitchen.

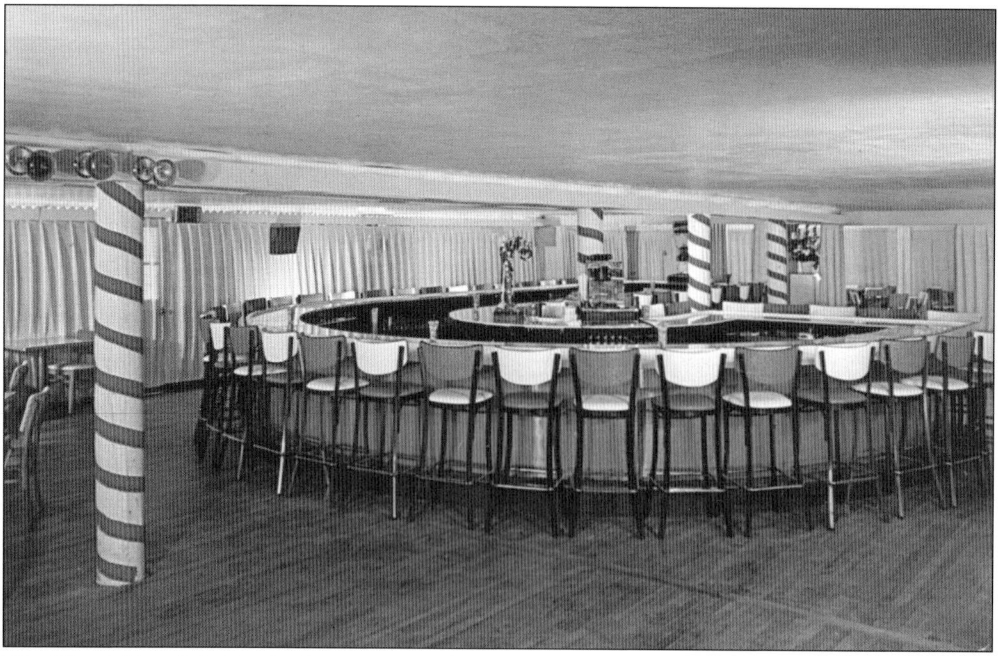

The Hotel Lincoln's Candy Cane Lounge had peppermint-themed décor that included a red-and-white bar surrounded by red-and-white chairs. Seen here in the mid-1960s, the lounge was short-lived. The Lincoln was torn down in 1969 to make way for a motel; today, the corner of Kingsley Street and Fourth Avenue is an empty lot.

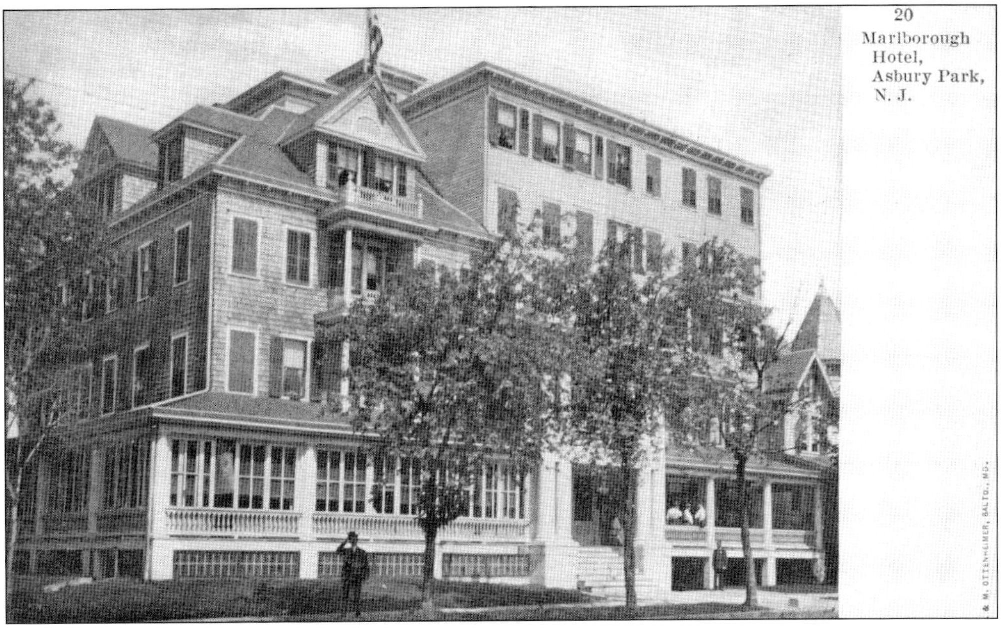


The Marlborough Hotel at 601 Grand Avenue was open year-round, and was advertised as a "fashionable center for winter patronage." The hotel, with a capacity of 300, had 46 baths and a telephone in each room. Allan E. Hughes was the hotel's operator in the late 1930s.

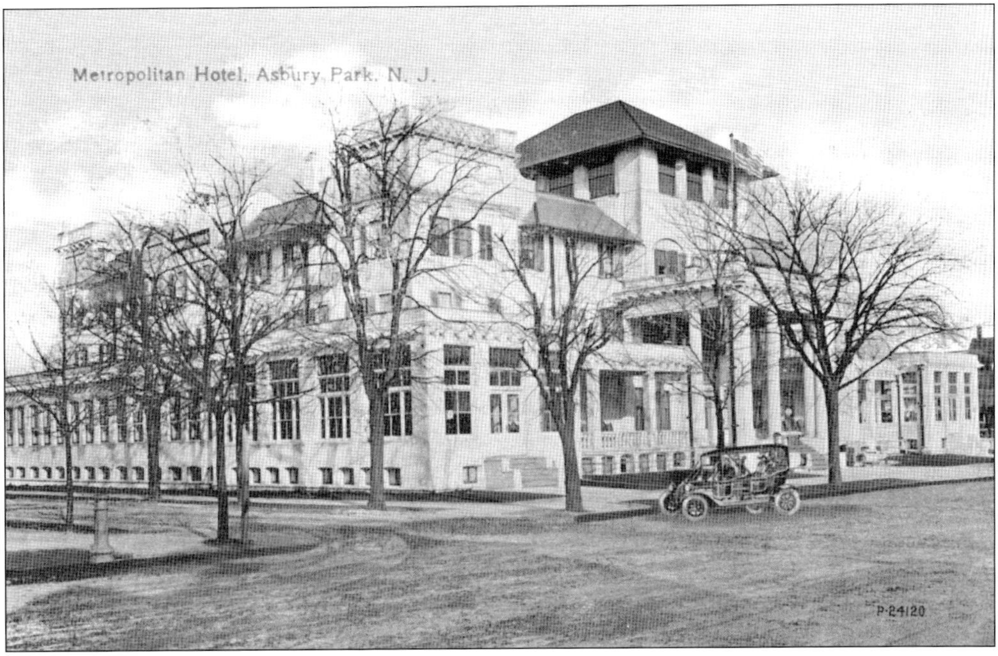


The Metropolitan Hotel was located on Asbury Avenue at the corner of Heck Street. An earlier wood-frame hotel bearing the Metropolitan name was operating at this location as early as 1880. This view captures the hotel as it stood in 1913, not long after being rebuilt. The manager was Francis Yarnell at this time.

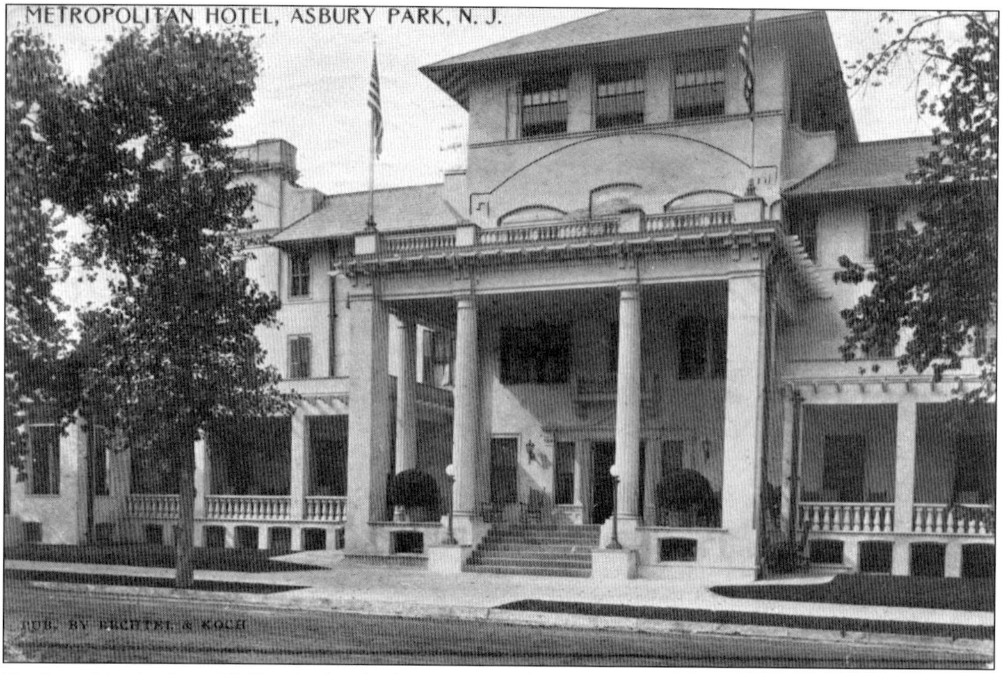


Designed in the Spanish Revival style that was popular in the early 20th century, the Metropolitan had glass-enclosed porches that were steam-heated in the winter. A solarium on the roof provided an expansive view of the surrounding area, including the ocean to the east and Library Square to the west.

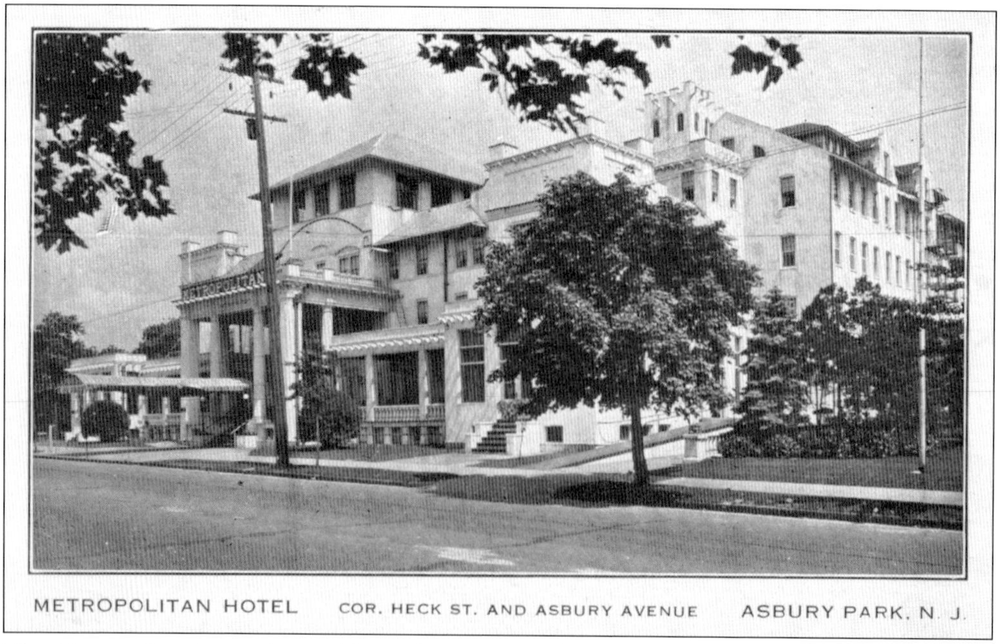


The Metropolitan boasted amenities such as two regulation-size tennis courts, a billiards room, and Asbury Park's first outdoor hotel swimming pool. At the time this postcard was produced, all of the rooms in the hotel had running water, but not all had baths. This image depicts the hotel prior to a motel addition in the 1960s.

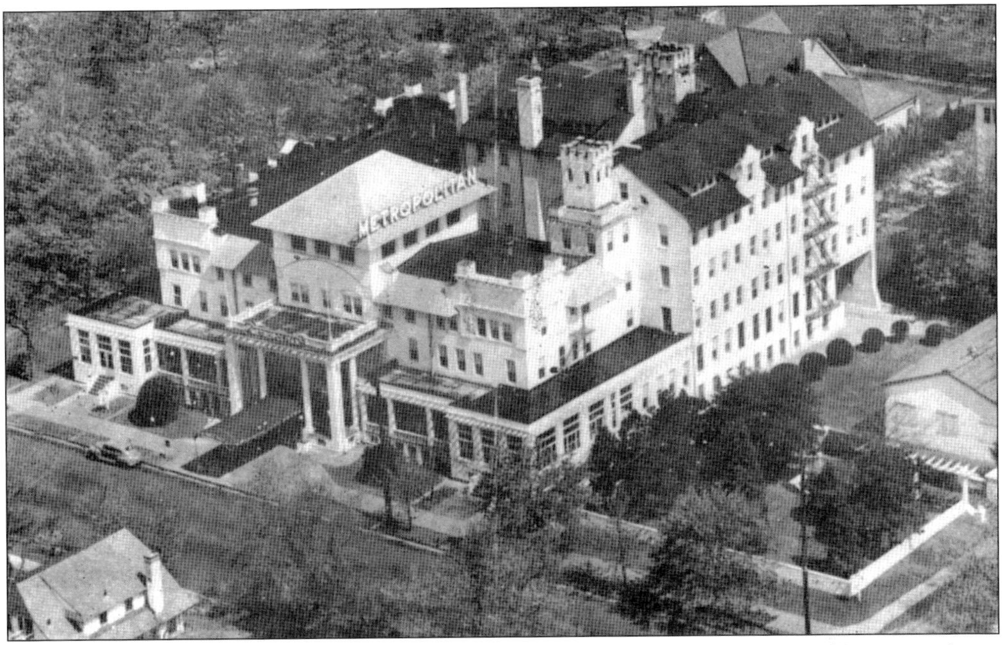


Sylvia and David Weinblatt were the owners of the Metropolitan at the time this postcard was produced in the late 1940s. With 180 rooms, the Metropolitan was the largest kosher hotel in Asbury Park. In addition to dining for 500, the hotel had a ballroom, beauty parlor, and barber shop. In 1967, the Metropolitan hosted Israel's future prime minister Golda Meir as she addressed a group of college students from all over the country.

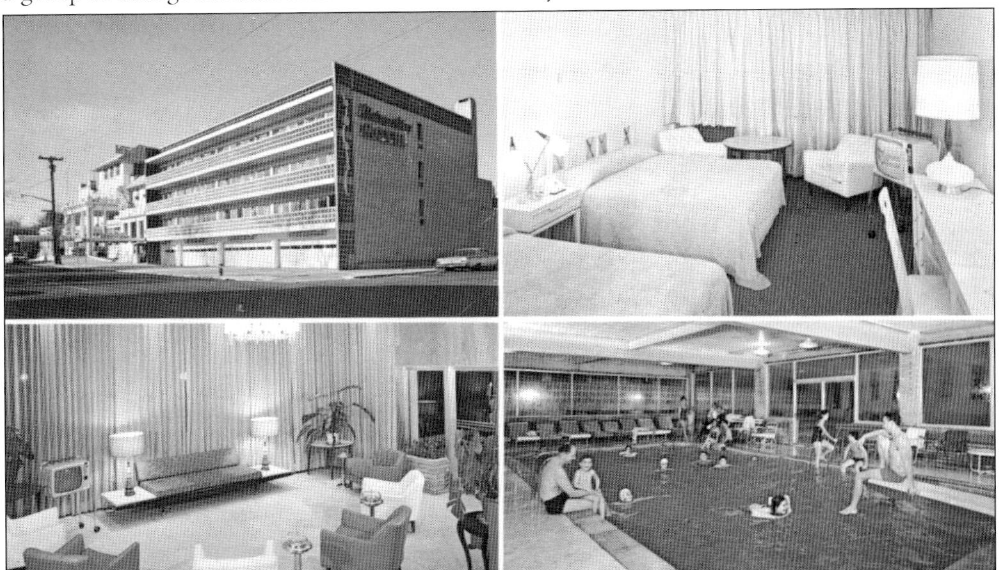

This postcard is the last one used by the Metropolitan up until the time the Weinblatts sold the hotel in 1987. The Metropolitan was one of the last grand hotels in Asbury Park when it closed in 1989. Despite being on the Monmouth County Register of Historic Buildings, it was demolished in March 2008. The motel portion stood standing until 2009, when it too was torn down.

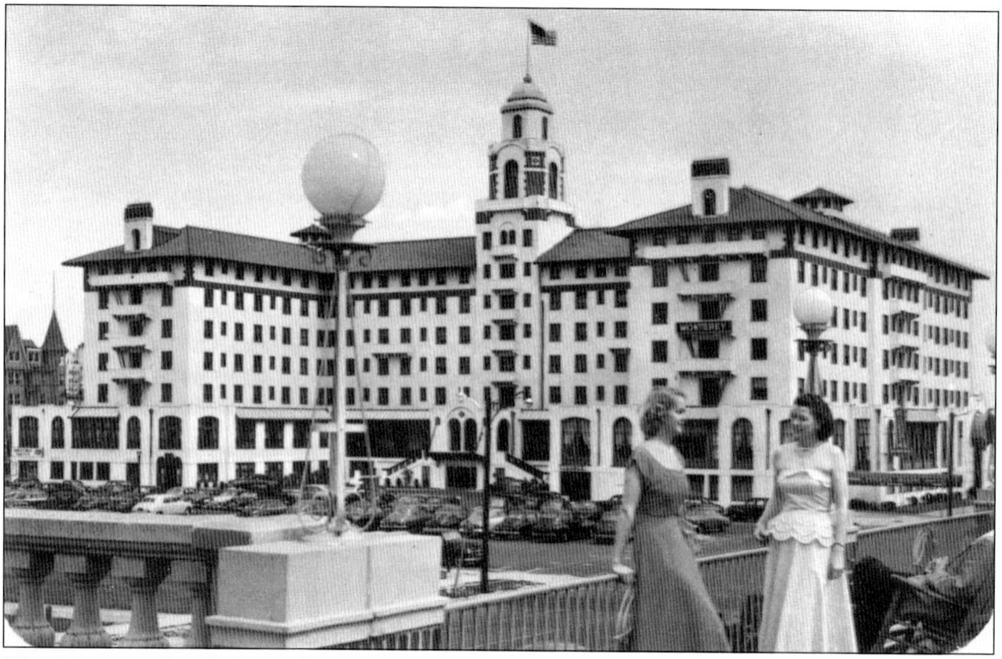

The Monterey hotel, located on Ocean Avenue at Sixth Avenue, was built in 1912. The six-story Spanish Revival building could accommodate 500 guests, making it the largest in the city until the Berkeley-Carteret hotel was built. Erected at a cost of $600,000, the Monterey was constructed of brick and steel and was advertised as the first fireproof hotel in Asbury Park.

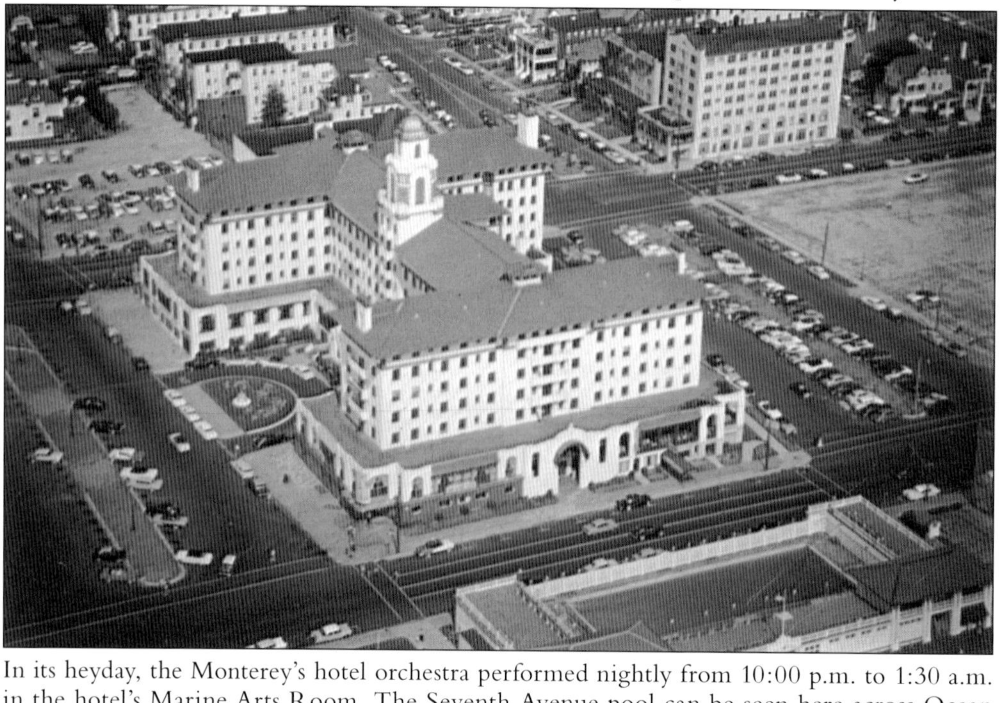

In its heyday, the Monterey's hotel orchestra performed nightly from 10:00 p.m. to 1:30 a.m. in the hotel's Marine Arts Room. The Seventh Avenue pool can be seen here across Ocean Avenue from the Monterey. In the 1950s, motels became more popular than grand hotels like the Monterey. After years of declining business, the hotel was demolished in 1963.

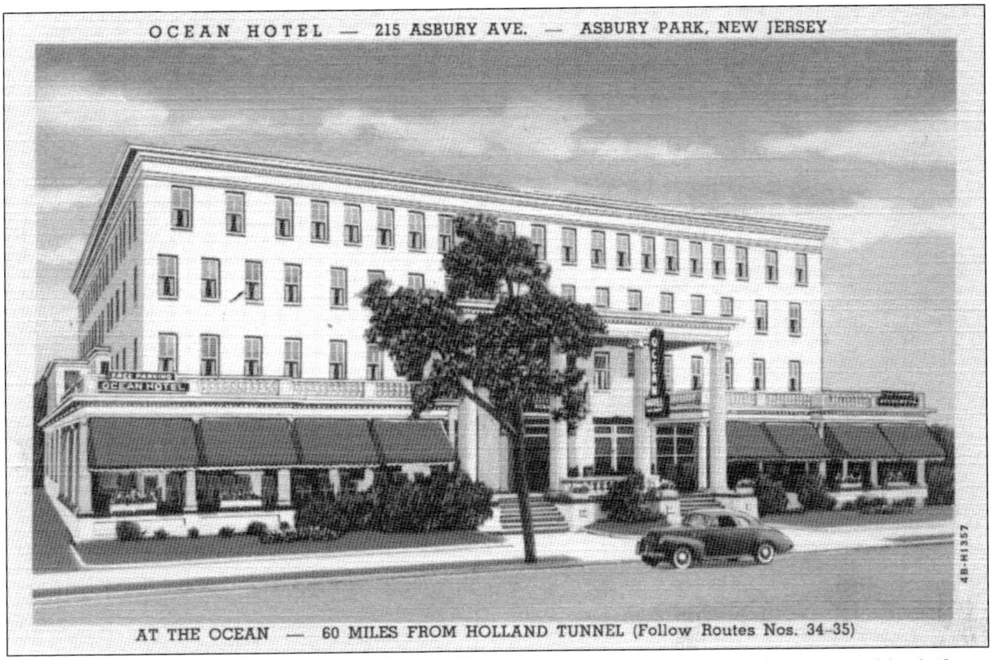


The Ocean Hotel, located on Asbury Avenue next to the West End Hotel, was one block from the beach. The structure seen here replaced an earlier wooden hotel that operated under the same name. The new building boasted 200 rooms, elevator service, a breakfast room, and a spacious porch. A room at the Ocean Hotel was $2 per day in the 1940s.

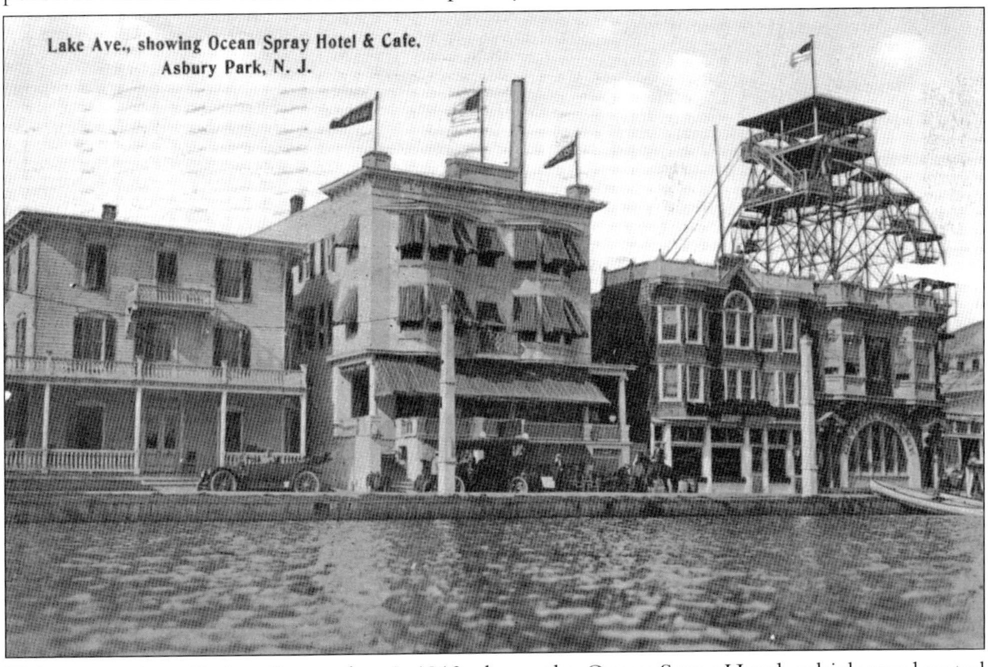


This postcard, mailed on September 1, 1913, shows the Ocean Spray Hotel, which was located on Lake Avenue across from Wesley Lake. The hotel was torn down in 1956 to make way for Palace Amusements' bumper-cars area. Palace Amusements' Ferris wheel and observation tower can be seen at right.

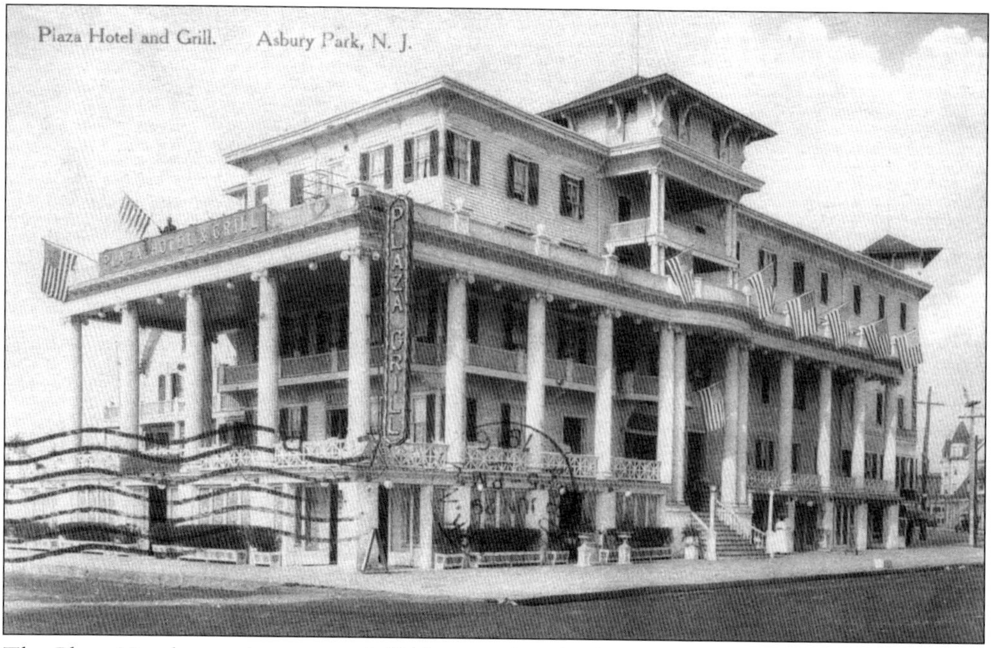


The Plaza Hotel, seen here around 1916, was advertised as "the show place of the shore." It boasted the Cactus Room, Sea View Terrace, and Garden Veranda, where patrons could enjoy dancing to music from famous bands and be entertained by Broadway stars. The Plaza's snack bar, which offered charcoal-broiled sandwiches, was open 24 hours in the late 1940s.

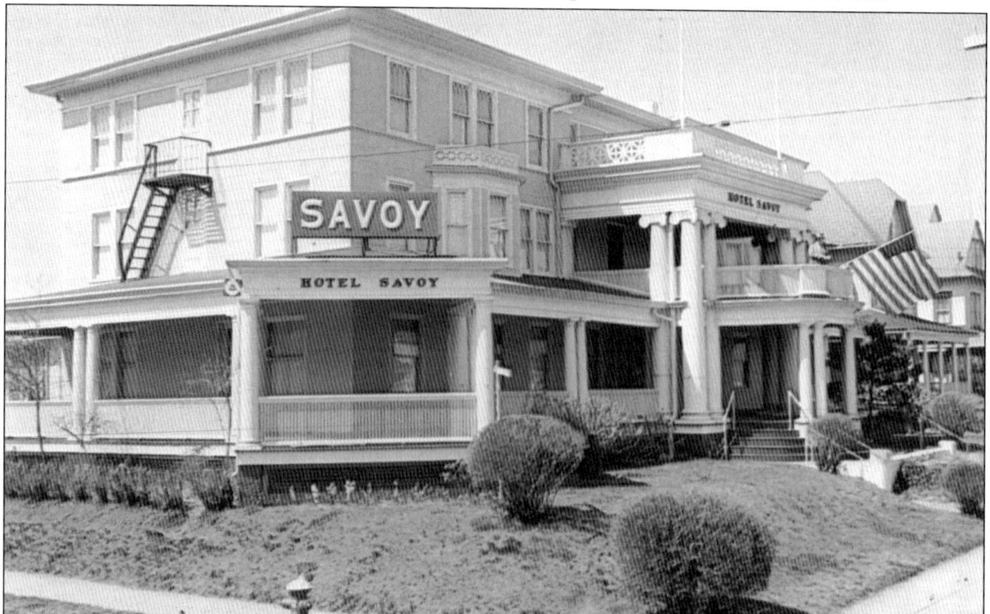


The 55-room Hotel Savoy was two blocks from the boardwalk at the corner of Fourth Avenue and Heck Street. In the 1940s, Mr. and Mrs. H.G. Wetlin owned and operated the Savoy. At that time, the cost of a room with meals included was $4. By the early 1960s, V. Mitre and his sons were the hotel's owner-operators, and the room rate, including meals, had increased to $7.50 per day.

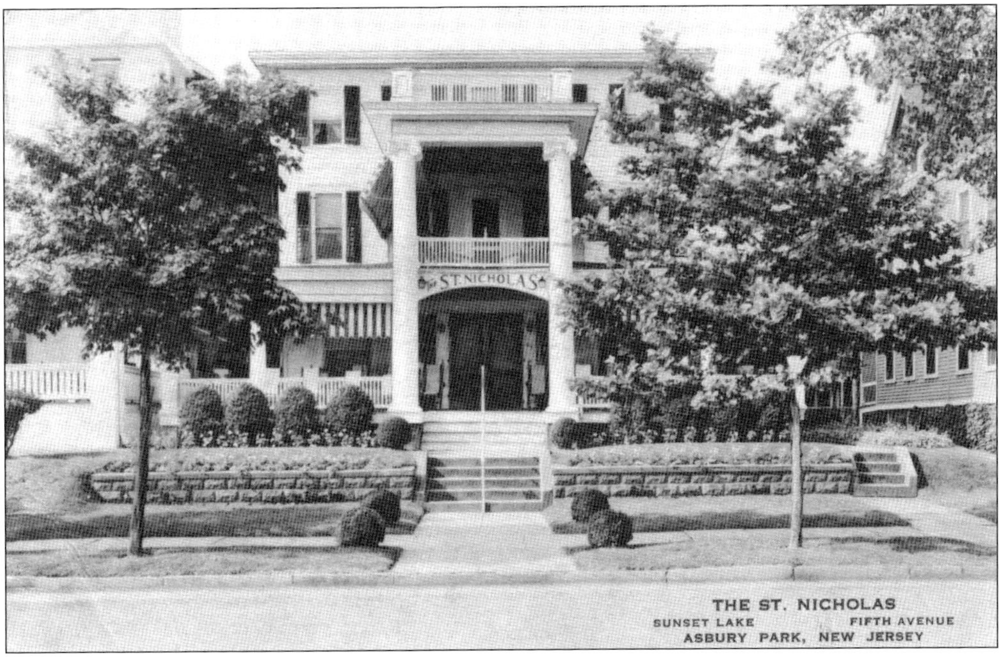


With room for a total of 60 guests, the three-story St. Nicholas Hotel was one of the smaller hotels in Asbury Park. This postcard shows the hotel as it appeared in the early 1940s.

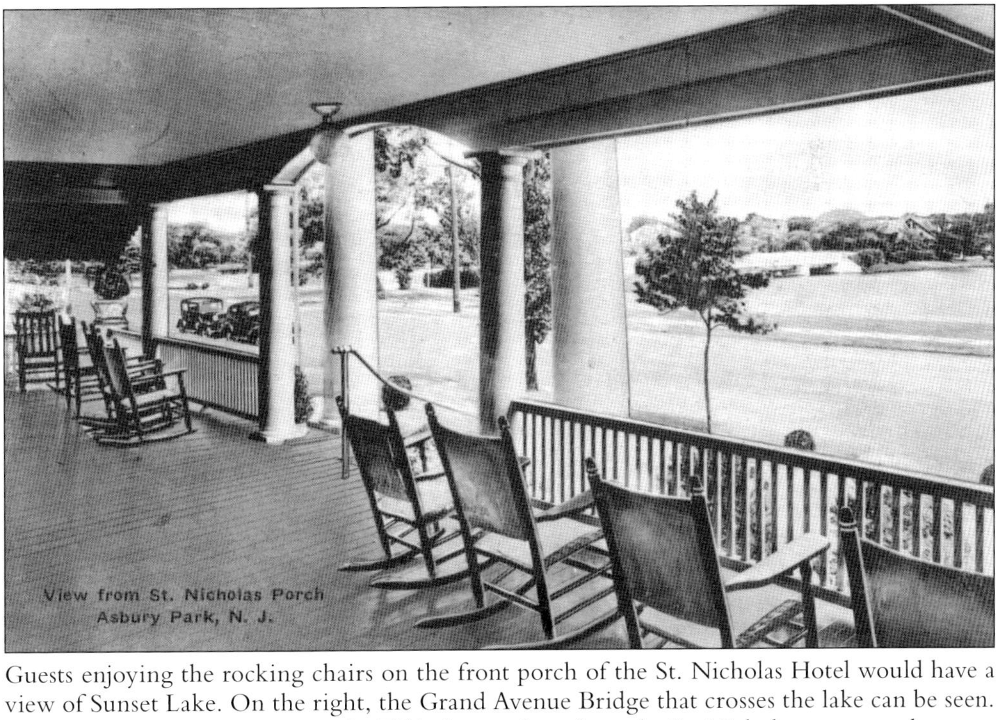


Guests enjoying the rocking chairs on the front porch of the St. Nicholas Hotel would have a view of Sunset Lake. On the right, the Grand Avenue Bridge that crosses the lake can be seen. Today, there are apartments on the Fifth Avenue lot where the St. Nicholas once stood.

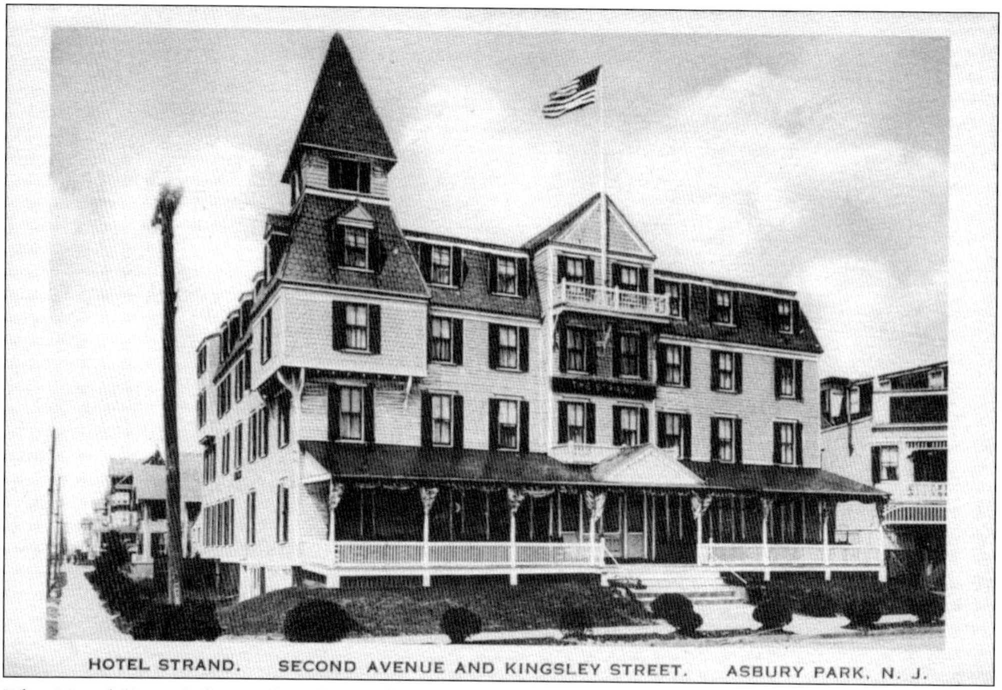


The Hotel Strand, located at Second Avenue and Kingsley Street, advertised reasonable rates in the early 1900s.

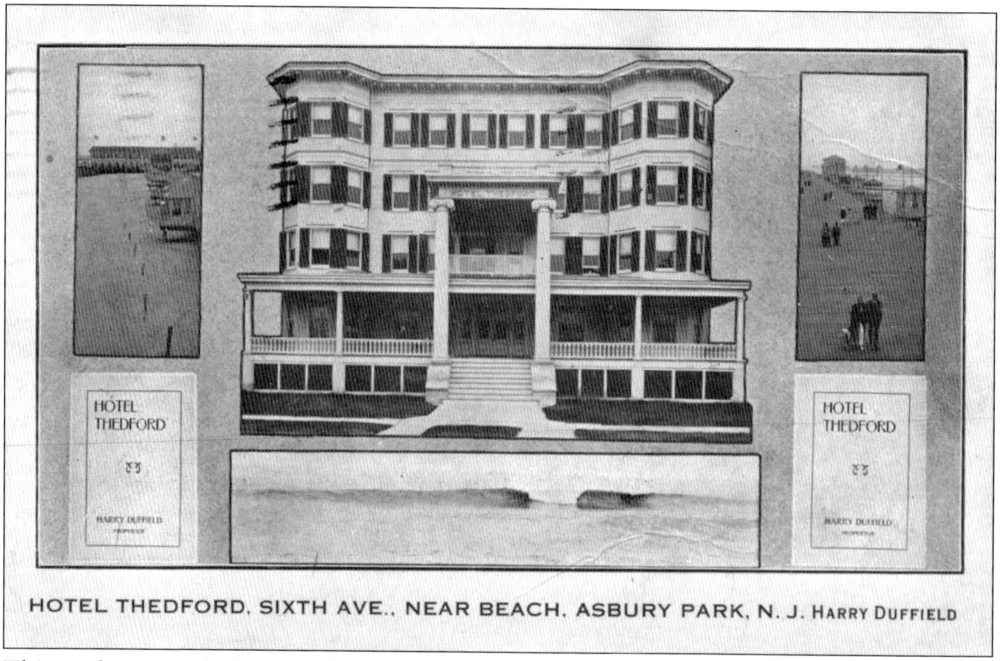


This card, postmarked September 15, 1915, shows the 75-room Hotel Thedford, which was located on Sixth Avenue. In the 1942 Asbury Park Chamber of Commerce guide, the hotel advertised that it catered to a "Christian clientele." The next year, they invited a "select clientele" to stay. In later years, the Thedford was known as the Van Hotel. A 1968 fire destroyed the Van and claimed the life of Varsenig Eretzian, the owner's wife.

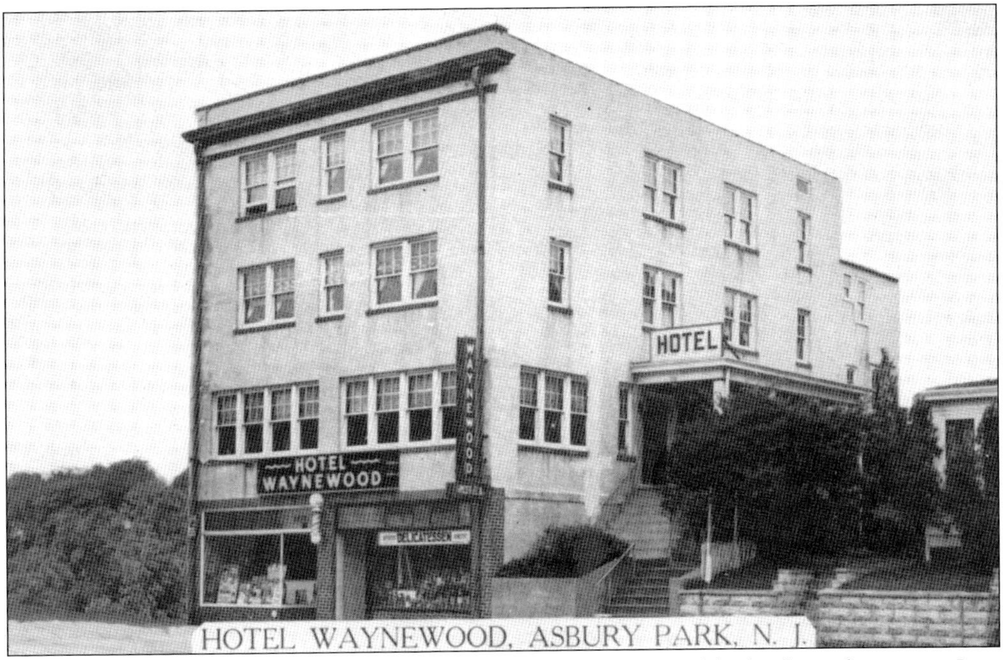


The Hotel Waynewood was located at 305 Sewell Avenue, two blocks from the ocean. Into the 1990s, the Waynewood operated as one of the many seaside hotels that had been converted into boarding homes for the mentally ill who were released from New Jersey institutions in the second half of the 20th century. The lot where the hotel stood is now empty.

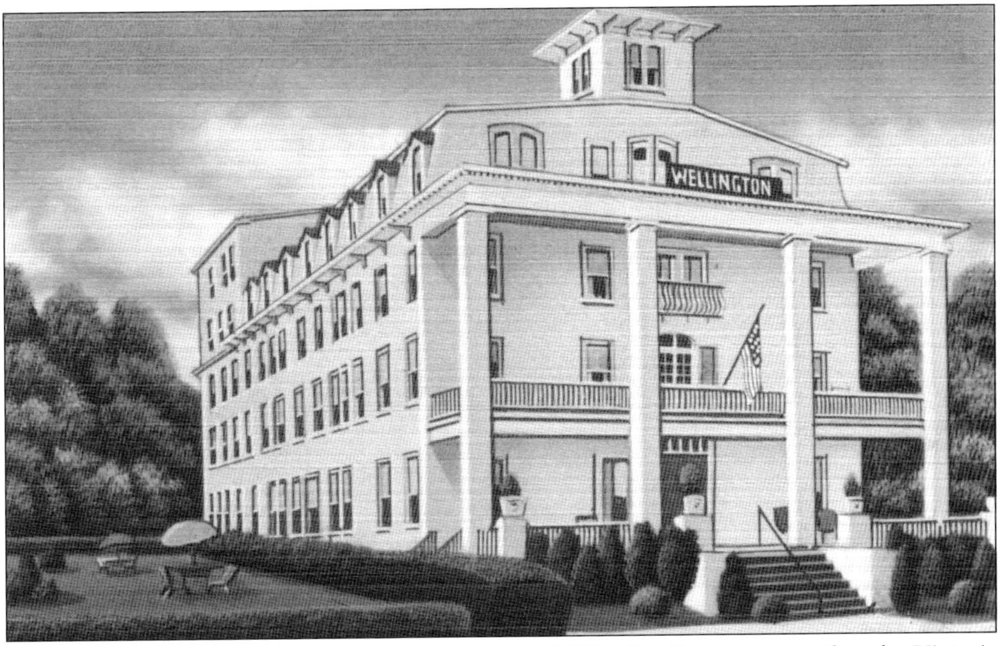


The Wellington Hotel, located at Sixth Avenue and Kingsley Street, operated as the Victoria Hotel prior to 1897. A 1902 advertisement boasted that it had "no malaria, no mosquitoes, no marshes or swamps." The hotel was destroyed in the fire that also ruined the nearby Van Hotel in 1968.

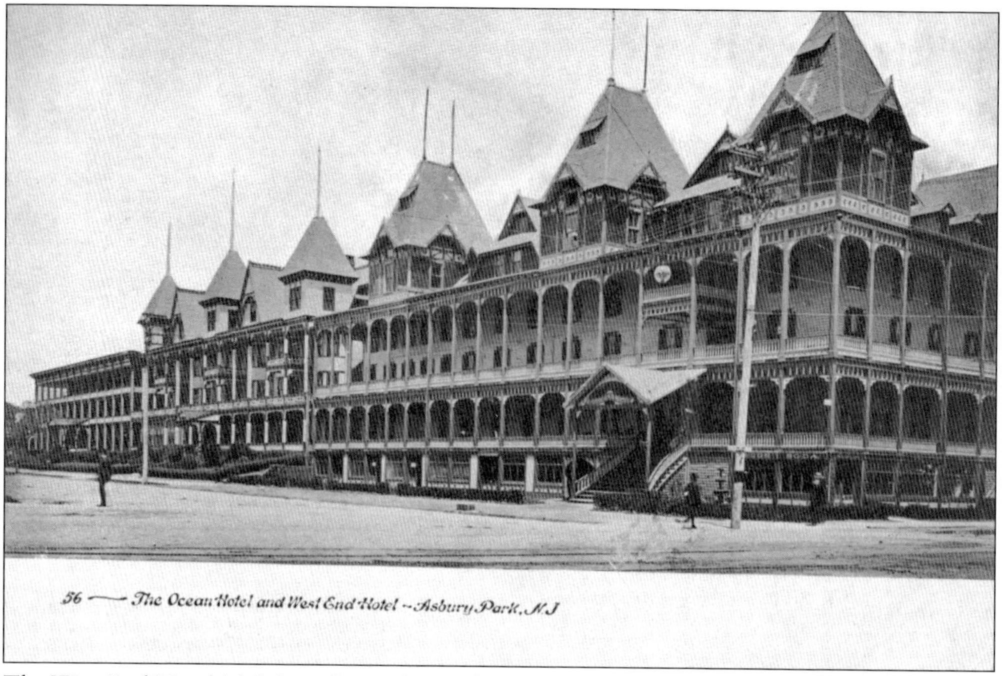


The West End Hotel (right) was located on Asbury Avenue next to the Ocean Hotel. In the early 1900s, the hotel was operated by Asbury Park's Frank Ten Broeck, who had been the city's first mayor. Around this time, the hotel advertised its "superior music and cuisine."

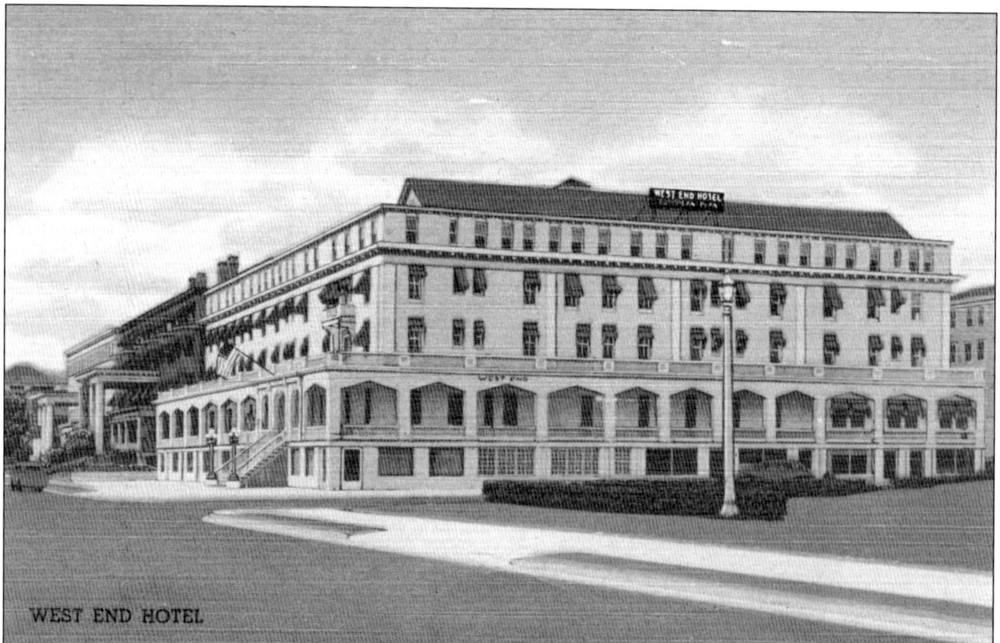


This is the West End Hotel (right) and Ocean Hotel as they appeared in 1950. L.T. Duane was the West End's proprietor at this time. Today, there are condominiums on the corner of Asbury Avenue and Kingsley Street where the West End Hotel once was.

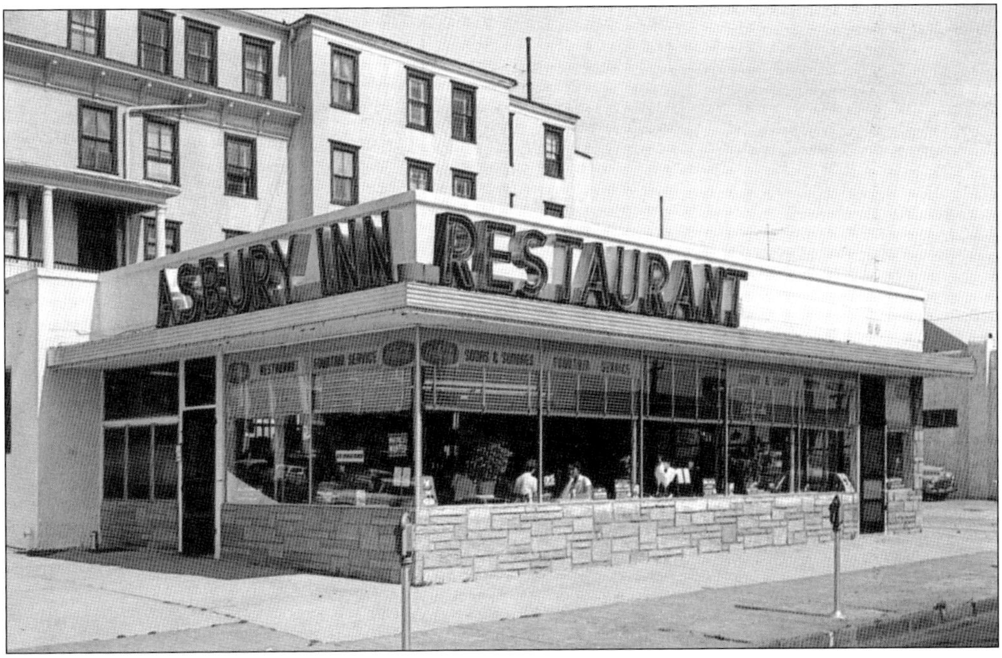


The Asbury Inn's restaurant, at the corner of Second Avenue and Kingsley Street, began serving vacationers in 1949. This postcard advertises the restaurant as a place "where cooking is an art—and eating is a pleasure," with specialties including steak, seafood, roast chicken, and Hungarian goulash.

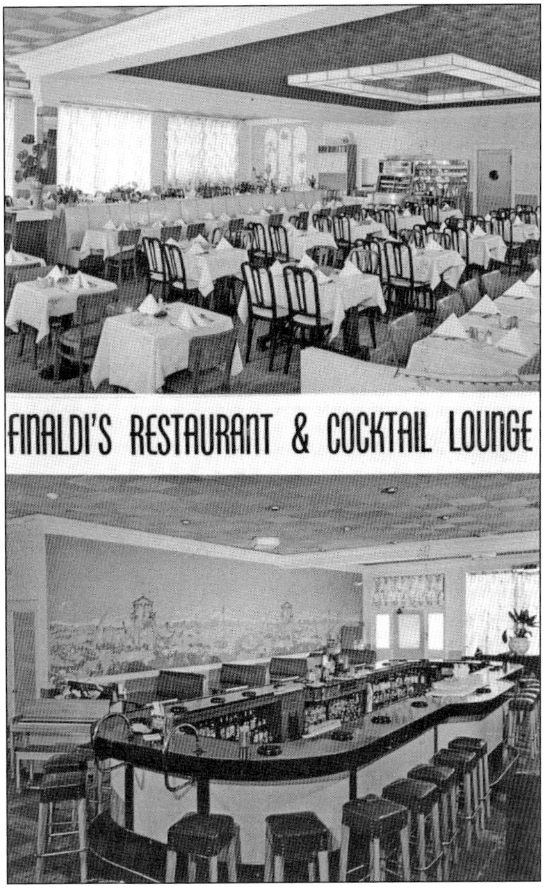


Finaldi's Italian restaurant and cocktail lounge was located at Fourth Avenue and Kingsley Street. The cocktail lounge's large oval bar and piano can be seen here.

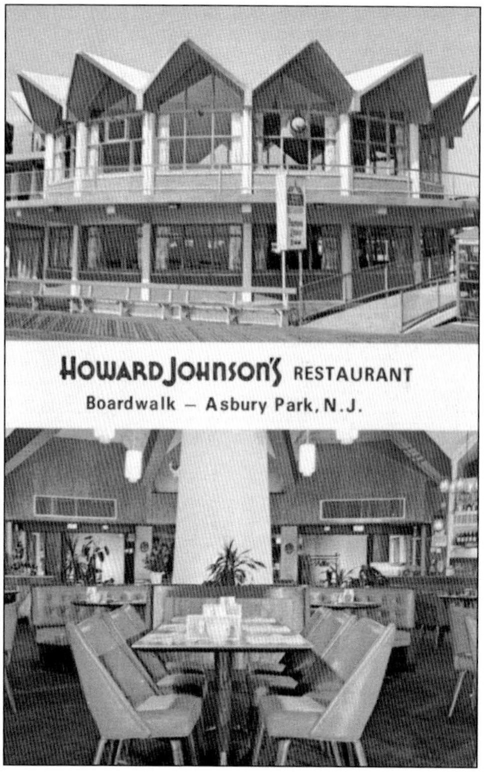


The Howard Johnson's attached to Asbury Park's Fifth Avenue pavilion was designed in the 1960s by the Philadelphia architectural firm of Fridy, Gauker, Truscott & Fridy. The Modernist style of the building was a departure from previous boardwalk architecture. In 2006, after years of declining business, owner George Panas finally closed Asbury Park's HoJo. At that time, it was the last one in New Jersey and one of only five in the country. Today, this building is home to Tim McLoone's Asbury Grille and Supper Club.

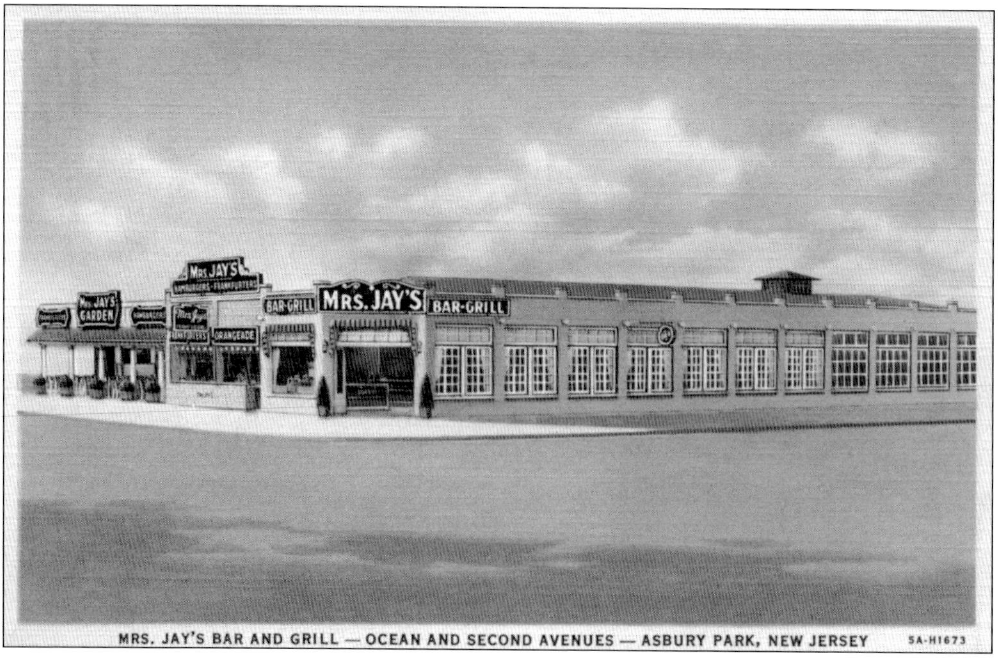


Mrs. Jay's Bar and Grill was on the corner of Ocean and Second Avenues, in what would become the location of the world-famous Stone Pony in 1974. Owners Ida and John Jacobs turned their hotdog stand into a permanent restaurant in the 1930s. They expanded the building to add a beer garden along Ocean Avenue, where they served 2-percent beer during Prohibition.

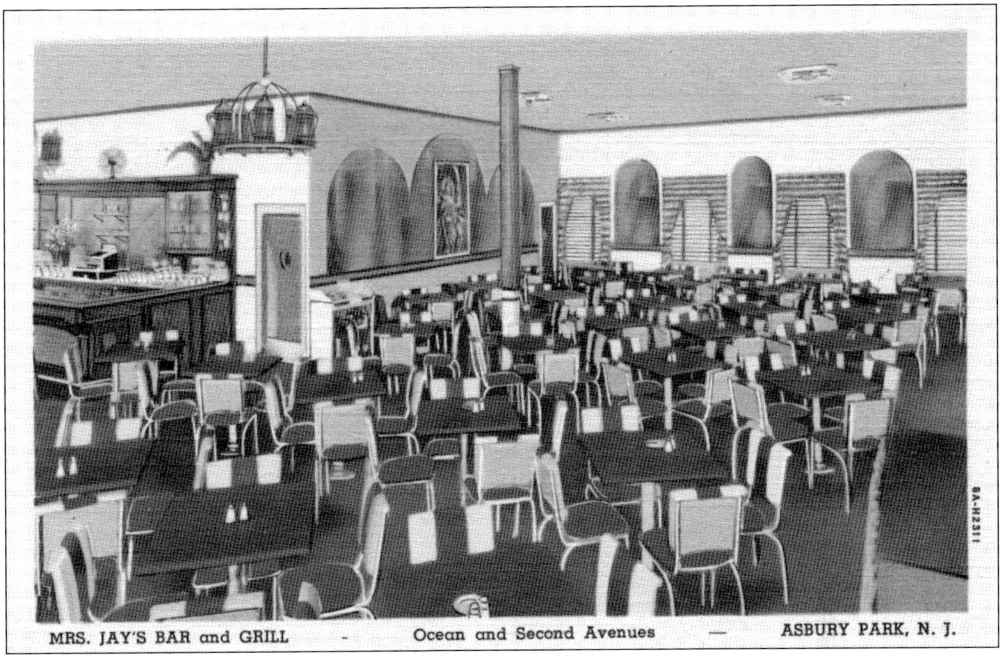


Mrs. Jay's dining room is featured in this postcard, which was mailed in 1938. Around this time, Mrs. Jay's advertised free parking, hot grilled sandwiches, and high-class entertainment every night.

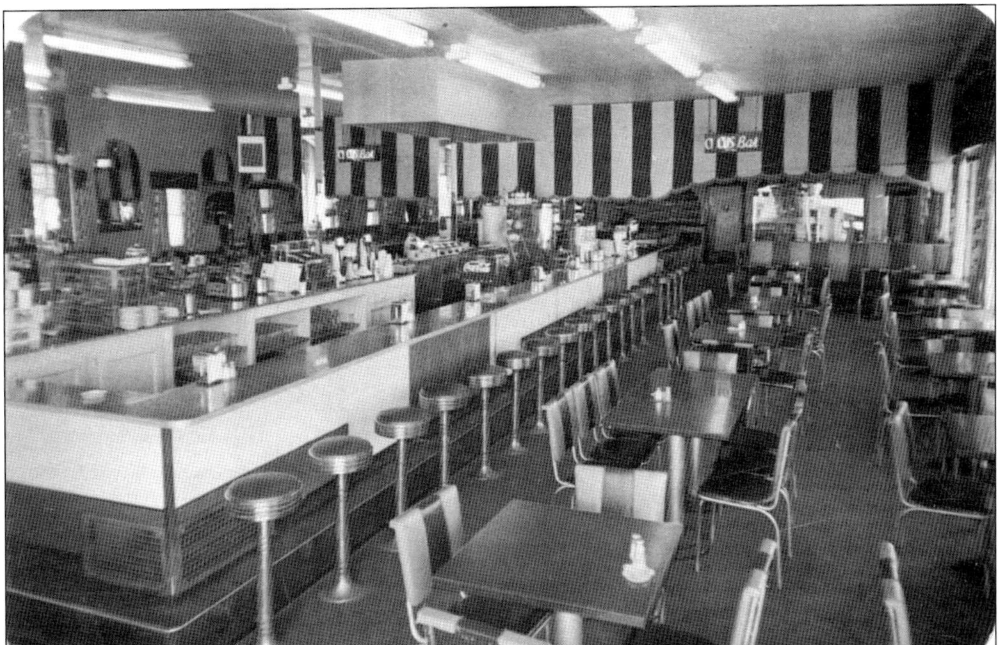

In later years, the Jacobs' daughter Jeanette and her husband, Murray Weiner, took over operating Mrs. Jay's. Shown here is the restaurant's Circus Bar. By the 1960s, Mrs. Jay's became a popular hangout for bikers.

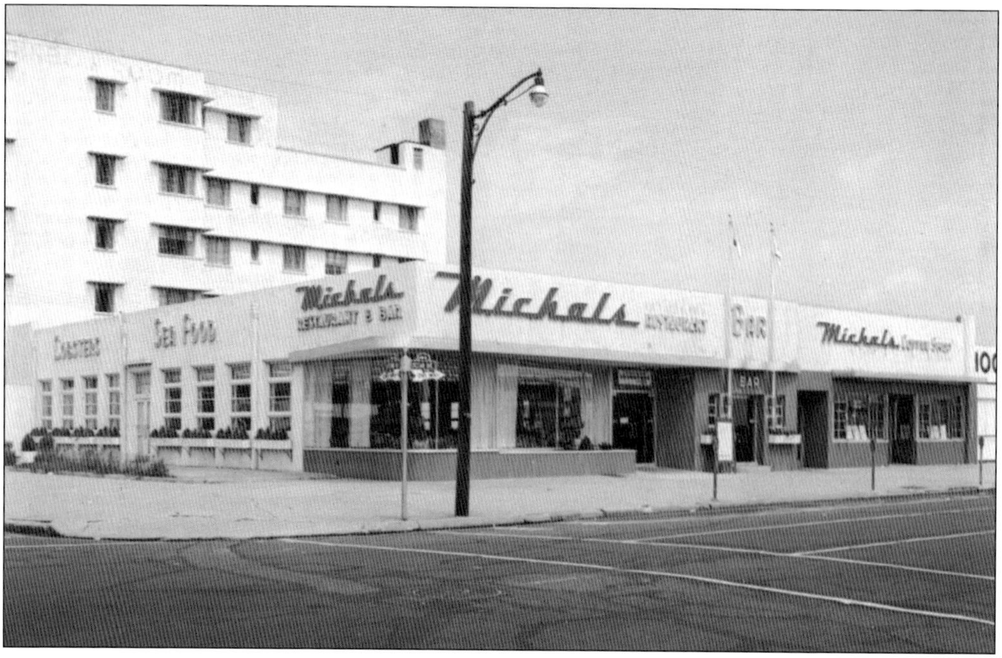


Spiros Michals originally owned a seafood restaurant in the Natatorium at First Avenue on the boardwalk. Later, he moved his restaurant to the location seen here at the corner of Ocean and Second Avenues. This building had previously been the Actaion Yacht Bar and Grill, and before that, this lot was the location of Asbury Park's Steeplechase Park.

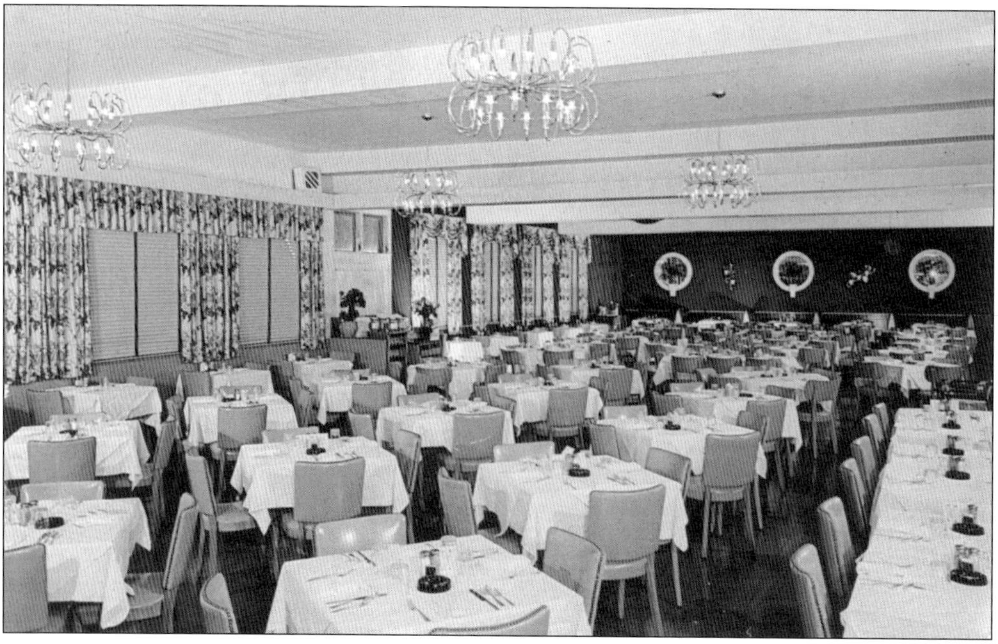

The interior of Michals Restaurant and Bar is seen here. The restaurant had three dining rooms and could seat up to 300 people.

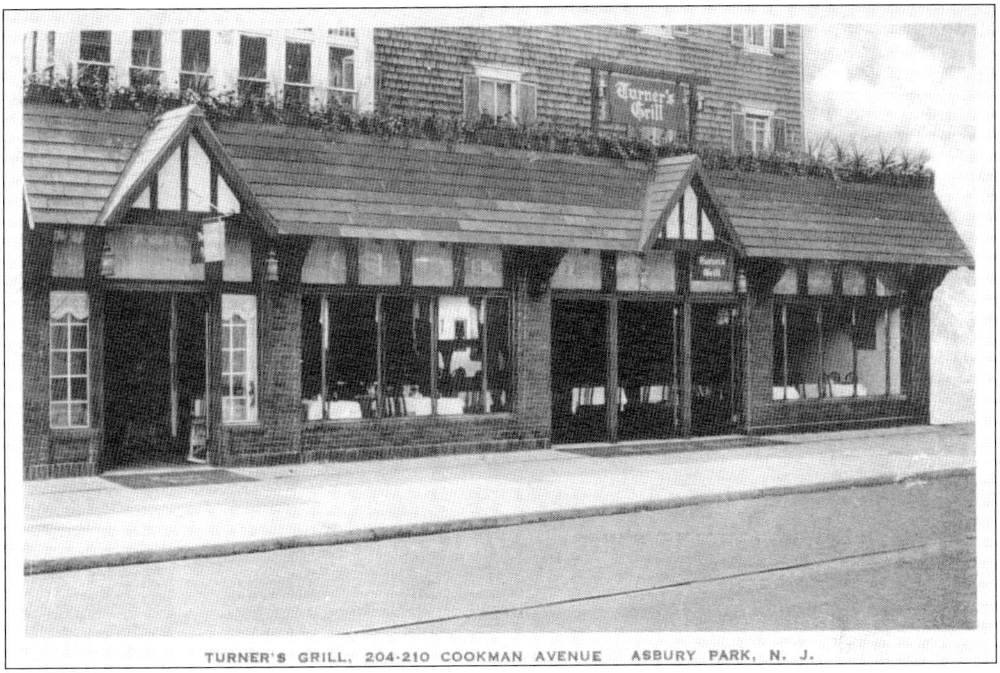


Turner's Grill was located on Cookman Avenue in the 1930s. Seafood, lobsters, steaks, chops, and chicken were all on the menu, and a full meal could be had for just $1.25. The restaurant's proximity to the Lyric and St. James Theaters made it popular with visitors.

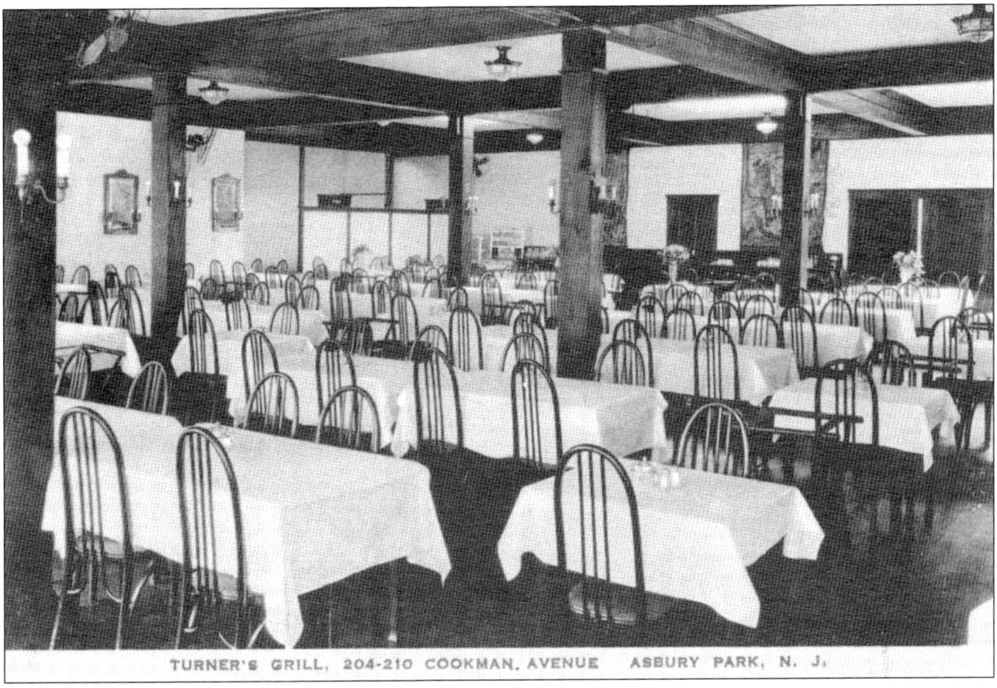


The interior of Turner's Grill is featured here. Not long after this postcard was mailed in July 1931, Turner's Grill became the Grand Atlantic Cafeteria. The building was torn down in the 1950s, when Palace Amusements underwent its final expansion.

# Asbury Park Postcard Publishers

Acme Print, Asbury Park, New Jersey.
Aladdin Business Service, Philadelphia, Pennsylvania.
The Albertype Company, Brooklyn, New York.
American Post Card Company, Brick Town, New Jersey.
American Post Card Company, Point Pleasant, New Jersey.
Arrow Advertising Specialty Company, Oakhurst, New Jersey.
Artvue Post Card Company, New York, New York.
Bechtel and Koch, Asbury Park, New Jersey.
Carol's Photo Service, Asbury Park, New Jersey.
C. Leighton Company, Portland, Maine.
Colourpicture, Boston, Massachusetts.
Curt-Teich, Chicago, Illinois.
Dexter Press, Pearl River, New York.
Dexter Press Inc., West Nyack, New York.
E.A. Burges, Burford, Ontario.
F.A. VonWeiding, Asbury Park, New Jersey.
F.G. Temme Company, Orange, New Jersey; Leipzig, Germany.
Franz Huld, New York, New York.
The H. Hagemeister Company, New York, New York.
Harry H. Baumann, New York, New York.
Ken Brown Cards, Cambridge, Massachusetts.
Lorenzo Harris, Asbury Park, New Jersey.
Lumitone Photoprint, New York, New York.
N.P.C. Studios, Avon, New Jersey.
Pappas Studios, Keyport, New Jersey.
Parlin Color Photo Company, Toms River, New Jersey; Boynton Beach, Florida.
The Post Card Distributing Company, Philadelphia, Pennsylvania.
Raphael Tuck & Sons, Asbury Park, New Jersey.
Samuel Strauss, Brooklyn, New York.
The Scheller Company, Hackettstown, New Jersey.
Service Print Inc., Asbury Park, New Jersey.
S. Langsdorf & Company, New York, New York.
Star Stationery Company, Irvington, New Jersey.
The Steinbach Company, Asbury Park, New Jersey.
Sunny Scenes Inc., Winter Park, Florida.
Theo E. Schulte, Ocean Grove, New Jersey.
Tichnor Brothers Inc., Boston, Massachusetts.
Tichnor Quality Views.
The Union News Company, New York, New York.
Valentine & Sons Publishing Company, New York, New York; Boston, Massachusetts.
Weston Publishers, Oakhurst, New Jersey.
W.H. Bechtel, Asbury Park, New Jersey.

# Bibliography


Africano, Lillian and Nina Africano. *You Know You're in New Jersey When . . . 101 Quintessential Places, People, Events, Customs, Lingo, and Eats of the Garden State*. Guilford, CT: Globe Pequot, 2006.

Ayres, Shirley. *Asbury Park*. Mount Pleasant, SC: Arcadia Publishing, 2005.

Bilby, Joseph G. and Harry F. Ziegler. *Asbury Park: A Brief History*. Charleston, SC: History Press, 2009.

———. *Asbury Park Reborn: Lost to Time and Restored to Glory*. Charleston, SC: History Press, 2012.

Chung, Nogin. "Transforming a Beauty Pageant: Mrs. America Contest in the Palisades Amusement Park and Asbury Park, NJ." *New Jersey History*, Vol. 126, No. 1, 2011.

Hicks, Brian. *When the Dancing Stopped: The Real Story of The Morro Castle and Its Deadly Wake*. New York: Free Press, 2006.

Linderoth, Matthew R. *Prohibition on the North Jersey Shore: Gangsters on Vacation*. Charleston, SC: History Press, 2011.

Nelson, William. *The New Jersey Coast in Three Centuries: History of the New Jersey Coast with Genealogical and Historic-biographical Appendix, Volume 3*. New York: Lewis Publishing Company, 1902.

noweverthen.com

palaceamusements.com

Pike, Helen C. *Asbury Park's Glory Days: The Story of an American Resort*. New Brunswick, NJ: Rutgers University Press, 2005.

Roberts, Russell. *Down the Jersey Shore*. New Brunswick, NJ: Rutgers University Press, 1993.

Salvini, Emil R. *Boardwalk Memories: Tales of the Jersey Shore*. Guilford, CT: Globe Pequot, 2006.

Schwartz, Rick. *Hurricanes and the Middle Atlantic States*. Alexandria, VA: Blue Diamond Books, 2007.

Wolff, Daniel. *4th of July, Asbury Park: A History of the Promised Land*. New York: Bloomsbury USA, 2005.